Native
South American
Discourse

Native
South American
Discourse

edited by
Joel Sherzer and Greg Urban

Mouton de Gruyter
Berlin · New York · Amsterdam

Mouton de Gruyter (formerly Mouton, The Hague)
is a Division of Walter de Gruyter & Co., Berlin.

Library of Congress Cataloging in Publication Data

Native South American discourse.
"Outgrowth of a conference held at the Institute of Latin American Studies
of the University of Texas in March of 1984"—Pref.
Includes bibliographies
1. Indians of South America—Languages—Discourse analysis—Congresses.
2. Indians of South America—Languages—Social aspects—Congresses.
I. Sherzer, Joel. II. Urban, Greg, 1948 – . III. University of Texas at
Austin. Institute of Latin American Studies.
PM 5027.N38   1986   498'.0141   86-12488
ISBN 0-89925-060-2 (alk. paper)

CIP-Kurztitelaufnahme der Deutschen Bibliothek

Native South American discourse / ed. by Joel Sherzer and Greg Urban. –
Berlin ; New York ; Amsterdam : Mouton de Gruyter, 1986. – & 1 Tonkassette
ISBN 3-11-010511-X

NE: Sherzer, Joel [Hrsg.]

Preface

Native South American Discourse is the outgrowth of a conference held at the Institute of Latin American Studies of the University of Texas in March of 1984. All of the papers in the volume have been extensively rewritten on the basis of discussions held at the conference and subsequent to it. The editors and authors are grateful to all of those who participated in the conference. We would especially like to thank Marie-Louise Liebe-Harkort for her perspicacious comments regarding the written representation of Native American texts. The conference was funded by the Institute of Latin American Studies and the University of Texas College of Liberal Arts. We would like to express our appreciation to William Glade, Director of the Institute, to Robert D. King, Dean of the College, and to William Livingston, Vice President and Dean of the Graduate School. Thanks also to the Center for Psychosocial Studies, Chicago for their support during the preparation of this book.

Since all of the participants at the conference felt that tape recordings of actual discourse are essential to our analysis, a cassette tape has been included with this volume. The tape contains sample portions of the texts which are represented and analyzed in the papers. We are grateful to Anthony Seeger and the Archives of Traditional Music at Indiana University for their help in producing this tape.

Joel Sherzer
Greg Urban

Contents

viii   Contents

Introduction

Joel Sherzer and Greg Urban

Native South American Discourse is intended as a contribution to the understanding of language use among indigenous peoples of South America, especially those groups occupying the Lowlands. The purpose is first and foremost empirical. The aim is to describe the actual nature of language use in these little-studied societies. This volume is simultaneously (1) an initial attempt to document language use in native lowland South America, (2) a model for research of its kind, and (3) a call to colleagues to direct their energies towards documenting the types of phenomena discussed here.

While this volume has a decidedly empirical bent, it also has a definite theoretical and methodological orientation. All of the papers demonstrate a commitment to a discourse-centered approach to the language, culture, and society relationship. The symbols and the meanings which characterize and constitute the cultures of lowland South America are not independent of the forms of discourse which are represented and analyzed on these pages. Rather it is precisely this discourse which constantly expresses and actually creates these symbols and meanings. And it is through the study of this discourse that we, as outsiders and analysts, can best penetrate and interpret them.

The study of discourse and language use intersects traditional academic boundaries. In particular it lies in the area of overlap between social and linguistic theories and redefines the boundaries of our knowledge about language and culture. This is reflected in the range of disciplinary identities of the contributors to this volume, some of whom consider themselves linguists, some folklorists, some ethnomusicologists, and some anthropologists. Within this latter discipline, some are identified as social anthropologists and some as linguistic anthropologists.

In most ethnographic descriptions of lowland South America, discourse is invisible, a glass through which the ethnographer comes to perceive the reality of social relations, of ecological practice, and of belief. Little attention is given to the glass itself. We are rarely informed about the structure of the discourse through which knowledge is produced, conceived, transmitted, and acquired - by members of societies and by researchers.

The authors of the papers in this volume take a wholly different tack. The assumption of *Native South American Discourse* is that we must treat the discourse through which knowledge is conceived and acquired as itself a datum, susceptible to scrutiny. We sense that a good portion of what is traditionally called culture is constituted by means of discourse, just as it is transmitted by means of discourse. Consequently, we must make that discourse itself the focus of research.

Simultaneously, the actual manifestation of language is not the phonemes and morphemes of conventional grammars, but utterances made by speakers under specific circumstances. These utterances themselves must be subjected to scrutiny, in order for us to achieve some understanding of their structure and function. The units of a discourse-centered analysis are both larger and smaller than the units of conventional linguistic analysis. The contributors to this volume pay attention to phonetic nuances not captured in traditional phonemicizations, finding in them functional units, meaning-bearing sign vehicles, which are often an important component of the message of the discourse. Simultaneously, attention is given to larger than sentence-level units, e.g. myth narrations, in which we find elaborate rhetorical structures, which prove also to be carriers of meaning.

All of the authors in this volume share as well a common methodological orientation, that the basic data for analysis are actual instances of language use, tape-recorded in natural contexts. The authors have endeavored to capture on tape forms of language use that occur when outside observers are not present. At the same time they have maintained a sensitivity to the impact of their own status as outside observers on the linguistic events they have recorded.

The investigation of discourse in lowland South America involves both an opportunity and an urgency. The opportunity resides in the fact that lowland South America provides a laboratory for the study of a wide variety of forms of oral discourse, still naturally occurring in ongoing traditional contexts. But at the same time there is an urgency, because these very forms of discourse are subject to radical change and disappearance due to the perilously delicate and fragile status of most lowland societies in the face of increasing and often brutal encroachments from the outside world.

While the focus of the papers in this volume is the structure of discourse in relation to social and cultural context and especially the role of discourse in the language-culture-society nexus, the texts which are represented and translated here are a reflection of the verbally artistic nature of language use in lowland South America. All of the papers deal to some degree with poetic aspects of discourse. By poetic we mean the organization of discourse into lines and other units, the employment of forms of repetition, especially parallelism, to create verbal patterns, the use of such symbolic processes as metaphor, the dramatization of the voice, and the development of distinctive narrative styles. In each of these cases, we view grammar as a resource in the performance of discourse.

In defining the poetic, it is crucial to take account of the native points of view, what audiences respond to, how they differentially evaluate different performers and performances, and what they believe makes for a good performance. It is important to point out that in native South America poetic discourse rarely occurs for purely esthetic purposes. Rather it is an aspect of and co-occurs with other functions of this discourse - ritual, ceremonial, political, curative, or magical. The esthetic function must always be viewed as integrated with these others.

No South American Indian has ever won the nobel prize for his oral performances of myths, legends, or political oratory.[1] Yet every day and every night members of societies in remote areas of Brazil, Ecuador, and Panama, living in nontechnological environments, are creating and performing a remarkable diversity of verbal forms characterized by metaphorical richness, complex poetic and rhetorical processes, and intensely personal styles, all of which are an intimate part of the replication and transmission of their cultural and esthetic traditions. In addition to the theoretical and methodological contributions these papers make to such fields as anthropology, linguistics, folklore, and ethnomusicology, we also hope they provide a feel for and an appreciation of the verbal art, the indigenous beauty, of the oral discourse of lowland South America.

The papers in this volume address a set of interrelated and intersecting topics. Centrally and predominantly there is the question of speech styles and patterns of speaking.

Greg Urban presents two stylistic aspects of mythological narrative among the southern Brazilian Shokleng - macroparallelism and ceremonial dialogue. Macroparallelism is the repetition with variation of whole blocks of discourse within a narrative. Ceremonial dialogue is the way in which myth is actually performed in a particular ritual context and involves syllable by syllable repetition by a second speaker of the utterances of a first. Urban describes the relationship of each of these stylistic aspects to both the semantic content of the myth and its social and cultural functions.

Anthony Seeger presents the major genres of verbal performance of the central Brazilian Suyá and classifies them according to several features - fixity of texts, relationship of linguistic style used to everyday speech, phrasing, voice quality, timbre, use of tonal structures, and social function.

Laura Graham contrasts three vocal styles in use among the central Brazilian Shavante - wailing, collective singing, and political oratory - along three parameters. She points out that these styles and the associated parameters shed new light on the nature/culture dichotomy so basic to Gê society.

Ellen Basso studies two speech styles of the central Brazilian Kalapalo. The first is the use of quoted speech embedded into narration. The other is the dialogic performance of narrative and in particular the existence of individuals, called "what-sayers" in Kalapalo, who respond in various ways during narrations and thereby contribute to their emergent structure. The use of quoted speech is also a predominant speech pattern among the Panamanian Kuna and is a central feature of the Kuna report analyzed by Joel Sherzer.

Harriet Klein investigates three basic styles of speaking among the Argentinian Toba, formal speaking style, narrative style, and informal conversational style, in terms of four levels of linguistic structure - the word, the phonological phrase, the line, and the episode.

Maurizio Gnerre is concerned with the role, traditionally and currently, of ceremonial dialogue among the Shuar and the Achuar of Ecuador.

It is interesting to note certain overlaps, intersections, and similarities among speech styles and patterns of speaking within lowland South America. Thus ritual or ceremonial dialogue, which is discussed in this volume with regard to the Shokleng, the Kalapalo, and the Shuar and the Achuar, has been reported for many other lowland South American groups, including the Kuna (see Rivière 1971, Sherzer 1983: 196-200, and

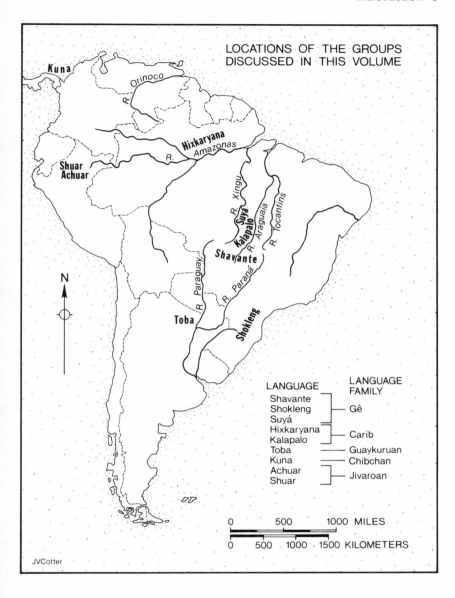

LOCATIONS OF THE GROUPS
DISCUSSED IN THIS VOLUME

Kuna

R. Orinoco

Hixkaryana

R. Amazonas

Shuar
Achuar

R. Xingu

Suyá

Kalapalo

R. Araguaia

R. Tocantins

Shavante

R. Paraguay

R. Paraná

N

Toba

Shokleng

LANGUAGE	LANGUAGE FAMILY
Shavante Shokleng Suyá	Gê
Hixkaryana Kalapalo	Carib
Toba	Guaykuruan
Kuna	Chibchan
Achuar Shuar	Jivaroan

0   500   1000 MILES

0   500   1000 · 1500 KILOMETERS

JVCotter

Urban 1986). The use of quoted or reported speech is a prominent feature of both Kalapalo and Kuna narrative. Parallelism seems to be a dominant feature in the ritual, ceremonial, and formal speech of many lowland South American societies.

Several of the studies of speech styles and patterns of speaking demonstrate quite clearly and effectively what we mean by a discourse-centered approach to the language-culture-society relationship. The performances of the Shokleng origin myth analyzed by Urban are not merely a reflection of Shokleng culture. Rather they are both a model of and an embodiment of Shokleng cultural continuity and replication. Basso shows that the meaning of a Kalapalo story cannot be arrived at without studying actual narrations. In fact, various interpretations and emphases are permitted, according to particular instances of performance involving specific tellers and specific responders. The story of Cuckoo, the text of a performance of which is the centerpiece of Basso's paper, constitutes a validation of goals, which are at the root of Kalapalo personal and social cooperation and solidarity. The report of a Kuna medicinal specialist, analyzed by Sherzer, is by no means marginal to Kuna curing practices. Quite the contrary. It is a central and in fact constitutive aspect of them. For it is this public report which actualizes its performer, Olowitinappi, as a snake-bite-curing specialist.

The authors in this volume are concerned with various aspects of the way in which discourse is organized, both in textual terms and in terms of the structuring of poetic and rhetorical features and units in actual performances. Urban shows that the Shokleng origin myth is constructed by means of repetitions of macro-units, coupled with micro-parallelism as well. Sherzer argues that the basic unit of Kuna narration is the line. The narrative he analyzes is furthermore organized into a series of episodes. Klein similarly finds the line to be the basic unit of Toba discourse. Toba line structure, as in Kuna as well, serves as a diagnostic feature distinguishing different styles of speaking. Desmond C. Derbyshire provides an analysis of Brazilian Hixkaryana discourse in terms of cohesion relations, studying the discourse distributions of grammatically-defined elements. His study of three Hixkaryana origin myths, which includes the only quantitative analysis in this volume, shows that Hixkaryana discourse is organized in terms of the use of specific grammatical devices to signal the pragmatic status of participants as they are referred to. The major unit of rhetorical structure with which Derbyshire deals is the episode. Hixkaryana episodes can be seen as semantically transparent, but they achieve as well a formal, textual distinctiveness through the cohesion relations. Both Klein and Derbyshire provide empirical evidence that aspects of Toba and Hixkaryana grammar respectively cannot be understood without reference to discourse.

Changing patterns of language use are the focus of several of the papers in this volume. The rapid transformations currently occurring in native South America constitute a threat not only to the future of research. They threaten as well the very objects of research.

Urban recorded several different tellings of the Shokleng origin-myth, which is supposedly memorized verbatim, syllable by syllable. Two tellings were by the same elder speaker, seven years apart, and one was by a somewhat younger speaker, maximally isolated in social terms from the former. While the tellings show remarkable consistency, the younger speaker's version indicates some systematic transformations of the older speaker's text, both in the pragmatics of intonation and rhythm and in the actual choice of morphemes. This is the kind of data on which analyses of discourse change, associated with social change, can be based.

Gnerre documents the disappearance of an entire discourse style, ceremonial dialogue, among the Shuar-Achuar. The Shuar Federation in Ecuador alone, with more than 25,000 members, contains villages (or centers) of varying degrees of acculturation. In remote centers, the ceremonial dialogues are still intact. In centers with more exposure to the national Ecuadorian society, the ceremonial dialogue is undergoing transformation, tending to be replaced by forms of verbal interaction more similar to those found in the national society. Ceremonial dialogue is viewed by the Shuar-Achuar as a diagnostic marker of their way of life. At the same time there has been a restructuring of forms of discourse and verbal interaction involving a decline in the salient use of ceremonial dialogue, which reflects increasing distance between traditional knowledge and current Shuar and Achuar beliefs, values, and verbal practices.

Klein's analysis of Toba discourse, in contrast, shows that, despite the almost total devastation of Toba society, certain elements of rhetorical structure persist, differentiating one type of narration from another.

A number of issues emerge from the papers in this volume, relating them to ongoing research in the study of oral discourse and verbal art in particular and to the concerns of anthropology, linguistics, folklore, and ethnomusicology more generally.

We know as yet relatively little about the structuring of participant roles in linguistically-mediated interactions in native South America, especially with regard to the comparative picture. All discourse in every society is ultimately interactional in that it involves people speaking to and with one another. But recent research in lowland South America and in particular the papers in this volume point to certain forms of verbal interaction that are particularly characteristic of the area. Probably most striking is ritual or ceremonial dialogue, which in a variety of forms is extremely widespread in lowland South America. Urban describes the *Wāñēklèn* style of myth narration among the southern Brazilian Shokleng, in which the myth is in effect told in dialogic fashion. One speaker recites one syllable and this is echoed by a second speaker, so that the myth is actually told syllable by syllable twice, but in staggered fashion. This is an extreme form of dialogue, in which the two speakers say the same thing. Yet there is obvious resemblance to the ceremonial dialogues of the Shuar-Achuar of eastern Ecuador, as recorded and described by Gnerre. Here, however, one speaker takes the lead, the other responds. The ensuing dialogue occurs in rapid-fire back and forth action and is unmistakably similar to the Shokleng *Wāñēklèn*. Similar ceremonial dialogues can be observed in Napoleon Chagnon's film, "The feast," dealing with the Yanomamo Indians of northern Brazil and southern Venezuela. These forms are evidently similar as well to the ceremonial dialogues reported by Rivière (1971) for the northern Brazilian Trio Indians. (See also Fock 1963, Sherzer 1983: 196-200, and Urban 1986).

More generally, it is becoming apparent that dialogue rather than monologue is the basic model for narrative performances in much of lowland South America. Basso describes the role of the "what-sayer" among the Kalapalo of the Xingu region of Brazil. This is a role that must be operationalized during narrations of myths. The myth teller recites a narrative, and his narration is punctuated with responses ("whats") from the "what-sayer." Such "what-saying" is rarely reported in ethnographic accounts and analyses of myths and is often edited out of transcriptions and translations. Among the Panamanian Kuna, the Brazilian Shavante, and probably other lowland South American societies as well, not only dialogic, but polylogic performances of narrative are quite common, in which two (or more) persons speak or chant simultaneously to a third person or to an audience.

It is impossible to study language use in lowland South America without paying attention to the intimate relationship between musicality and speech. Many forms of discourse, especially ritual and ceremonial discourse, are sung or chanted, with or without the accompaniment of musical instruments. The distinction between speech and music, spoken speech and sung speech, is by no means obvious and in fact may vary considerably from society to society and event to event.

Seeger in particular stresses the intimacy of the speech-music relationship in his analysis of Suyá verbal genres and styles. Certain styles, such as ritual chanting, have especially pronounced musical characteristics in rhythm and intonation. Music is a more or less prominent part of all discourse, becoming more prominent here, receding into the background there. The Suyá tell myths about the origin of particular songs, in which the telling leads gradually to the actual singing of the song. In this way, the singing is both reported by means of the discourse, and performed as part of the discourse.

Graham shows that the interplay between linguistic structure and musicality is essential to the expression of the language, culture, society relationship in Shavante. She examines the formal connections among Shavante verbal styles, ranging the three styles along continua of musicality and semanticity. Shavante ritual wailing employs only a few vowels (in addition to the glottal stop). There are no true words or even syllables, so that the verbal style lacks semanticity altogether. Yet it is highly musical, with a developed melodic structure exhibiting microtonal rising. Collective singing, in contrast, involves the entire repertoire of Shavante syllables, and even makes use of some words; yet the songs are not propositionally meaningful in the true sense. Such singing actually possesses less melodic structure than ritual wailing, and some of the syllables show more speech pitch (shouting) than true musical pitch. Finally, political oratory involves full propositional discourse. However, its musicality is confined to the parallelistic repetition of lines and the metering of phrase units.

The analysis of music-discourse interrelationships requires careful attention to formal detail, to intonation, to metering and rhythm, and to stress. However, as both Graham and Seeger make apparent, the relationship is one that in native South America is actually reflected upon, through myths about music and music about myths, and through the mapping of the interrelationships onto social space. (See also Basso 1981, 1985 and Sherzer and Wicks 1982).

Several of the authors pick up on issues that have been raised by William Bright, Dell Hymes, Dennis Tedlock, Joel Sherzer, and Anthony Woodbury concerning the determination and representation of such discourse units as lines, verses, and episodes, and such textual patterns as parallelism, as well as how best to translate oral discourse into written form and into a language which retains the essences of the original native oral performance and yet is both accessible to and able to be appreciated by readers. (See Bright 1984, Hymes 1981, Tedlock 1983, Sherzer and Woodbury 1987). The authors, each in their own way, provide transcriptions of texts which capture and visualize in written form the intersection of syntactic, semantic, lexical, and paralinguistic features essential to the oral performances they have recorded. In this sense these papers constitute significant contributions to ethnopoetics, for they reflect a variety of lowland South American verbally artistic forms and performances as well as a variety of techniques for representing, translating, and analyzing them.

Native South America is an ideal laboratory for ethnopoetics. Many of the cultures are sufficiently intact so that we can obtain, insofar as research conditions permit, in situ recordings, which capture something closely approximating traditional poetic and rhetorical structures. It is thus possible to experiment with different textual transcriptions, translations, and analyses, based on different structuring criteria - syntactic, semantic, lexical, and paralinguistic - and, especially, to develop ways of representing the intersection of these features that occurs in actual performances.

Ethnopoetics, as we envisage it, depends crucially on actual tape recordings of in situ data. These recordings should be made available to those wishing to see where our analyses come from. The tapes will also make it possible for others to propose alternative analyses more readily.

Tapes provide reproductions of specific instances of discourse. As field researchers, most of us have heard numerous instances of the specific type of discourse we have chosen to analyze. However, the type is an analytical abstraction. In moving from token to type, we filter out a great deal of the specificity of discourse - coughs, hesitations, false starts, interjections, and inserted comments. Some of these seem fortuitous or variable. Yet, as we increase the depth of our analyses, we appreciate that these supposed vagaries actually form part of the pragmatic meaning of the discourse.

In insisting upon tapes, we do not mean to blur the distinction between type and token, between general form and concrete instance. None of us feels that the instance should be taken for the type. The specific instance contains a richness, a wealth of nuance, that we can imagine is less than fully reflected in the general form. However, we feel strongly that the process of moving from instance to form is itself an analysis, which must be justified. If we make claims about general forms, we must be willing to show how these forms grow out of a study of instances.

The graphic representation of a snippet of tape in the form of a transcription is itself an analysis. Within this purview, however, there is considerable room for disagreement. In just what does transcription, as analysis, consist? Is there a single correct transcription of a given stretch of discourse, or are there alternative possible transcriptions?

Some of the authors in this volume feel that there should, in principle, be a single way of transcribing a given stretch of discourse. After all, there is a single string of sound substance acting as sign vehicle. If the mind decomposes the stretch of spoken discourse into its constituent signals, so ought the reader to decompose the transcription. One needs only a set of rules, a kind of discourse grammar, for interpreting the transcription.

It is possible to argue with this position, however. In actuality, it is only a supposition that discourse presents itself as a single sign vehicle. In fact, as a number of the papers here point out, discourse is from the start multi-channel, involving gestural and contextual input, simultaneously as it involves sound substance. Even the sound substance itself may actually be presented to the mind as multiple, if the view that language is inherently multifunctional indeed has some validity. It may be, for instance, that the mind processes pragmatic input separately from semantic input.

Whatever the case in this formal area, it is important to recognize that the functions of a transcription are not identical with the functions of the original spoken discourse that the transcription is designed to represent. A transcription is not a communication of the same type as the original discourse. Its purpose is rather to analyze or foreground some facet of the discourse.

This being the case, we can readily appreciate that certain kinds of transcription would be more appropriate than others for certain analytical tasks. Thus for purposes of displaying a morphological analysis, a careful morpheme by morpheme transcription, with interlinear translation, would be especially appropriate. However, given the nature of such transcriptions, it would be difficult to employ them as a means of highlighting poetic and rhetorical structure, wherein one wishes to give a graphic representation of lines, verses, stanzas, scenes, and episodes. Nor would it prove suitable for highlighting parallelism. Transcriptions of discourse organized into lines, with attention paid to groupings of lines or parallels between them, would be more appropriate for these latter chores. Again, if one wishes to show parallels between (non-phonemic) intonation contours, one needs to devise a method for displaying those contours, and for juxtaposing the relevant lines to exhibit the parallels.

While the authors do not agree on all aspects of the theory of transcription, we do agree that rigid rules should not be established in this regard. Consequently, the papers in this volume reflect a range of approaches to the transcription problem. Each approach is designed for the specific task chosen by the author. At the same time, because of our insistence on tape recordings, data are present for the construction of alternative analyses and of alternative transcriptions. This is in keeping with the general philosophy of this volume - that transcription is analysis and that alternative transcriptions must be argued for and against on a case by case basis.

This volume is a reflection of a significant transformation that is in the process of occurring in anthropology. We no longer consider the populations with which we deal as objects, in the classical scientific sense. Research consists instead in interactions with other subjects, in engaging in a dialogue with those other subjects. In this regard as well, discourse occupies a central position. Those of us who make discourse our research focus are dealing with the very voices of the people with whom we work. Our data are the sign vehicles by means of which they represent themselves. The tapes we analyze, the texts we transcribe and translate, can become a forum through which native South Americans speak to a larger world. There is a sense in which students of discourse occupy a unique position, among anthropologists, in being able to facilitate a dialogue between native South Americans and the world at large.

The authors of this volume share deep concerns in this regard. The papers all deal with indigenous verbal art forms. When one focuses purely on the cultural (i.e. semantic) content of these forms, as in the case of ordinary myth analysis, or purely on the linguistic content, as in conventional grammatical analysis, one misses a good deal of what this verbal art is all about. Much of its power resides in the discourse structures themselves, in the poetics of line and verse, in the parallelisms, in the rhythms and intonations, in the metaphors and allusions, and in the relationships among speakers, hearers, and audiences. It is up to us to find ways of representing these discourse structures, such that they become intelligible to a broader audience.

This is the first collection of papers dealing with Native South American discourse in its social and cultural context. Our aim is to show the validity of a discourse-centered approach for a deeper understanding of the social, cultural, verbal, and esthetic worlds of lowland South America. Discourse is a part of ongoing social and cultural behavior. It is embedded in a concrete context shaped by actors pursuing multifarious goals. It is a general frame of reference through which ongoing social and cultural activity is construed. It is the active manifestation of both language and culture. Yet, simultaneously, it is also the creator of language and culture, which, otherwise, subsist in a purely individual mental realm. For this reason, the authors of this volume share a sense of excitement about their research. They consider themselves to be working in an area that might redefine the boundaries of classical social and linguistic theory. We hope that this excitement has been carried over into the papers of the volume.

Note

1. The closest is Miguel Angel Asturias, Guatemalan Nobel laureate, whose writing poetically incorporates the oral discourse of the Mayan Indians of Guatemala.

References

Basso, Ellen B.
   1981   A "musical view of the universe": Kalapalo myth and ritual as
          religious performance. *Journal of American Folklore* 94: 273-
          291.
   1985   *A musical view of the universe: Kalapalo myth and ritual
          performances*. Philadelphia: University of Pennsylvania Press.
Bright, William
   1984   *American Indian linguistics and literature*. Berlin: Mouton
          Publishers.
Fock, Niels
   1963   *Waiwai: religion and society of an Amazonian tribe*.
          Copenhagen: National Museum.
Hymes, Dell
   1981   *"In vain I tried to tell you": essays in Native American
          ethnopoetics*. Philadelphia: University of Pennsylvania Press.
Rivière, Peter
   1971   The political structure of the Trio Indians as manifested in a
          system of ceremonial dialogue. In *The translation of culture:
          essays to E.E. Evans-Pritchard* , T. O. Beidelman (ed.), pp. 293-
          311. London: Tavistock.
Sherzer, Joel
   1983   *Kuna ways of speaking: an ethnographic perspective*. Austin:
          University of Texas Press.
Sherzer, Joel, and Sammie Ann Wicks
   1982   The intersection of music and language in Kuna discourse. *Latin
          American Music Review* 3: 147-164.
Sherzer, Joel, and Anthony Woodbury, eds.
   1987   *Native American discourse: poetics and rhetoric*. Cambridge
          University Press. To appear.
Tedlock, Dennis
   1983   *The spoken word and the work of interpretation*. Philadelphia:
          University of Pennsylvania Press.
Urban, Greg
   1986   Ceremonial dialogues in South America. *American
          Anthropologist* 88. To appear.

The Semiotic Functions of Macro-parallelism in the Shokleng Origin Myth

Greg Urban

This paper purports to analyze, from a semiotic point of view, the parallelistic structures of the Shokleng origin myth, known as the *wãñēklèn*. The term "parallelism"[1] is associated in western poetry with phonologically-based rhyme schemes. Traces of this kind of parallelism can be found in the Shokleng origin myth, as I will discuss below. However, the primary parallelism is of a distinct sort. It involves the formal similarity or parallels between larger blocks of discourse, wherein a cluster of sentences, occurring at one point in the narration, is repeated with certain substitutions at a later point. These repetitions supply the basis for an intricate and rather remarkable structure, about whose significance we must wonder.

I propose in this paper to explore the semiotic functions of this "macro-parallelism," and to examine the relationship between these functions and the broader purposes of origin-myth telling as a component of ongoing social activity. To do so, it is important to scrutinize the formal characteristics of the myth as narrative discourse. A considerable portion of this paper does just that. However, assessment of semiotic function requires consideration as well of how formal design relates to (1) semantic content, and (2) the broader social and even non-linguistic world. Simultaneously, social purpose must be assessed through an analysis of context -- the matrix of activity within which origin-myth telling occurs. I hope to show that there is a crucial linkage between macro-parallelism as a sign vehicle and the encompassing world of social purpose.

Specifically, I argue that macro-parallelism, as a sign vehicle, brings within the scope of intellectual scrutiny the question of cultural continuity. It focuses attention upon (1) the formal replicability of origin-myth telling, which itself both embodies cultural continuity and is a model of it, and (2) the continuity inherent in the semantic meanings of the myth text itself, a continuity that again models the broader processes of cultural continuity in the world. Simultaneously, the meanings suggested by macro-parallelism, as a sign vehicle, are linked to the social purposes of origin myth telling. Indeed, it is possible to see in macro-parallelism a kind of "blueprint" for the construction of social purpose, a component of discourse that indicates how that discourse itself is to be situated with respect to an encompassing social world.

Micro-parallelism

I will refer to the classic type of parallelism, where there is similarity between two lines based upon rhyme and/or meter, as well as to extentions of the classic type that are based upon other kinds of parallels between lines as the principal unit (cf. Hymes 1981), as "micro-parallelism." The Shokleng *wãñēklèn* has traces of this type of parallelism, as can be detected through listening to the tapes. It is in part through micro-parallelism that the units are constructed which form the constituents of macro-parallel structure.

An examination of B.2.1 (1975) (Appendix I and tape) will reveal instances of such poetic structuring of the *wãñēklèn*. Lines 5 and 6, for example, form a rhymed couplet:

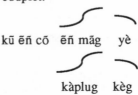

The *yè* ("for") in Shokleng rhymes with *kèg* ("to fashion"), and there is as well a parallel in the meter. The major stress in each line occurs on the penultimate syllable, and this stress corresponds with a tonal peak.

A similar couplet occurs in the following two lines:

mū lõ ti kï   tū

ēñ cõ wèg   mū

Once again it is the final syllables of the two lines that rhyme. However, here primary stress is on the final syllable, and this corresponds with the tonal peak. In other words, lines 7 and 8 represent, insofar as stress and intonation are concerned, an inversion of the pattern found in lines 5 and 6.

We find the pattern of lines 5 through 8 reflected in the pattern of lines 9 through 12. Lines 9 and 10 are identical to lines 5 and 6 but for the substitution of a single word:

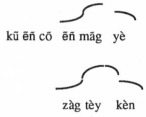

kū ēñ cõ   ēñ māg   yè

zàg tèy   kèn

Here there is similarly a primary penultimate stress corresponding with the tonal peak and a secondary final stress corresponding with a falling intonation. Lines 11 and 12 are wholly distinct in semantic terms from lines 7 and 8, and, indeed, the final syallables do not even rhyme. However, in terms of intonation and stress they are identical to lines 7 and 8:

kū ēñ cõ ti làn ke

kū   kàgnāg

Listening to the tape, indeed, one quickly appreciates that there is a parallel as well between lines 11 and 12, on the one hand, and line 13, on the other, which represents a continuation, without pause, of this entire sequence. Line 13 as well shows the rising tone accompanied by a final stress.

The general formula may be represented as follows:

$$5=6 : 7=8 :: 9=10 : 11=12$$

We may wonder whether there is any semiotic meaning associated with this purely formal structure. I would suggest that it does indeed have some significance. If we examine the semantic content of these lines, it is apparent that 5 and 6, like 9 and 10, make a positive affirmation, in response to the earlier question (line 4): "what is the cause of all of this noise?" In lines 5 and 6, the speaker asserts that he had attempted to fashion a certain type of wood, known as *kàplug*, into an animal, in particular, as we learn later in the narrative, into a jaguar. Lines 7 and 8 point to the failure of this attempt: "however, it did not call out (properly), I saw." In lines 9 and 10, the speaker refers to his second attempt to make a jaguar, this time using wood from the majestic araucaria pine (*Araucaria brasilienses*). This attempt again fails, because, as lines 11 and 12 indicate, the speaker was about to paint it but he made a mistake. So in line 13 he declares: "and that is what all of the noise is about."

The pragmatic discourse variables, therefore, pattern in a manner analogous to the relationships between the semantic meanings of the corresponding lines. The intonational and stress inversions mirror the semantic inversion associated with "attempt" and "failure."

There is a rhetorical structure for the entire episode B.2.1 (1975) that grows out of this micro-parallelism. However, it does not involve lines of fixed length. Nor is the micro-parallelism found uniformly throughout the episode. Rather, the latter occurs at the center of the episode, and it involves very short lines with no pauses in between, lines being isolated here primarily by parallelism in intonation, meter, and stress, and by phonological rhyming. In the opening and closing portions of the episode, the lines are longer and are marked by pronounced pauses (> 1.0 sec. in duration). Indeed, if one were to isolate lines purely on the basis of pause marking, lines 5-8 would be regarded as a single line, just as would lines 9-13.

The rhetorical structure I propose for this text is given in Fig. 1. The numbers stand for what I have isolated as lines. They correspond with the line numbers in the transcription (Appendix, B.2.1 (1975)). The letters here correspond to the major, formally-defined groupings of lines. Thus, from a formal point of view, lines 1 and 2 are unmarked descriptive statements made by the narrator. Line 3 is set off from them through its formal characterization as a quotation by means of the final *ke mū*. Hence, 1 and 2 are grouped as A, and 3 is grouped as B. The particle *iwo* sets off lines 4-13. It indicates a change of speaker within a quotation, so we know that these lines, and, indeed, line 14 as well, were spoken by someone distinct from the person quoted in line 3. Consequently, 4-13 are grouped together under D. 14, like line 3 and line 17, is set off by the quotative *ke mū*. Moreover, the quoted material in line 14, like the quoted material in line 3, is set off formally as a question, in opposition to lines 4-13 and 15-16. Consequently, it is assigned the letter D. Lines 15 and 16 are set off by the change of speaker particle and also by their formal parallelism. They are grouped as E. Finally, 17 is set off by the quotative, and is formally marked as a command. The internal organization of lines 5-12, indicated in Fig. 1, has already been discussed.

It should be noted that the major segmentation of this episode into five parts has a semantic correlate, as indicated in Fig. 1. In A, the narrator states an event, the arrival in the dance plaza of Zàgpope Patè. The latter is quoted as having asked a question in B: "what is all of this noise about?" In C, this question is answered at length by the main character, who himself in D asks a question of the newly arrived Zàgpope. This question is answered in E, and in F the main character issues a polite command to Zàpope.

I have endeavored to capture this rhetorical organization, insofar as was possible, in the transcriptions that are to be found in the appendix. Thus, the absence of indentation indicates that the material is a statement made by the narrator. One level of indentation indicates that the line is quoted. A second level of indentation indicates that the line shows evidence

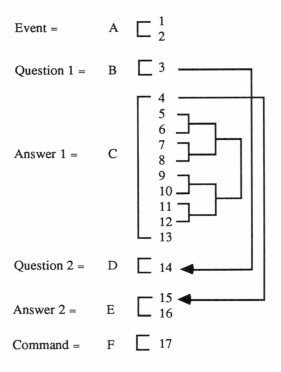

Fig. 1: Rhetorical Structure of B.2.1 (1975)

of micro-parallelism with a preceding line. Other than this, *ke mū* at the end of a line marks completion of a quote.

Since there has been something of a controversy in the literature over the method for isolating lines (cf. Hymes 1981 and Tedlock 1983), it is relevant to note that the lines I have isolated do not always correspond with pause boundaries. The significant pauses in the episode range from 0.7 to 2.4 seconds in duration. Such pauses occur after what I have isolated as lines 1, 2, 3, 13, 14, 15, 16, and 17. They may be said to set off those lines. However, the pauses sometimes occur internally to what I have isolated as lines. This can be noticed through a careful listening to the tape. In line 1, there is a 1.6 second pause between *Patè* and *ēñ*. Yet grammatically the two halves of this rather long line go together, and there seems to be no parallelistic reason for separating them. The change of speaker particle *iwo* is also followed by a pause, but for reasons of economy I have chosen to place it in the same line with the following quoted material.

An interesting problem occurs in connection with the phrase *kū ēñ cō* ("and I"). A pause occurs after it in lines 5 and 9, so that we might construe the phrase as attached to preceding line. However, the connective *kū* is a frequent marker of the beginning of a line, as in 14, and, indeed, it can be used to define many of the lines between 5 and 14. On the basis of this parallelism, I have chosen to place *kū ēñ cō* regularly at the beginning of lines.

From an artistic point of view, there is even arguably a significance to the tension between lines marked by pauses and lines marked by parallelism. In readings of western poetry, one senses a monotony, a dullness if pauses are regularly inserted at the end of lines. Good poetry readings typically involve a skillful interweaving of lines defined by pause and those defined by other parallelistic means. A similar art may be involved in rendering of the Shokleng origin myth.

It may be remarked that from the middle of line 5 to the middle of line 9 there is no significant pause, just as there is no pause between the middle of line 9 and the end of line 13. Indeed, the pause within line 9 itself is exceedingly short, only 0.7 seconds. Listening to the taped narration of this episode, one will readily appreciate that the pace of narration reaches a peak here in this middle phase. The pace begins slow, with lengthy pauses, gradually increases, and then slows back down towards the end. This corresponds with the shortening of lines towards the center, and, indeed, it would not be unreasonable to speak of the narrative's reaching an "artistic peak," where there is (1) a density of micro-parallelism, (2) relatively short lines, and (3) the rapid production of syllables with little or no pause.

Replicability

The Shokleng tacitly believe, and on occasion explicitly aver, that the *wāñēklèn* must be memorized and recited verbatim, syllable by syllable. Each instance should be a perfect replica, insofar as morphemic composition is concerned, of some ideal type. In proportion as distinct tellings actually approach identity, therefore, the *wãñēklèn* constitutes maximally pure evidence of the continuity of culture, of the ability of individuals over time to replicate socially learned activities. This ideology of language use can be compared with the actual facts regarding replicability.

The *wãñēklèn* is actually told or peformed in two distinct ways. The versions on tape in Selections 1 through 6 are instances of one such style -- the ordinary narrative style, which is employed in telling stories around the campfire at night. In this style, there is some room for embellishment. A narrator will occasionally slip in a *kū yi tã wū* ("and, it is said, he ..."), as in line 2 or B.2.1 (1981), or a didactic aside, such as line 18 of B.2.1 (1981) -- "that is, Pata, Patè who shot the falcons" -- a remark addressed to me as someone learning the *wãñēklèn*. Nevertheless, even here the principal text should be rendered faithfully.

In the other style, there is no room for even these kinds of deviation, at least in principle. This other style is the *wãñēklèn* proper, a special ceremonial form through which the origin myth is performed. This performance style, indeed, makes narration of the Shokleng origin myth a true art form. The performance involves two men, who sit facing each other in the dance plaza. Such performances occur most frequently near the conclusion of the the *ãgyĩn* ceremonies for the dead. One speaker, using laryngeal and pharyngeal constriction, shouts out one syllable of the myth, and he is echoed by the second speaker, who repeats that syllable, and so forth, as they proceed through the entire narration.

Speaker 1:	ū	yè	kõñ	gàg	ū	yè
Speaker 2:		ū	yè	kõñ	gàg	ū	yè

An excerpt from an actual performance of the *wãñēklèn*, which gives some idea of the acoustically stunning effect, is included on the tape.

Evidently, in such a performance, a number of the variables determining micro-parallelistic structure, e.g., intonation contour, stress, and pause structure, become irrelevant. The style involves a largely constant pitch, primarily even stress, and a finely-tuned metering of syllables. This makes rhetorical structure considerably less prominent than in the ordinary narrative style.

In what follows, I have chosen the ordinary style as providing the greatest insight into the overall question of continuity. Just how closely do distinct tellings actually resemble one another? For these purposes, I recorded the eldest living ritual specialist in 1975 and then again in late 1981 reciting the entire *wāñēklèn* sequence. I also recorded a somewhat younger specialist in 1982, one, moreover, who was maximally removed in social terms from the first. Through a comparison of these three narrative "tokens," or instances, it is possible to assess just how constant is the *wāñēklèn* as a poetic "type" across social space and across time.

B.2.1 (1981) is an excerpt from the 1981 narration by Nil. It corresponds to the 1975 excerpt analyzed in the preceding section, which is actually only a 50 second fragment of an approximately 70 minute narration. It will be apparent from listening to the tape, that Nil had aged considerably during this period.[2] The general pace is slower and the delivery is less vigorous. This has probably affected the pause structure in some measure. Nevertheless, the overall similarities between these two instances are remarkable. It is apparent that the *wāñēklèn* indeed constitutes a fixed type, memorized verbatim, and transmitted across the generations.

Still, there are some differences even as regards the semantically segmentable text. For example, in the 1981 version, line 2 of the 1975 version has disappeared altogether. It has been replaced by a typical narrative-style filler, almost as though the general rhythm of delivery suggested to Nil that something should go there, but he could not remember what. Another difference occurs in line 4. Here in 1981 Nil has evidently forgotten a portion of the line, and skipped ahead. So in line 5 he starts over again, putting in the proper line. From there on the two versions parallel each other until line 18 of the 1981 version, which is a didactic aside to me.

It will be observed that the 1981 lines are generally, from a semantic point of view, exact replicas of the 1975 lines. However, occasionally there is an extra morpheme here, a deleted morpheme there. This is true, for example, of the connective particle *kū*, which appears in line 14 of the 1975 version, but not in the corresponding line 15 of the 1981 version. Similarly, *kū* is employed at the beginning of line 19 in 1981, even though it did not occur at the beginning of the corresponding line 17 in 1975. These discrepancies have been noted on the 1981 transcription.

It is remarkable that even the intonational and stress patterns show continuity from 1975 to 1981. The basic elements of the micro-parallelism discussed above for the 1975 version apply as well to the 1981 version. There are a few differences here, e.g., the *mū lō* of line 8 in the 1981 version receives more stress and participates in the rising intonational contour more than its counterpart in the 1975 version. Nevertheless, the general structure present there is preserved in the 1981 telling.

Interestingly, the patterning of pauses shows somewhat more variability than the patterning of other pragmatic variables. Some of this is evidently a matter of pause length. For example, there is a pronounced pause in in the 1975 line 1 after Patè, which lasts some 1.6 seconds. In 1981 this has been reduced to a barely noticeable 0.5 seconds. Correspondingly, in 1981 the pause at the end of that line is greatly augmented (3.0 seconds). However, in some cases the differences would affect the general rhetorical structure, were we taking pauses as primary structural markers. For example, in 1975 there is no noticeable pause after *wū* in line 15, and the line is followed by a pronounced (1.0 second) pause. In 1981, however, the corresponding line 16 has a major (0.8 second) pause after *wū*, and an almost imperceptible (0.3 second) pause at the end of this line. Were we employing pause as the basis of text segmentation, the 1975 and 1981 variants would look quite distinct. Grammar, phonological rhyming, and intonation and stress, however, yield an identical segmentation of the two texts.

This is not to suggest that there is no constancy in the pause structure. In 1981, lines 1,3,13,14,15,17,18, and 19 are still marked by pronounced pauses. Moreover, the relative pacing of syllables with respect to pauses is the same in each case. Just as in 1975, in 1981 the initial and concluding portions are delivered at a relatively slower rate than is the middle, which again constitutes a kind of artistic peak, maximally parallelistic, with little interruption of the sound flow. Nevertheless, pause patterning does show considerable variation between tellings.

These observations cast a slightly different light on the Hymes-Tedlock debate (Hymes 1981, Tedlock 1983; cf. Woodbury 1985). Tedlock has proposed that pauses and other discourse pragmatic features are the principal sign vehicles for rhetorical structure. Hymes, in contrast, argues for the role of grammatical parallelisms. Given the materials at their disposal, the argument perforce focuses on discourse instances or tokens.

There are really no criteria for extracting rhetorical structure as a type, i.e., as a replicable patterning of the semantico-referential material. In the present case, however, because the semantico-referential material should be repeated verbatim in each telling, we have a method for determining just how constant are the discourse pragmatic features associated with it. Thus far, the evidence would seem to weigh against pause patterning as the basis of replicable rhetorical segmentation.

An examination of the narration of a distinct speaker, maximally removed in social terms from Nil, adds another dimension to the problem of continuity. In Wāñēkï's 1982 narration, while the semantic content is nearly identical to that in Nil's narration, the micro-parallelistic structure has all but broken down. The rhyme in lines 5 and 6 is still present, but in lines 7 and 8 it has been destroyed by the addition of the morpheme *hà* ("really") to the end of 7. The only remaining parallel between lines 7 and 8 is the final stress. Moreover, Wāñēkï has omitted what is Nil's (1975) line 9, a repetition of line 5. Consequently, there is here no 9-10 parallel. Lines 10 and 11 still parallel one another in terms of final stress, but they lack the global structure against which they could assume significance.

It is evident from the tape that Wāñēkï is a somewhat younger and more vigorous narrator than Nil. Indeed, his narrative style is an imitation of the tough, aggressive style traditionally used by mature men during the initial stages of inter-group encounters. His concern with this style seems to override his dedication to the almost delicate poetic structuring characteristic of Nil's narration.

There are other differences as well. In line 1, for example, Wāñēkï uses the expression *ti kòñka hà* instead of the expression *wāgyò*, employed by Nil. The term used by Wāñēkï, meaning "his relative," is apparently synonymous with the term used by Nil. However, *wāgyò* is considered to be an "ancient" form, one no longer used in everyday communication. It is confined to origin-myth telling. The expression used by Wāñēkï, on the other hand, is still current, and is considered to be less "ancient." One senses here the processes of unidirectional change through replacement at work.

The remaining textual differences are of the same order as those found between the two Nil tellings. For the most part, however, it is striking how closely Wāñēkï's and Nil's narratives parallel one another in morpheme by morpheme terms. There is a nearly perfect one-to-one mapping of lines between the two versions. Where there are differences, they generally involve only single morphemes, e.g., Wãñēkï's use of *ti* ("his") at the beginning of line 2, Nil's use of *hã* (focus) in lines 14 and 15, and so forth. Overall, from a semantic point of view, the texts are nearly identical. Where there is difference, it is a matter of pragmatics.

These similarities between instances provide evidence of a shared culture among the Shokleng, of continuity over space and time. Such evidence is, I believe, important to the Shokleng themselves. Through the replicability of the origin myth, they are able to glimpse the essence of cultural continuity itself, the reality of collective representations. By telling the origin myth -- a fixed, memorized form -- continuity is in effect performatively constituted. There is something concrete about precise replication that the mind is able to grasp.

However, the significance can easily go unnoticed, if there is no sign vehicle, no metacommentary, to bring it into intellectual focus. I propose that the macro-parallelism of the origin myth fulfills this function. It acts as a kind of sign vehicle or model of replication. It causes one to take note of the processes that resemble it. Those processes occur at two levels: (1) at the level of linguistic form, i.e., the morpheme by morpheme instantiation of the myth "type," and (2) at the level of the semantic meaning of the texts themselves, i.e., the purported reference to continuities among events occurring in the world.

Macro-parallelism

The B.2.1 excerpt is merely a fragment of the total origin myth. It requires between 38 seconds (Wãñēkï's 1982 version) and 60 seconds (Nil's 1981 version) to narrate, i.e., roughly 1.2 % of the total narration time. However, it is one building block of a larger macro-parallelistic structure. In fact, this fragment is repeated mutatis mutandis four times, and there are reduced echoes of it in two other parts of the origin myth as well.

The nature of macro-parallelism in the origin myth is something that requires further explication. What is involved is not simply repetition, but rather repetition with certain key semantic changes. In the case of the parallelism between B.2.1, B.2.2, and B.2.3, for example, the episodes are identical, except as regards the character who arrives. The variation in this area can be seen by examining line 1 in each of these versions. In B.2.1, reference is to the arrival of Zàgpope Patè, in B.2.2 to a relative of Zàgpope known as Zēzē, and in B.2.3 to another relative of Zàgpope known as Nūklèg Kïy.

From a semantic point of view, the different episodes linked together by macro-parallelism involve the same events. In each case, the character arrives, asks "what is all of this noise about," and is told about the making of the animal. He is in turn asked his name, and a request is made that he help paint the newly created animal. The differentiation between episodes, insofar as semantics is concerned, focuses solely upon the major participant.

There are other kinds of semantic difference between parallel units as well. For example, B.1.1 and B.2.1 involve the arrival of the same character, Zàgpope Patè. However, in B.1.1 the action centers on the making of the tapir, which was fashioned from *kàplug* wood. In B.2.1 the action centers on the making of the jaguar. This latter episode builds upon the former. When the main character is asked "what is all of this noise about," he refers first to the making of the tapir, mentioning the use of *kàplug* wood. However, he continues by noting that the animal made during the early episode did not call out properly, so he began making another animal, this time with araucaria pine wood. After this, the lines again proceed in perfectly parallel fashion.

From a formal point of view, the similarities between parallel episodes are marked by the use of the same words in the same syntactic arrangements. Here is formal replication, just as we find in two distinct tellings of the myth. However, the replication is internal to the narration itself. Moreover, the replication process involves by design some formal and semantic change.

A careful inspection of the transcriptions and tapes shows that, aside from changes present by design, the differences between parallel units are of the same kind as those between the analogous episodes in different tellings. Indeed, the variation is also of the same order, in quantitative terms. I have endeavored to measure this by means of a morpheme by morpheme comparison. The two episodes of the 1975 telling that are parallel with B.2.1, i.e., B.2.2 and B.2.3, show respectively a 20% and 10% variation with respect to B.2.1.[3] In comparison, Nil's 1981 B.2.1 and Wāñēkï's 1982 B.2.1 both show a roughly 15% variation with respect to Nil's 1975 B.2.1.

From the point of view of pragmatic features -- pause structure, intonation contour, and stress -- there is also variation between parallel episodes. However, significantly, the patterning responsible for the micro-parallelism described above (Section 2) remains in place for B.2.2 and B.2.3. There are only minor disruptions. Thus, in B.2.2 the phrase *kū kàgnāg* does not occur between lines 12 and 13, as it should, according to the pattern in B.2.1 and in other tellings -- both Nil 1981 and Wāñēkï 1982. One can sense the slight disruption in the rhythm of narration. In B.2.3, Nil includes the *kàgnāg* but fails to include the *kū*. Again, there is a slight but noticeable disruption of rhythm.

In other respects, however, the micro-parallelism remains intact, despite the differing lines that precede this poetic core. We find again the initial couplet with penultimate stress correlated with the tonal peak. It stands in contrast to the following couplet, which has final stress correlated with a tonal peak. This pattern is then repeated again, mutatis mutandis, in the next two couplets.

It is interesting to observe how these poetic structures build upon the micro-parallelism of B.1.1. Here there is an analogous rhymed couplet in lines 4 and 5, with penultimate primary stress, followed by a couplet with final primary stress in lines 6 and 7. However, this is the entire extent of the internal micro-parallelism. There is no subsequent repetion of this pattern. The overall comparison can be summed up in the following schema:

B.1.1   4=5 : 6=7

B.2.1   5=6: 7=8 :: 9=10 : 11=12

Thus, B.2.1 builds upon B.1.1 not only in terms of semantic incorportation, but as well in terms of a kind of poetic incorporation. The poetic structure of B.2.1 is an amplification of the structure in B.1.1.

This description gives us some idea of the nature of macro-parallelism, looked at up close. We are able to see how, from a formal point of view, macro-parallelism models the relations between distinct tellings. From a semantic point view, macro-parallelism describes the world in terms of a linear unfolding in which the events and situations at one point in time are comparable to and even identical with the events and situations occurring at some later point in time.   It is as if history regularly repeated itself. Of course, from the point of view of culture, history does indeed repeat itself, insofar as culture is transmitted across the generations. Situations and events are recreated generation after generation. Although the actors change, the patterns remain the same. Macro-parallelism in the Shokleng origin myth provides an icon of this kind of replicability. However, to fully understand the macro-parallelism, it is necessary to step back and behold the entire origin myth, seeing how an elaborate structure is built up from this internal repetition.

Global Structure

The Shokleng origin myth is a huge and complicated work of art.   It tells the story of humankind (i.e., the Shokleng) from the beginning of time -- the emergence of the earliest ancestors from beneath the earth -- to the historical period. Consequently, one can think of it as a kind of chronicle, and in some measure the narrative line follows an historical sequence.   The origin myth is a repository of the collective memory.

However, the myth is not simply a chronicle. In fact, there are four distinct myths that make up the *wāñēklèn* cycle, and each can be told independently. It is true that, when the myths are told together, they invariably follow a fixed order. However, each of the first three myths goes back to the "creation," to the earliest period of humankind, and traces events up to the historical period, i.e., roughly 150 years ago. These three form the core of the *wāñēklèn* cycle. Indeed, the last myth, which deals with comparatively recent events, is also the shortest myth and it is one that is not known by everyone. It seems not yet to have won a place as an accepted component of the cycle. The first three myths, however, are shared, and these tell independent, albeit parallel, stories of tribal history.

Each of these three myths shows an internal macro-parallelistic structure, of the sort described in the previous section. If we label each distinct episode with a capital letter, and indicate each parallelistic repetition by means of an attached number, the linear unfolding of the first *wāñēklèn* may be represented as follows:

A.1 A.2 A.3 B.1.1 B.2.1 B.2.2 B.2.3 C.1 C.2 C.3 C.4

This is the global macro-parallelistic structure of the first of the Shokleng origin myths.

Each of the episodes in this sequence has a semantically-describable coherence. The A episodes all deal with discovery of the world after the emergence. In each case, someone ascends, goes forth into the world to discover some aspect of it, e.g., grass or a kind of bird, and brings evidence of this discovery back with him to show the others. The B episodes, similarly, all involve the making of an animal, B.1 the tapir and B.2 the jaguar, as we have seen above. In C preparations are made for a great war among the Shokleng themselves. Each parallel episode describes the arrival of a new figure, who explains that he is mad because there are no women left to marry, and talks about how he is preparing for war.

Despite the semantic coherence of these episodes, it is important to note that the global structure emerges from local relations, viz., from formal macro-parallelisms such as were described above. In other words, the discourse structure is based upon the textual distributions of actual morphemes and syntactic arrangements of those morphemes. Global structure, in this sense, is an aspect of the discourse as a meaning-bearing sign vehicle.

This first origin myth is the basic one, and it is also the longest of the four, taking up 40.5% of the total narrative time or some 28.3 minutes in Nil's 1975 version. It is rivalled by the second myth, which takes up 37.3% of the narration or 26.1 minutes. In contrast, the third myth takes up only 14.6% of the total narration time or 10.2 minutes, and the last myth is a mere 7.6% of the total cycle or 5.3 minutes.

The second *wañēklèn* myth has its own global structure, distinct from that of the first myth, but related to it. If we continue with the representation of episodes by means of an alphabetic sequence, that structure may be formalized as follows:

D.1 D.2 D.3 D.4   E   F.1 F.2 F.3   G   C.1 C.2 C.3 C.4

The D episodes describe the arrival of different personages, shortly after the initial emergence, each of whom bestows some gift, e.g., a particular kind of fiber blanket or dance ornament. Importantly, episode E shows no internal macro-parallelism. It deals with a boy whose father died falling from a tree while trying to fetch fledgling birds for his son. The G episode similarly shows no internal macro-parallelism, dealing with an encounter with the Guaraní Indians. In F, there is a contest in which different persons test their skill at eluding arrows. The person in F.3 gets hit, terminating the sequence.

Finally, the last part of this myth is identical to the concluding set of episodes in the first two myths. By means of this sequence, the first two myths themselves are brought into parallel alignment. They begin differently, but they conclude with the same events, leading to the great war among the Shokleng and the dispersal of the bands, which is coupled with the entry of the historic Shokleng bands into the forest, i.e., their abandonment of the savannas. The global structure, built up from formal relations at the local level, thus extends across the individual myths that make up the cycle, giving shape to the entire *wañēklèn* sequence.

This inter-myth structuring is continued with the third component of the *wañēklèn* cycle, whose opening portions are parallel to, albeit not identical with, the opening parts of the first myth. Interestingly, both the second and third myths hark back to the first myth. However, they show no parallelism with one another. This would seem to confirm the prominence of this first myth within the cycle. The global structure of the third myth may be represented as follows:

A.4 H.1 H.2 B.3 B.4 I

The opening episode A is a discovery of the world episode, perfectly parallel to the beginning of myth I. The H episode concerns fire. Two times in succession the fire goes out at night, and the main character suffers the bites of mosquitoes. In each case, fire is later restored, in the first instance by the arrival of someone who possesses fire, in the second by the main character having mastered the art of making fire himself. B.3 and B.4 concern the making of animals -- a wild cat and a snake, respectively -- and these episodes run parallel to those in myth I. Finally, the concluding episode is again one with no internal macro-parallelism. It deals with the transformation of a man into a capibara.

The myth IV of the *wañēklèn* cycle shows, so far as I have been able to detect, no evidence of internal macro-parallelism. There are obvious ways in which this myth could be transformed and brought into alignment with the other three. However, it has presently all the earmarks of a recent addition to the *wãñēklèn* cycle. Moreover, the events it recounts seem to pick up where myths I and II left off.

I consider the non-parallelistic character of this myth, and of some episodes in myths II and III, to be significant. If we think of the problem of cultural continuity, it seems obvious that not all historical events can be seen as replicas of certain general "types," at least not initially. There is a kind of unilinearity or idiosyncrasy to history. This is especially true with respect to relatively recent events, which have not had time to undergo interpretation and assimilation into a larger scheme. The non-parallelistic portions of the myth capture this idiosyncrasy.

I consider it likely that the Shokleng origin myth itself grew by a process of historical accretion, as the forces of poetic ordering operated to shape the old materials into more refined poetic form. Simultaneously, new materials would have been added, as we may be witnessing in the case of myth IV. This new material would be gradually assimilated into the older structures. If so, then, in addition to reflecting the processes of cultural continuity and change, the Shokleng origin myth would also embody them.

In any case, the general macro-parallelistic structure of the entire cycle is layed out in Fig. 2. This is a rather remarkable structure, for we must remember that it has never been presented to the Shokleng themselves in this overt form. Instead, the structure is for them something that the mind comes to apprehend only gradually through innumerable tellings. Each of these tellings is a linear unfolding. The mind must pick out of these tellings the regularities -- the parallels -- and fit these regularities into a global structure.

This is not the kind of task that is within the intellectual competence of every native speaker. Indeed, there is good evidence for a kind of hierarchy of mastery. Some Shokleng men, even prior to the first peaceful contact with White Men in 1914, had failed to adequately memorize the myth, and were never able to perform it in the ceremonial sphere. Of those who did memorize it, there were differing degrees of certainty with which they had internalized the structures, and differing levels of appreciation for the art form itself. The two individuals whose narrations I have employed for this paper were clearly masters of the art form. Moreover, of these, Nil clearly had the highest level of appreciation.

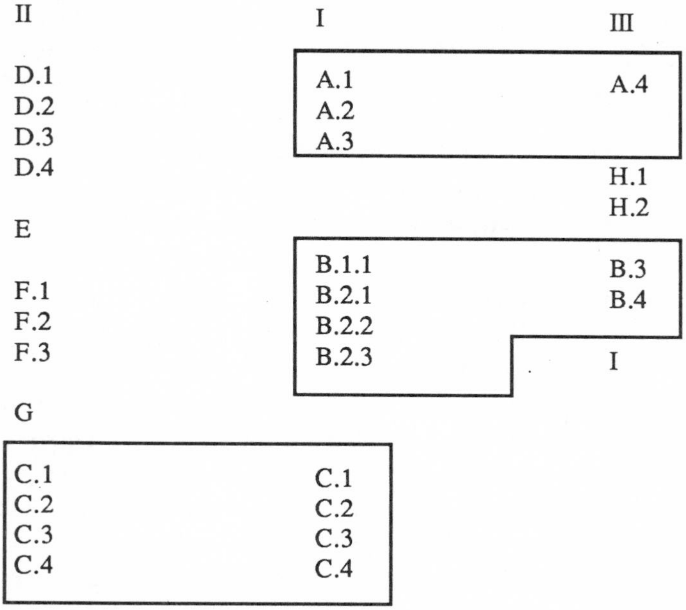

II	I	III
D.1	A.1	A.4
D.2	A.2	
D.3	A.3	
D.4		
		H.1
E		H.2
	B.1.1	B.3
F.1	B.2.1	B.4
F.2	B.2.2	
F.3	B.2.3	I
G		
C.1	C.1	
C.2	C.2	
C.3	C.3	
C.4	C.4	

Fig. 2: Global Structure of the Wãñēklèn

Nevertheless, even for those who are not capable of fully understanding it, the *wãñēklèn* exercises a kind of fascination. Hearers always know that they are in the presence of something important, something whose significance is linked to the overall significance of Shokleng culture.

Function

The question of what functions the macro-parallelistic structures fulfil can be addressed from an analytic point of view. This is what I attempt here, deferring questions of the native point of view on efficacy until the next section. From such a perspective, the following functions of macro-parallelism in the Shokleng origin myth may be proposed:

1. *Mnemonic function.* The macro-parallelistic structure can be seen as an aid to memory. In the Shokleng origin myth, there is ideally a fixed text, which must be memorized and repeated verbatim. Parallelism can facilitate this memorization process in two ways: (1) by furnishing clues as to the proper location of textual materials, i.e., by situating them within a global structure, and (2) by cutting down on the total amount of textual material that must be memorized -- obviously, the amount of repetition is inversely proportional to the amount of text that must be memorized. In this way, macro-parallelism functions as a semiotic device facilitating the processes that underlie textual replicability.

2. *Aesthetic function.* Macro-parallelism can also be construed as a device that focuses attention upon the origin myth as a sign vehicle. This is what Jakobson (1960: 356) has referred to as the "poetic function," i.e., the function of language whereby there is a "focus on the message for its own sake." The sign vehicle as object in itself becomes a source of fascination, apart from whatever semantic meaning it communicates.

This process is the result of sign vehicle-internal iconicity. A given fragment of the discourse becomes itself a sign vehicle standing for another fragment, with which it shares formal similarity. This second fragment then becomes in turn itself a sign vehicle formally similar to yet another fragment, and so forth, as the interpreter begins to discern the outlines of a global structure, itself the residue of a multiplicity of such semiotic recognitions. Through this process, there is generated a kind of fascination for the overall discourse as a sign vehicle itself.

Within the Shokleng origin myth, this global structure operates over a considerable stretch of discourse, forming a vast labyrinth into which the mind is inevitably drawn. One hearing produces recognition of certain parallels, but is insufficient for a thorough comprehension of the phenomenon. The interpreter is led to seek subsequent hearings, and from these begins to gradually discern the outlines of a global structure. The discovery of intricacy leads to a quest for new intricacies. A significant work of art is able to serve as a focus of fascination in this way. It continually draws attention to itself. In this regard, I believe that the Shokleng *wañēklèn* is a significant work of art.

3. *Metapragmatic function.* Another possible function of macro-parallelism resides in its ability to bring into question the nature of the

relationship between the meanings attached to the formally parallel units. Parallelism challenges the mind to compare these semantic meanings and to draw from this comparison some conclusion about the relationship. In the Shokleng case, the conclusion is invariably the same. Comparison leads to a recognition of similarity. Despite the unilinear unfolding of events, the narrative consists of repetitions of events of the same type.

Sometimes two events of the same type can have very different implications. For example, the events associated with A.1, A.2, and A.3 all have to do with discovery of the world. In A.1, a man goes forth and discovers the savanna, bringing with him upon his return a tuft of grass. The people look on admiringly and proclaim: "surely you are a chief; only a chief could have brought back such a wonderous and strange thing." In A.2, however, another man goes forth, but along the way he loses the path. He burns down a house and returns with the ashes, attempting to pass these off as his discovery, but his ruse is discovered. The people look on in scorn and proclaim: "surely you are not a man; that is why you burned down the house and brought back the ashes."

Nevertheless, the dominant theme of Shokleng macro-parallelism is similarity. The discourse line represents a unilinear unfolding, isomorphic with the unfolding of the story line. The parallels at the level of discourse point to the parallels at the story level, leading to an appreciation that the story is really an assemblage of replicable episodes. Each episode may be unique by virtue of the individual involved or some characteristic of the event. However, episodes are also similar. Events seem to repeat themselves. The formal parallelism is a device designed to bring out this similarity and to make it salient.

4. *Diagrammatic function.* All of the functions discussed thus far technically involve the iconic sign mode. However, in none of the above cases does macro-parallelism as a sign vehicle reach outside of the origin myth itself and convey information about the broader world of which origin-myth telling forms one part.

Yet, it can be readily appreciated that macro-parallelism, as discussed in some measure earlier, actually models the real-world processes of cultural continuity. The replication of units within the origin myth is an icon of the replication of the origin myth in its different instances or tellings. This latter process is the very stuff of which cultural continuity is made. Macro-parallelism can thus be seen as a "diagram" of the process of cultural continuity itself.

5. *Metaphorical function*. A special case of this iconic function is the "metaphorical function," which involves a similarity between the semantics of the *wãñēklèn* text and the real-world processes of cultural continuity. Insofar as formal macro-parallelism plays a metapragmatic role in relation to the interpretation of the semantic meaning of the text, it is implicated also in metaphorical connection between semantic meaning and the non-linguistic world. Formal parallels facilitate the comprehension of semantic parallels. Semantic parallels in turn model the real-world processes of cultural continuity.

6. *Numerical function*. A final possible function of macro-parallelism concerns the actual number of repetitions. The number itself may assume significance, as in the case of the sacred numbers reported for some North American tribes. In the Shokleng origin myth, there is a tendency for threefold repetition to dominate, although various aspects of twofold (e.g., the sequence B.1, B.2 in myth I) and fourfold (e.g., C.1-C.4 in myths I and II) repetition are found as well. There is no evidence that this corresponds with a sacred number.

However, it is of interest that Lévi-Strauss (1967a, 1967b) originally pointed to the problem of number as a social structural issue in central Brazil. He remarked that the moiety structures in many Gê societies suggested the operation of a binary cross-cousin marriage system. However, there were numerous pieces of contradictory evidence, and there was much to suggest the operation of ternary and quaternary structures, i.e., of a system of generalized exchange. It is just possible that the playing off of two's, three's, and four's in the Shokleng origin myth may be related to the social structural facts. This is an argument that requires further investigation. It cannot yet be supported for the Shokleng case.

Context

The consideration of function thus far has centered upon the possible analytical connections between parallelism as a sign vehicle and its object.

In most cases, we are dealing with iconicity, with the resemblance between the sign vehicle and its object, e.g., between repetition within a myth and distinct tellings of that same myth. Such a connection can be readily apprehended by an outside observer. However, the analytic connections are established in the absence of contextualizing ethnographic data. We have no idea from an examination of them alone precisely how they are fit into a scheme of ongoing social action. To determine this, we must pay attention to the context of use and to native perceptions of purposefulness.

Regarding context, some information has already been given above. The *wãñẽklèn* can be told around the campfire in ordinary narrative style. The two occasions on which it is actually performed are: (1) the *ãgyïn* ceremonies for the dead, and (2) the planned violation of a food taboo. Finally, aside from the contexts of telling and performing, there is the context in which the *wãñẽklèn* is actually taught.

The *ãgyïn* ceremony is a celebration of community, of social integration. Following the death of a spouse, a widow or widower is sent into seclusion for a period of some two weeks to one month. This seclusion is followed by a reintegration into the community, and it is in connection with this reintegration that the *ãgyïn* ceremony is held. The ceremony involves body painting, collective singing, and the drinking of mead. At its conclusion, mature men pair off in the center of the dance plaza and perform the *wãñẽklèn*.

For the Shokleng, death is a disruption, something that threatens the continuity and persistence of the community. Correspondingly, the *ãgyïn*, and the *wãñẽklèn* performance within it, is conceptualized as a method for re-establishing that community, for asserting continuity with the past. The origin myth is a mythical history, a history of the Shokleng people, but also of the community. The myth deals with the ancestors, those men who first emerged into this world, and who were the forefathers of the presentday Shokleng. To tell this myth is to bring the ancestors into the present, to assert the existence of a community with traditions, to bring about continuity with the past. This establishment of continuity may be considered the socially-defined purpose of origin-myth telling.

One will readily appreciate the similarity as regards food taboo violation. Violation of a taboo -- of a rule set down by the community -- is similarly a disruption of that community. In some instances, unfortunately, such a disruption is necessary, as when there is a scarcity of food. In such instances, the Shokleng who are about to violate the taboo perform the *wãñēklèn*. The performance makes it possible, or so I have heard Shokleng aver, to violate a taboo without suffering the inevitable consequences. We can readily appreciate this from the point of view of cultural rules. Performing the *wãñēklèn* reaffirms the community, together with its rules of conduct and ways of acting. It re-establishes continuity with the past, reasserts the behaviors that have been learned socially. The *wãñēklèn* has a perceived efficacy, and that efficacy has to do with cultural continuity.

Establishment of cultural continuity is evidently the purpose that the Shokleng themselves see in origin-myth telling as a form of social action. Their "awareness" of this purpose is strikingly confirmed in the fact that the *wãñēklèn* is actually taught.[4] Indeed, this myth is the only one among the Shokleng repertoire that is actively taught. The others are learned passively through the process of repeated hearing. In the case of the *wãñēklèn*, however, adolescent boys are taken aside and made to memorize the myth verbatim. Indeed, they memorize it on a syllable by syllable basis, repeating after the elder who functions as teacher. This process resembles and may have actually suggested to the Shokleng the dyadic performance style itself (Urban 1985b). In any case, the fact of teaching strikingly confirms the awareness Shokleng have of the role of this myth in cultural continuity.

From the analysis given above, it can be appreciated that the perceived purpose of origin-myth telling is not at all discordant with certain of the analytically isolated meanings of its constituent macro-parallelism. The metapragmatic, diagrammatic, and metaphoric functions all have to do in some way with cultural continuity. Formal macro-parallelism is the sign vehicle that makes salient, brings into intellectual focus, the very idea of continuity -- semantic continuity between episodes, continuity in the token replicability of the myth itself, and continuity within the encompassing culture for which the myth is a metaphor.

In this regard, it should be noted that origin-myth telling, at its lowest level of functionality, is not a sign vehicle standing for cultural continuity. At this level, where an individual repeats verbatim something that he himself has learned, origin-myth telling is an instance of cultural continuity. However, every instance of culturally learned behavior is also an instance of cultural continuity. In this respect, the origin myth is nothing special. What sets it apart from other cultural behavior is that, in its very design, the myth as discourse contains sign vehicles that point to its telling/performance as an instance of cultural continuity.

Through iconicity, macro-parallelism, as a design feature of origin myth telling, suggests to the mind that the instance of telling is simultaneously an instance of cultural continuity. Through the shaping of the discourse as a sign vehicle, a kind of "signal reflexivity" is created. The interpreter is given a clue -- indeed, numerous clues -- through the sign vehicle itself as to how that sign vehicle is to be interpreted. I believe that there is something significant in this fact.

It is possible to see how the purposeful character of origin-myth telling grows out of, or is shaped by, the very design characteristics of the discourse itself. Macro-parallelism, as a design feature of the origin myth, suggests an interpretation of that myth. It suggests to interpreters that the myth is "about" continuity. As a seeming consequence of this suggestion, the interpreters employ the myth within a system of ongoing social action in such a way that its imputed purpose is to actually establish continuity. Social purpose is linked to perceived meaning and perceived meaning is linked to discourse design.

The analysis of parallelism here suggests an amplification or refinement of Jakobson's (1960) original conception of the "poetic function." Parallelistic structures may focus attention upon the message, but they may also, through the mechanisms discussed earlier, comment upon the message, suggest how the latent possibilities for interpretation residing within the semantics are to be actualized. If this is so, then we can see the attention-getting function as only the lowest level of a more elaborate signal-reflexive functioning.

From a semiotic point of view, the attention-getting function is a basic indexical function. The parallelistic structure "points to" the discourse of which it forms part, but conveys no further information. If there were different types of parallel structure, pointing to different types of associated discourse, the index would convey information about genre or narrative type. Such a system does not appear to be operative in the Shokleng case. However, here parallelistic structures function also in the iconic sign mode. They can serve as a direct "diagram" of some aspect of the world, or they can operate through the metapragmatic function to some metaphorical relationship with the world. Whatever the type of connection, these formal parallelisms, grounded in relationships of similarity, suggest a search for similarities among those aspects of the world with which they are compared.

Analytically, we can think through the possible uses to which parallelism, as a signal-reflexive sign vehicle, can be put. However, it is clearly preferable to have empirical research in this regard. The question will remain open whether the hypothetical connections we imagine are actually realized in specific cultures. Moreover, even if we can establish certain semiotic functions through de-contextualized analyses of texts, we still need ethnographic data such as will show us the encompassing social purpose which motivates a particular analysis.

An understanding of the signal reflexive properties of parallelism, therefore, requires a close-up study of specific texts that have been (1) situated relative to their contexts of use and (2) illuminated from the point of view of a broader ethnographic understanding. In this regard, native South America provides an ideal laboratory. If the Shokleng data are any indication, we can expect to find here an incredible richness of parallelistic structuring, the semiotic functions of which are almost entirely unexplored. Moreover, it is still possible to collect the necessary materials in context, something that cannot be said for many other parts of the world. If we are to make any headway in the broader empirical endeavor -- an endeavor intimately linked to the theoretical issue of semiotic functioning and social purpose -- native South America would seem to be the logical focus for our research. The present paper constitutes one attempt to advance research along these lines.[5]

Appendix 1: Transcriptions and Translations

This appendix contains the transcriptions referred to in the paper, and their associated translations. The transcriptions are numbered according to the global structure (see Section 5) discussed there, i.e., B.1.1, B.2.1, B.2.2, B.2.3. In addition, I have indicated the particular telling in parentheses. Where there is no name included, the narrator is Nil. Thus, B.2.1 (1975) is Nil's narration of the B.2.1 episode in 1975. B.2.1 (Wãñēkï: 1982) indicates Wãñēkï's 1982 narration of episode B.2.1. For each of the three 1975 episodes that are parallel with B.1.1 (i.e., B.2.1, B.2.2, B.2.3), I have set off in italics those portions that are by design semantically distinctive from the preceding parallel episode. Other differences may be presumed to be the result of performance variation.

The translations are done on a line by line basis and correspond closely with the Shokleng texts themselves. I have indicated the change of speaker particle by the abbreviation "sp.ch."

B.1.1 (1975)

1 wãgyò tõ zàgpope tõ patè ēñ yo katèle
2   ne to agèlmēg wũ mũ ke mũ
3 iwo   ēñ cõ kõñgàg kale yògï mã
4   kũ ēñ cõ ēñ mãg yè
5   ēñ cõ kàplug kèg
6   kũ ēñ cõ ti làn ke
7   kũ kàgnãg
8   kũ tõ gèlmēg nē wã
9   kũ ã yïyï tē hãlike tē ke mũ
10   ēñ yïyï hã wũ zàgpope ke tē
11   ēñ yïyï hã wũ patè ke tē
12   ke mũ mò yè ēñ ñõ ēñ mãg làn yè kala ke mũ

B.2.1 (1975)

1 wãgyò tõ zàgpope tõ patè ēñ yo katèle
2 glè yò ki kala
3   kũ ne to agèlmēg wũ mũ ke mũ
4 iwo   ēñ cõ kõñgàg kale yògï mã
5   kũ ēñ cõ ēñ mãg yè
6   kàplug kèg
7   *mũlõ ti kï tũ*
8   *ēñ cõ wèg mũ*
9   *kũ ēñ cõ ēñ mãg yè*
10   *zàg tèy kèn*
11   kũ ēñ cõ ti làn ke
12   kũ kàgnãg
13   kũ tõ gèlmēg nē wã
14   kũ ã yïyï tē hãlike tē ke mũ
15 iwo   ēñ yïyï hã wũ zàgpope ke tē
16   ēñ yïyï hã wũ patè ke tē
17   ũ ke mò yè ēñ ñõ ēñ mãg làn yè kala ke mũ

B.1.1 (1975)

1   relative Zàgpope Patè arrived in front of me
2   "what is all of this noise about" he said
3   sp.ch.   "I hear the sound of many men coming
4   and so for my creation
5   I fashioned kàplug wood
6   and I painted it
7   and (I) erred
8   and that is what all the noise is about
9   and what would your name be" he said
10   "my name would be Zàgpope
11   my name would be Patè"
12   "well then come help me to paint my creation" he said

B.2.1 (1975)

1   relative Zàgpope Patè arrived in front of me
2   (he) arrived in the middle of the dance plaza
3   and "what is all of this noise about" he said
4   sp.ch.   "I hear the sound of many men coming
5   and so for my creation
6   (I) fashioned kàplug wood
7   *however he did not call out*
8   *I have seen*
9   *and so for my creation*
10   *(I) fashioned araucaria pine wood*
11   and I painted it
12   and (I) erred
13   and that is what all the noise is about
14   and what would your name be" he said
15 sp.ch.   "my name would be Zàgpope
16   my name would be Patè"
17   "well then come help me to paint my creation" he said

B.2.2 (1975)

1   wãgyò tõ zàgpope tõ patè *wãmõhà tõ zẽzẽ* ti no katèle
2   ne to agèlmẽg wũ mũ ke mũ
3   iwo   ẽñ cõ kõñgàg kale yògï mã
4   kũ ẽñ cõ ẽñ mãg yè
5   ẽñ cõ kõñgàg kòmãg nẽ hà we
6   kũ ẽñ cõ ẽñ mãg yè
7   kàplug kèg
8   mũlõ ti kï tũ
9   ẽñ cõ wèg mũ
10   ẽñ mãg yè
11   ẽñ cõ zàg tèy kèn
12   kũ ẽñ cõ ti làn ke
13   kũ cõ to gèlmẽg nẽ wã
14   kũ ã yïyï tẽ hãlike tẽ ke mũ
15   (ẽñ yïyï hã wũ zàgpope ke tẽ (throat clear))
16   iwo   ẽñ yïyï hã wũ *zẽzẽ* ke tẽ
17   hà we kũ nũ ti mõ
18   ũ ke mò mã ẽñ ñõ ẽñ mãg làn yè kala ke mũ

B.2.3 (1975)

1   wãgyò tõ zàgpope tõ patè wãmõhà tõ *nũklèg tõ kïy* ti no
         katèle
2   ne to agèlmẽg wũ mũ ke mũ
3   iwo   ẽñ cõ ẽñ mãg yè
4   ẽñ cõ kõñgàg kale yògï mã
5   ẽñ mãg yè
6   kàplug kèg
7   mũlõ ti kï tũ
8   ẽñ cõ wèg mũ
9   kũ ẽñ mãg yè
10   ẽñ cõ zàg tèy kèn

B.2.2 (1975)

1	relative Zàgpope Patè's *companion Zēzē* arrived in front of him
2	"what is all of this noise about" he said
3	sp.ch.	"I hear the sound of many men coming
4	and so for my creation
5	I truly fear the men
6	and so for my creation
7	(I) fashioned kàplug wood
8	however he did not call out
9	I have seen
10	for my creation
11	I fashioned araucaria pine wood
12	and I painted it
13	and that is what all the noise is about
14	and what would your name be" he said
15	("my name would be Zàgpope (throat clear))
16	sp. ch.	my name would be *Zēzē* "
17	truly it is and I (said) to him
18	"well then you come help me to paint my creation" I said

B.2.3 (1975)

1	relative zàgpope patè's companion *Nūklèg Kïy* arrived in front of him
2	"what is all of this noise about" he said
3	sp.ch.	"I for my creation
4	I hear the sound of many men coming
5	for my creation
6	(I) fashioned kàplug wood
7	however he did not call out
8	I have seen
9	and so for my creation
10	I fashioned araucaria pine wood

11   kū ēñ cō ti làn ke
12   kàgnāg
13   kū tō gèlmēg nē wā
14   kū ā yïyï tē hālike tē ke mū
15   ēñ yïyï hā wū *nūklèg* ke tē
16   ēñ yïyï hā wū *kïy* ke tē
17   ū ke ēñ māg làn yè kala ke mū

B.2.1 (1981)

1   wāgyò tō zàgpope tō patè no katèle
2   kū yi tā wū
3   ne to agèlmēg wū mū ke mū
4   iwo   ēñ cō ēñ māg yè
5   kōñgàg kale yògï mā
6   kū ēñ cō ēñ māg yè
7   kàplug kèg
8   mūlō ti kï tū
9   ēñ cō wèg mū
10 kū ēñ cō ēñ māg yè
11   ēñ cō zàg tèy kèn
12 kū ēñ cō ti làn ke
13 kū kàgnāg
14 kū tō gèlmēg nē wā
15   ā yïyï tē hālike tē ke mū
16   ēñ yïyï hā wū zàgpope ke tē
17   ēñ yïyï hā wū patè ke tē ke mū
18 (tō pata tō   patè tō yugug pènū hā wā)
19 kū tā ke mò mā ēñ ñō ēñ māg làn yè kala ke mū

11   and I painted it
12   and erred
13   and that is what all the noise is about
14   and what would your name be" he said
15   "my name would be *Nūklèg*
16   my name would be *Kïy* "
17   "well come help me to paint my creation" he said

B.2.1 (1981)

1   relative Zàgpope Patè arrived in front
2   and it is said he said
3   "what is all of this noise about" he said
4   sp.ch. "I for my creation
5   (I) hear the sound of many men coming
6   and so for my creation
7   (I) fashioned kàplug wood
8   however he did not call out
9   I have seen
10   and so for my creation
11   I fashioned araucaria pine wood
12   and I painted it
13   and erred
14   and that is what all the noise is about
15   what would your name be" he said
16   "my name would be Zàgpope
17   my name would be Patè" he said
18   (pata   patè who shot the falcon)
19   and he said "well then come help me to paint my creation"
              he said

B.2.1 (Wāñēkï: 1982)

1   ti kõñka hà tõ zàgpope ti no katèle
2   ti glè yò ki kala
3   ne to agèlmēg wũ mũ ke mũ yi tã
4   iwo   ēñ cõ kõñgàg kale yògï mã
5   kũ ēñ mãg yè
6   kàplug kèg
7   mũlõ ti kï tũ hà
8   ēñ cõ wèg mũ
9   kũ ēñ cõ zàg tèy kèn
10   kũ ēñ cõ ti làn ke
11   kũ kàgnãg
12   kũ tõ gèlmēg nē wã
13   ke tã ti mõ mũ
14   ã yïyï tē hãlike tē
15   ēñ yïyï hã wũ zàgpope ke tē
16   ēñ yïyï hã wũ patè ke tē
17   ke ñãg hà we kũ yi tã
18   ũ ke mò ēñ ñõ ēñ mãg làn yè kala ke mũ

B.2.1 (Wãñēkï: 1982)

1   kinsman Zàgpope arrived in front of him
2   (he) arrived in the middle of his dance plaza
3   "what is all of this noise about" he said it is said
4   sp.ch.   "I hear the sound of many men coming
5   and so for my creation
6   (I) fashioned kàplug wood
7   however he really did not call out
8   I have seen
9   and so I fashioned araucaria pine wood
10   and I painted it
11   and erred
12   and that is what all the noise is about"
13   he said to him
14   "what would your name be"
15   "my name would be Zàgpope
16   my name would be Patè"
17   thus it truly was it is said
18   "well then come help me to paint my creation" he said

Appendix 2:   Pause Structure

This appendix contains transcriptions with lines based on pause segmentation. I compare the pause structure for two parallel episodes within the same telling (B.2.1 (1975) and B.2.3 (1975)), and for three distinct tellings of the same episode (B.2.1 (1975) versus B.2.1 (1981) versus B.2.1 (Wãñēkï 1982)). Pause lengths have been determined by the measurement of tape and are indicated in seconds inside of square brackets at the end of lines. The length of lines excluding line final pauses is given in parentheses at the end of lines. I have recorded all pauses of 0.4 seconds or greater. However, line cutoffs were arbitrarily established at pause junctures of 1.0 seconds or greater. This somewhat skews the segmentation of B.2.1 (Wãñēkï 1982), which is a faster-paced narration with correspondingly shorter pauses. However, I have noted all pauses of less than 1.0 second that occur within lines, so that the reader can experiment with different segmentations.

B.2.1 (1975)

1	wãgyò tō zàgpope tō patè	[p=1.6]	(2.9)
2	ēñ yo katèle	[p=1.1]	(1.6)
3	glè yò ki kala kū	[p=1.3]	(2.5)
4	ne to agèlmēg wū mū ke mū	[p=2.4]	(2.4)
5	iwo	[p=1.5]	(0.6)
6	ēñ cō kōñgàg kale yògï mã kū ēñ cō	[p=1.0]	(3.0)
7	ēñ mãg yè kàplug kèg mūlō		
	ti kï tū ēñ cō wèg mū kū ēñ cō [p=.7]		
	ēñ mãg yè zàg tèy kè kū ēñ cō		
	ti làn ke kū kàgnãg kū tō		
	gèlmēg nē wã	[p=1.3]	(10.1)
8	kū ã yïyï tē hālike tē ke mū	[p=1.4]	(2.6)
9	iwo	[p=1.7]	(0.6)
10	ēñ yïyï hã wū zàgpope ke tē	[p=1.0]	(2.8)
11	ēñ yïyï hã wū patè ke tē	[p=1.7]	(1.7)
12	ū ke mò yè ēñ ñō ēñ mãg làn yè		
	kala ke mū		(3.0)

16.0   (33.8)

49.8 sec.

B.2.3 (1975)

1   wāgyò tō [p=0.8] zàgpope [p=0.4] tō
     patè wāmō tō nūklèg tō kïy ti no katèle   [p=2.7]   (8.2)
2   ne to agèlmēg wū mū ke mū   [p=2.0]   (2.6)
3   iwo   [p=1.6]   (0.6)
4   ēñ cō ēñ māg yè ēñ cō   [p=1.5]   (1.8)
5   kōñgàg kale yògï mā [p=0.6] ēñ māg yè
     kàplug kèg mūlō ti kï tū ēñ cō wèg mū kū
                                                    [p=1.0]   (6.4)
6   ēñ māg yè ēñ cō   [p=1.1]   (1.2)
7   zàg tèy kèn kū ēñ cō ti làn ke kàgnāg
     kū tō gèlmēg nē wā   [p=2.8]   (4.7)
8   kū ā yïyï tē hālike tē ke mū   [p=1.1]   (2.4)
9   ēñ yïyï hā wū nūklèg ke tē [p=.4] ēñ yïyï hā
     wū kïy ke tē   [p=3.0]   (4.9)
10 ū ke ēñ māg làn yè kala ke mū   (2.5)

                                                    16.8   (35.3)

                                                    52.1 sec.

B.2.1 (1981)

1	wãgyò tõ zàgpope tõ patè [p=.5] no katèle	[p=3.0]	(4.9)
2	kū yi tã mū ne to agèlmēg wū mū ke mū	[p=2.4]	(3.6)
3	iwo	[p=1.5]	(0.9)
4	ēñ cõ ēñ mãg yè kõñgàg kale yògï mã		
	kū ēñ cõ ēñ mãg yè kàplug kèg mūlõ	[p=1.5]	(6.1)
5	ti kï tū ēñ cõ wèg mū kū ēñ cõ ēñ mãg yè		
	ēñ cõ zàg tèy kèn kū ēñ cõ ti làn ke		
	kū kàgnãg [p=0.5] kū tõ gèlmēg nē wã	[p=2.9]	(9.4)
6	ã yïyï tē hãlike tē ke mū	[p=2.1]	(2.6)
7	ēñ yïyï hã wū [p=0.8] zàgpope ke tē	[p=0.3]	
	ēñ yïyï hã wū [p=0.5] patè ke tē ke mū	[p=1.1]	(7.7)
8	(tõ pata tõ	[p=1.4]	(1.1)
9	patè tõ yugug pènū hã wã)	[p=1.5]	(2.2)
10	kū tã [p=0.7] ke mò mã ēñ ñõ ēñ mãg làn yè		
	kala ke mū		(3.9)

_____

17.7   42.4

_____

60.1 sec.

B.2.1 (Wãñēkï: 1982)

1	ti kõñka hà tõ zàgpope ti no katèle ti glè		
	yò ki kala	[p=1.6]	(3.9)
2	ne to agèlmēg wũ mũ	[p=1.5]	(1.6)
3	ke mũ yi tã iwo	[p=2.2]	(1.3)
4	ēñ cõ kõñgàg kale yògï mã kũ ēñ mãg yè		
	kàplug kèg mũlõ ti kï tũ hà ēñ cõ wèg mũ		
	kũ ēñ cõ [p=0.7] zàg tèy kèn kũ ēñ cõ		
	ti làn ke kũ kàgnãg kũ tõ gèlmēg nē wã	[p=2.7]	(11.5)
5	ke tã ti mõ mũ [p=0.9] ã yïyï tē hãlike tē		
	ēñ yïyï wũ zàgpope ke tē		
	ēñ yïyï wũ [p=0.6] patè ke tē [p=0.9]		
	ke ñãg hà we kũ yi tã [p=0.9] ũ ke mò ēñ		
	ñõ ēñ mãg làn yè kala ke mũ		(12.4)

8.0	30.7

38.7 sec.

Notes

1. According to Jakobson (1980: 23), "'parallelism' as a characteristic feature of all artifice is the referral of a semiotic fact to an equivalent fact inside the same context, including the case where the aim of the referral is only an elliptic implication." This is the general definition I employ here. Indeed, the present work has been considerably influenced by Jakobson's poetics (1960, 1966, 1968, cf. Fox 1977). Nevertheless, I have not fully subscribed to his view that "artifice," based upon parallelism, as a sign mode "is to be added to the triad of semiotic modes [i.e., icon, index, and symbol] established by Peirce" (Jakobson 1980: 22). Instead, I view parallelism as a unique clustering of iconic and indexical functioning, as will become apparent subsequently.

2. Nil -- pronounced [ndíli] -- was probably around 80 years old in 1975. He was married and had one child at the time of the first peaceful contact with White Men in 1914. To my great sadness, he died in 1983, reportedly in the throws of visions of animal spirits (see Urban 1985a).

3. Variation was calculated by taking one variant as the base and seeing how the other compared with it. There are roughly 100 morphemes in each episode. If the variant lacked a morpheme that was found in the base, or if it had a morpheme not found there, that was counted as one morphemic variation. The morphemes had also to be in the same structural position within the text. If the two versions were maximally different, therefore, they could exhibit a theoretical maximum of 200 morphemic variations. In fact, the versions here generally exhibit between 20 and 40 such variations.

4. Actually, by 1975 the *wāñēklèn* was no longer being actively taught, except in a few sporadic cases. It is likely that the form will disappear altogether as a performance style by the end of this decade.

5. The research on which this paper is based was assisted by grants from the Doherty Foundation Program in Latin American Studies, the Committee on Latin America and the Caribbean of the Social Science Research Council, the University Research Institute of the University of Texas at Austin, and the Institute of Latin American Studies of the

University of Texas at Austin with funds from the Mellon Foundation. I gratefully acknowledge the help of these institutions. I would also like to thank Des Derbyshire, Dell Hymes, Joel Sherzer, and Michael Silverstein for their helpful comments on earlier drafts of this paper.

References

Fox, James J.
1977   Roman Jakobson and the comparative study of parallelism. In *Roman Jakobson: echoes of his scholarship* , D. Armstrong and C.H. van Schooneveld (eds.), pp. 59-90. Lisse: Peter de Ridder.

Hymes, Dell
1981   *"In vain I tried to tell you": essays in Native American ethnopoetics*. Philadelphia: University of Pennsylvania Press.

Lévi-Strauss, Claude
1967a [1956] Do dual organizations exist? In *Structural anthropology*, C. Jacobson and B.G. Schoepf (trans.), pp.116-127. Garden City, New York: Anchor.
1967b [1952] The social structures of central and eastern Brazil. In *Structural anthropology*, C. Jacobson and B.G. Schoepf (trans.), pp.116-127. Garden City, New York: Anchor.

Jakobson, Roman
1960   Concluding statement: linguistics and poetics. In *Style in language,* T.A. Sebeok (ed.), pp. 350-377. Cambridge: M.I.T. Press.
1966   Grammatical parallelism and its Russian facet. *Language* 42: 399-429.
1968   Poetry of grammar and grammar of poetry. *Lingua* 21: 597-609.
1980   *The framework of language.* Ann Arbor: Michigan Studies in the Humanities, no. 1.

Tedlock, Dennis
1983   *The spoken word and the work of interpretation.* Philadelphia: University of Pennsylvania Press.

Urban, Greg
  1985a   Nil do Macuco. *Revista do Museu Paulista* 27/28: 445-446.
  1985b   The semiotics of two speech styles in Shokleng. In *Semiotic mediation: sociocultural and psychological perspectives*, E. Mertz and R. J. Parmentier (eds.), pp. 311-329. New York: Academic Press.
Woodbury, Anthony
  1985   The functions of rhetorical structure: a study of central Alaskan Yupik Eskimo discourse. *Language in Society* 14: 153-190.

Oratory Is Spoken, Myth Is Told, and Song Is Sung, But They Are All Music to My Ears

Anthony Seeger

The separation of the various disciplines that deal with vocal and verbal art has had a disastrous effect on the development of our thinking about them. Not only have linguistics, musicology, and studies of oral literature developed separately, they each have their own journals, their own professionals, and they rarely communicate among themselves. Since research usually begins from the perspective of an academic discipline rather than from the speech/music event itself, it is often difficult to reconstruct the original from the analyses of it. Linguists typically ignore the features of oral style that are not grammatical or syntactic, literary scholars ignore the linguistic; and while ethnomusicologists spend years analyzing sound structures, they usually do so in isolation. The failure to recognize the interrelationship of verbal and musical genres and the importance of the way they are used can result in a dry formalism that reifies the text, performance, or melody and does not account for the richness and use of verbal art forms.

My systematic consideration of the genres discussed in this paper started from an inability to distinguish between what the Suyá Indians of Mato Grosso, Brazil, glossed as "song" and what they glossed as "telling." Some examples of their speech seemed more "musical" in the traditional western sense of tonal structuring than examples of song, yet they insisted that those performances were not song. The only satisfactory approach was to consider the verbal genres together, and analyze some of the interrelationships among the genres as a preliminary to further research on the songs themselves - to which the Suyá attach tremendous importance. This paper presents some of the results of my attempt to relate song to the other forms of verbal performance.

The paper is divided into two parts. In the first part, the major genres of Suyá verbal performance are presented and compared. This section examines the similarities and differences among the genres with respect to textual fixity, the alteration of speech, phrasing, timbre, and tone. In the second part, a single example of one of those forms - a curing song - is translated and analyzed.[1] The brevity of the curing songs permits a presentation of an entire performance; certain anomalies in the structure and performance of the songs provide particular challenges to the scheme developed in the first half of the paper. Short examples of each of the verbal forms are provided on the accompanying tape.[2]

The Suyá are a part of the Northern branch of the Gê linguistic group. The Northern Gê traditionally occupied a large area in what are now the Brazilian states of Maranhão, Pará, Mato Grosso, and Goiás, and share many features of social organization and language. The Suyá are probably most closely related to the Apinayé and Kayapo, although in some ways their social organization more closely resembles that of the Eastern Timbira groups. They live in a single village of approximately 130 members in the Parque Nacional do Xingu. During the last 150 years they interacted frequently with the native societies in the Upper Xingu, adopting many material and symbolic forms from them. Extensive discussions of Suyá social organization and some of their symbolic forms have already appeared, and it is unnecessary to discuss them here.[3]

kapérni, iarén, ngére

There are three nouns (and, a slightly different form, verbs) that are central to an understanding of the way Suyá formulate different genres. These are *kapérni, iarén, and ngére. kapérni* I translate as speech, and to speak. It is modified by a number of other words which describe kinds of speech, e.g. "plaza speech," "bad speech," and "angry speech." Speech itself is contrasted with *iarén*, which I would translate as "to tell." A form of *kapérni* is never a *iarén*. As with the *kapérni*, there are various kinds of *iarén*. *iarén* forms include everything from formal exhortations to children to recitative solos in public ceremonies to myths. The third major term is *ngére*, which the Suyá translate as music (the Portuguese term "*música*"), but which in their case is entirely song. There are many different genres of *ngére*, associated with specific singing styles and also with specific ceremonies. Some of the different forms are listed below. Examples of *kapérni, iarén* , and *ngére* may also be heard on the accompanying tape (examples 1 - 5).

Some Suyá Vocal Genres

1. *kapérni* refers to speech of all kinds.   There are a number of specifically named forms of speech, among them the following:

   1.1 *kapérni* ("speech") at the most general level refers to everyday speech forms, spoken by men, women, and children.   In *kapérni* there is little formality, and phrases are of variable length . Example one is a short excerpt from an interview with three men discussing a ritual.

   1.2 *kapérni kasaga* ("bad speech") refers to the jealous speech of witches and selfish people.   It is a private, rather than a public form, without a particular structure, hour, or place of performance.   It is probably more talked about than spoken.

   1.3. *Grútnen kapérni* ("angry speech") refers to public speech made by any man (old or young) who is angry and chooses to use it to make his feelings known publicly. It is only spoken by men.   When men perform in the plaza they usually walk in a circle carrying a weapon. It is a style characterized by short, rapidly spoken phrases and abrupt tone contours.

   1.4. *kapérni kahr ĩdo* ("slow speech") refers to the exhortative speech of any older adult man addressing the entire village from the village plaza.   "Slow speech" contrasts with "angry speech" in the slow delivery of the phrases and the intonation.   It is hard to distinguish from the "everybody listens speech" except that more men may use it. Example 2 is an excerpt of "slow speech" spoken by Peti.

1.5. *Mē mbai hwa kapérni* ("everybody listens speech") is highly structured public speech, with long phrases and cadences. It is said to be spoken by political and ceremonial leaders, and exhorts the community to behave "correctly."

2. *iarén* is "to tell," "to relate," or "to instruct." It is often used in the sense of a parent instructing a child, or reporting on an entire, concluded, event. There are various levels of formality which are given below.

2.1. *iarén* of an unspecified sort usually refers to a kind of instruction. A father tells a child how to behave; a man relates the events of a fishing expedition; or a mouse (in a myth) gives instructions regarding the cooking of maize. There is no specific time or place for these events, and the phonetics and grammar are usually that of everyday speech.

2.2. *Mētumji iarén* ("What the old people tell") refers to narratives we would call myths. They are stories with clear narrative coherence (plot), but only a moderately predetermined performance style, which varies by the age of the man, woman, or child telling it, and the nature of the audience. Anecdotes about more recent events are not called by this term. They are often performed in a question and answer form in the houses or in the village plaza, but without restrictions as to time and place. Example 3 is an excerpt from the myth of the origin of maize, told by Mbeni, an elderly woman considered to be an excellent performer.

2.3. *Huru iarén, ngatu iarén, gaiyi iarén* refer to recitative-like addresses in ceremonies in which certain members of the village are publicly instructed to take certain ritual steps with respect to gardens, boys, or girls in specific ceremonies. All of these are performed by men (usually recently initiated) in the village plaza.

3. *ngére* refers to music, especially song, of any type. They have textual fixity and a similar overall structure of textual presentation, but there are quite a few different genres of song.

   3.1. *Akia* ("shout song") refers to individual shout songs sung only by boys and adult men until they have several grandchildren. Example 4 is a single verse of an adult *akia* sung by Uetagu.

   3.2. *ngére* ("song") refers to songs sung usually in a lower register, and often in unison. The singers may be men, women, boys, girls, and the aged together or as separate groups. Some are sung by certain moieties. There are quite a number of variations in song style. The songs from different ceremonies are known by the name of that ceremony, e.g. "deer song," "wild pig song," and "turtle song." Example 5 is a verse from a "turtle song" sung by the adult men of the Suyá community.

4. *Sangére* ("curing song") is a quietly recited form with a song-like structure which is performed over patients by adults of either sex in a number of different locations - although usually not in the plaza. Example 6 is a curing song to relieve fever and convulsions in a child. It is sung by Robndo; example 7 is the same song at a slower speed.

5. *Ngwa Iangraw* ("burity log invocation") is a kind of recitative which is spoken quietly at the head of a log racing track in order to make the heavy burity logs "light" and to keep them from injuring the runners. It has a song-like structure, and is performed by the ritual specialist.

There are a number of ways these three distinct verbal forms can be contrasted. Among the most important of these are the relative fixity of the texts, the alteration of speech, phrasing, voice quality or timbre, and the use of tonal structures.

Textual Fixity

The three forms differ quite markedly in the degree to which their texts are considered by the Suyá to be fixed.

kapérni is not fixed in terms of its content. Everyday speech can obviously serve as a vehicle for everything the Suyá discuss. While not everything is considered fit for public speech, the speaker has quite a lot of latitude in his presentation, even in the more formal public speech forms. He or she is not simply repeating the text of a previous speaker. Compared with the *iarén* and the *ngére*, the texts of even the most formal *kapérni* are quite variable.

The *iarén*, which includes certain formal exhortations, myths, and recitatives, appears to be relatively more fixed. The performer knows the entire *iarèn* as a unit before he or she starts. So, too, does most of the audience. The performer adjusts the performance to the particular situation - in myths it is the audience, in exhortations the specific attributes of the person being exhorted, and in recitatives according to the particular people addressed - but the general form is known by everyone and can be judged by the audience as a complete entity in a way a performance of *kapérni* cannot.

The *ngére* texts are entirely fixed, and they are all learned from animals or plants. They tend to be quite short, dense, and should be performed identically every time. In this case there is a clear source for the entire text. While some *iarén* also have a non-human origin, the precise performance varies according to the circumstance. The performance of a *ngére* text is said by the Suyá to be entirely fixed.

Alteration of Speech

kapérni are all spoken in what could be called "everday language" in the sense that they generally conform to modern usage. The more formal types of speech do employ some rhetorical forms rarely heard in everyday conversation, but phonetically they are all examples of "modern" Suyá. One could think of the relationship of the formal speeches to everday speech as similar to that between a presidential candidate's speech and kitchen conversation in our own culture - while they differ stylistically, they are phonetically similar.

iarén sometimes use archaic forms of certain words, and occasionally require interpretation for younger audiences unfamiliar with the content. The similarity here might be with the King James version of the Bible. The speech has its unusual phonetic and semantic features, but it clearly adheres to the same patterns of grammar and expression as everyday speech. The performances do not insert additional syllables in common words. Instead, syllables are sometimes drawn out, glissando is frequent, and the pitch of the voice is very important.

ngére present a rich complexity of linguistic alterations. While text and melody have a simultaneous origin (in the initial "composition"), the melody of the song clearly dictates the way language is employed in it. Each note in a melodic line has a syllable, and there are specific "song syllables" which can be inserted into the words. Many song words are pronounced in a way that is now archaic but which is similar to pronunciations recorded in Karl von den Steinen's 1886 word list (Steinen 1942) and to the way the Western Suyá (known as the Tapayuna or Beiços de Pau) still pronounce them. The song syllables and phonetic alterations make the songs somewhat hard to understand. There is, however, a fairly consistent system which, once it is learned, makes it relatively easy to understand recently composed songs. This is similar to understanding that Ha-le-lu-u-u-u-u-u-u-u-u-u-ia means Haleluia.

Song texts are also symbolically dense, with opaque meanings. Songs the Suyá say are quite old may escape interpretation altogether. The Suyá often say that only the beings that taught the song to the Suyá originally knew what it meant (and it is hard to get translations from jaguars, extinct enemies that lived under the earth, bees, and birds). For the

Suyá it is enough that they are singing the songs as they say they were taught - whether in an archaic language, in an inexplicable form, or, when the composition is recent, in complete clarity.   This is not unlike Americans participating in a Latin Mass or a service in Hebrew.   The apparent indifference of the Suyá to the semantic meaning of their songs is especially striking in the songs they have learned from other Indian and non-Indian societies.   They know songs in at least eight languages - three from groups now extinct - and sing them in the original language, whether it be Iaruma or English.   They consider themselves to be the true tradition bearers for certain Upper Xingu ceremonies.[4]   It does not seem to bother them at all that they do not understand the words of the foreign songs.   The Suyá can often give a gloss on what they are singing in the unknown language, but they are not concerned with the specific referents of the words or details of the text.   It is enough to get them inserted correctly into the musical line and to sing them with the correct timbre and associated with the correct movements.

The differences between the three genres with respect to their language, then, can be summarized as going from completely modern, unaltered forms to fairly archaic forms and even foreign languages which are performed according to dictates of melody, rhythm, and movement.

Phrasing

The structuring of time is different in the different genres.   One of the most obvious temporal structures is phrasing.   In addition, songs have smaller units dictated by their internal structure and the dance that accompanies them.

As the different forms of *kapérni* get more and more public and formal, their phrases become more and more regular in the temporal sense. This is especially clear in the oratory, where the thumping of a club (or the slapping of the arm against the trunk in the case of the Western Suyá) provides a kind of percussion accompaniment.   The phrases are extremely long, compared to everyday speech, and are what we might call melodic. Subject changes are also marked by a long syllable held on a single note (in music, a *fermata*).

The *iarén* can also be internally differentiated with respect to the way time is structured. When a myth is told by a good teller, there are also long, carefully constructed phrases. This is less clear in performances by less experienced tellers. When a soloist is performing a public ceremonial recitative, the phrases are fixed and extremely melodic. The rhythm is what we would call musical: the relationships among the time values for each syllable are very regular.[5]

Within the *ngére* genre there is not much variation among the styles in terms of their overall structure. Each structure is timed in ways that we call musical. Phraseology is determined by the melody and by dance, rather than by the words. Tempo is one of the distinguishing features among songs - some are considered to be "slow" and others "fast." In certain ceremonies slower songs are sung by one moiety, and faster ones by the other. The internal time is quite clearly established and maintained by a song leader, and sudden changes in tempo are signs of arrivals at a new part of the song structure (Seeger 1980a).

Timbre

Timbre is a word used in music to indicate sound quality. It is a difficult concept for western musicologists to work with, as so much of our musicology is based on structures of harmony and rhythm. Ethnomusicologists have recognized the importance of timbre but have not done extensive work with it, partly because it is so difficult to describe.

Voice quality is not commented upon much in performances of *kapérni* and *iarén* (where knowledge is usually stressed), but it is very important in Suyá evaluations of *ngére*. Discussions of the aesthetics of song involve descriptions of the singer's throat. Singers are described as having "good throats" when they sing loudly and well, "big throats" when they sing with a full, rich, sound at a relatively low pitch, "small throats" when they sing high and with a tense voice. These qualities are discussed during ceremonies, and when the Suyá listen to tapes.

Timbre is, therefore, a very important part of Suyá singing, but is not discussed in performances of the other genres, where content is much more often discussed rather than performance style.

Tone

Since the western conception of music is predominantly harmonic and melodic, tone is often taken to be the distinguishing feature of music. Of all the features examined so far, tone is the least useful for distinguishing among Suyá genres. Suyá is not a tonal language, but no speech act is without pitch change. The recitative (*ngatu iarén*) is in some ways more melodic than many of the songs (*ngére*). But, according to the Suyá, the *iarén* is not song (*ngére*). Nor are myths music, although when musical texts are sung in the course of telling a myth there can be songs within myths. Within a given genre, distinctions according to tone may be useful.

There are some differences in the use of tone in the different genres. Tone is extremely important to a person performing a myth. Many myths are practically entirely in dialogue form. Without the use of tone and timbre it would be virtually impossible to follow them. Tone is also used by speakers who wish to insert drama into their speech. But tone is a question of style in those forms, not a question of essence the way it is for a song. A speech or myth without tone would be a badly performed speech. But a recitative or song without tone would be incorrect. Even this distinction between essential tonality and competence tonality does not distinguish the Suyá genres, however. It places some *iarén* together with all of the *ngére*, rather than distinguishing them.[6]

All the genres structure time, tone, text, and timbre in a way that is "musical." The "musical" features of most oral genres have consistently been ignored, however. Regardless of whether the Suyá are making political speeches, telling an animated version of a myth, or singing a song, the sounds are "music to my ears." The ethnomusicological perspective on verbal arts is that the structures of time, tone, and timbre must not be ignored. We must not strip the world's verbal forms of their sounds if we are to come to any appreciation of the nature of verbal art itself.[7]

Summary of Suyá Genres

All three of the verbal genres discussed structure phonetics, time, tone, and timbre and also have semantic content. But the degree of structuring, and the priority of semantic meaning over time and tone, or vice versa, is crucial in distinguishing them. One could speculate as to the distribution of such distinctions among the Native South American societies, but there is still very little information to work with. The points I have made above are summarized in Figure 1.

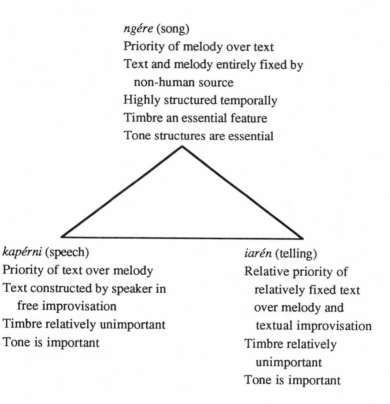

ngére (song)
Priority of melody over text
Text and melody entirely fixed by
   non-human source
Highly structured temporally
Timbre an essential feature
Tone structures are essential

kapérni (speech)
Priority of text over melody
Text constructed by speaker in
   free improvisation
Timbre relatively unimportant
Tone is important

iarén (telling)
Relative priority of
   relatively fixed text
   over melody and
   textual improvisation
Timbre relatively
   unimportant
Tone is important

Fig. 1: Song, Speech and Telling Compared

Sangére: Unheard Melodies are Effective

The word for a large group of Suyá curing songs is *sangére*.[8] It is possible to consider them to be a kind of *ngére* or song (*sa-ngére*). The Suyá, however, do not accept this etymology. They say curing songs are different from songs (*ngére*). In terms of the tripartite scheme above, the curing songs are anomalous: their texts are hardly heard at all, they are not learned from animals, and yet performances are highly structured by time, tone, timbre, and text. Perhaps they are, in fact, a style borrowed from the Upper Xingu, although the Suyá consider them to be traditional. In spite of their difference from the *ngére*, I will continue to call the *sangére* "curing songs" for convenience.

Curing songs are more important than herbal medicines in the pharmacology of the Suyá. Herbal medicines are generally collected by family members. *Sangére* are often sung by family members, but some people have a specialized knowledge of them. If the patient recovers, the singer of a *sangére* is given a present by the people who asked him or her tosing it. That is not the case for most herb medicines. While I have called them curing songs, *sangére* are not restricted to curing. They not only reduce fevers, swellings, pain or convulsions, some of them stimulate quick growth, give strength to parts of the body, and in other ways act on the healthy body.

Curing songs operate through an intricate system of metaphors. The central element of a *sangére* is the insertion of an attribute of an animal, plant, or other natural object into the body of a human in order to give a particular body part or function the properties of the animal. For instance, in the example below, the *sangére* for a child with a high fever and convulsions names the white cayman. According to the Suyá, the cayman lies very still in the water without a tremor and never gets hot. The implication is that the *sangére* will give the feverish child the quietness and coolness of the cayman. For a toothache the *sangére* most often used names the wild pig - it eats roots and its teeth do not hurt. The *sangére* for an easy birth names a small fish, which slips easily out of the hands. There is another one which can be used also, which names a manioc "pancake" (*beiju*). Just as women turn these pancakes quickly and take them off the fire rapidly, so the child will come out of her womb. In the prophylactic sphere, the *sangére* to make a child grow straight and tall names the wild banana plant, which grows swiftly to tower over the other vegetation; the song about the giant otter will give a child strong wind; one about the forest deer will make it swift.

For the Suyá, the interpretation and translation of *sangére* usually consists of establishing what animal attributes are described and which animal is eventually named. After listening to my taped examples, and knowing that I wanted a translation into colloquial Suyá, most adults would say "That is the *sangére* of the _____ (an animal); you know, it has very _____ (the trait)." It was extremely difficult to get an exact translation of every line and each metaphor. To the Suyá I worked with, who were themselves performers, after the initial metaphor and the animal had been deciphered, the rest was unimportant. Indeed, the areas of variation within the performances of the same *sangére* by different people or by the same person at different times seem to be in the number and type of different metaphors employed after the initial one, which is relatively fixed.

The best parallel for the efficacy of a curing song I can imagine is an injection. The blowing injects a particular powerful essence of animality, distilled through metaphor, through the skin of the patient into his or her body. Once in the body it either rectifies weaknesses or strengthens tendencies which have an effect on the physical well-being of the patient.

Curing songs are performed by men or women, who usually blow onto the patient as they perform the curing song very quickly and very quietly. The time and place of their performance depends on the objective: *sangére* for growth are usually performed in the early morning after bathing; those for alleviating specific symptoms (pain, fever, bleeding, etc.) are performed when the symptoms are manifested. *Sangére* are extremely hard to hear for persons standing more than three feet from the patient, and they are very difficult to record except in special circumstances. My recordings were all made in the forest or gardens surrounding the village, far form the domestic noises and the "noise of children." Even so, the volume had to be turned up very high and the microphone placed near the mouth of the singer to get an adequate recording.

Curing songs are usually learned by older children and adolescents who listen to adult performances. Children are able to move in close to performances in a way that adults rarely do or can. They learn most of the *sangére* by being close enough to actual performances to learn the style. The youths do not usually perform what they have learned until they have children of their own. According to the adults, youth is the time when the ear is "unclogged" and learning is easy. Most *sangére* are quite widely known, and have been passed down through tradition. Some have been composed by known individuals. Certain of the composed *sangére* are considered very valuable by the people who know them, and they are only taught with the understanding that a gift will be given in exchange. The *sangére* for scorpion bites, for example, was so jealously guarded by its "master" that it died with him. Now the Suyá can only use a general pain *sangére* to treat scorpion and spider bits.

Although the older men told me that people no longer use *sangére* as much as they used to before they encountered western medicine, it was still an active form throughout my fieldwork. A curing song performance was often the equivalent of "first aid" and prophylaxis. Certain older men were also asked to perform *sangére* on children from other tribes in the Xingu, for which they received some gift in return. When the Suyá visited the local FUNAI administration post (Diauarum) they would often be requested to perform *sangére* on members of the groups at the post.[9]

The example given below, examples 6 and 7 on the tape, is a fairly typical curing song in terms of structure and performance style. It was sung in a recording session in the gardens, but it was apparently identical to a version I heard in an actual cure. It has been transcribed using longer pauses as line breaks. I have not tried for an exact phonetic transcription, but rather attempt a readable approximation. Multiple vowels indicate lengthened syllables. Some diacritical marks have been used to indicate emphasis; the drawn-in marks above the words indicate tone patterns. It is impossible to imagine what the form sounds like without listening to the tape, and I recommend that that be done first. Then listen to the slow version of the same *sangére* (example 7) and try to follow the transcription.

Sangére for a Child With Fever, sung by Robndo,1972:

> hen sangére?
> Will you sing a curing song?

> hūūū ne
> (agreement)

> 1. ffffff, fff-fff, ffffff
> (Blowing on the patient.)

2. (blow once) ngo iasu kandé
   (blow once) Water still master

3. (blow once), ngo iasu kandé
   (blow once) Water still master

4. (blow once) ngo iasu kandeeeeee
   (blow once) Water still master

5. ngo iasu kandeeeee
   Water still master

6. wa iō ngo su kandé
   Our water still master

7. mī saka-chi   da kaw kurā ti
   Cayman white-(aug.) with skin rough (aug.)

8. sikra wikenti, sō kwa kitchi anitaaaaaaaw
   His hand spread out, trembles not, how come?

9. mbru tō, mbru tō, kot ga kuré ne naw.
   Animal, animal   lying there

10. wa iō ngo iasu kandé, mi saka chi da
    Our water still master, cayman white (aug.)

11. Ngo tu kandé so kaw ku   daw,
    Water shallow master   his rough skin

    whare da kot ga kuré ne naw
    lying there in the stream

12. (blow once) ngo su kandé
    (blow once) Water still master

13. (Blow once) ngo iasu kandé
    (blow once), Water still master

14. (blow once) ngo su kandé
   (blow once) Water still master

15. ngo iasu kandeeeee mmmmm
   Water still master (hum)

16. wa iõ ngo iasu kandé
   Our water still master

17. mī saka-chi da ngo tu kanti
   Cayman white-(aug.), is water still master

18. kra ti wikenti, mbut kaw wikenti,
   Hand spread out, neck skin spread out,

   sikra wikenti, anitaaaaw.
   his hand spread out, how come?

19. mbru tõ, mbru tõ, kot ga kuré ne naw.
   Animal, some species, animal some species, lying there

20. (blow) ngo su kandé
   (blow), water still master

21. (blow) ngo su kandé
   (blow) water still master

22. (blow) ngo su kandé
   (blow) Water still master.

This can be freely translated as:

1. Blowing
2. Master of the still waters
3. Master of the still waters
4. Master of the still waters
5. Master of the still waters

6. Master of our still waters
7. Rough-skinned white cayman his hand is spread out. How come?
8. Animal, Animal, that lies there still.
9. Master of our still waters
10. Master of our still waters, white cayman
11. Master of the still waters, with his rough skin,
    lying there in the stream.
12. Master of the still waters
13. Master of the still waters
14. Master of the still waters
15. Master of the still waters
16. Master of our still waters
17. White cayman, master of still waters
18. His hand is spread out, his neck skin is spread out, his
    hand is spread out, he trembles not. How come?
19. Animal, animal, lying there
20. Master of the still waters,
21. Master of the still waters,
22. Master of the still waters.

There is a structure to the curing song, involving a parallelism between certain parts. This curing song can be divided into six parts as follows:

A: lines 1, 2, 3, 4, 5, 6,
B: lines 7, 8, 9,
C: lines 10, 11
D: lines 12, 13, 17, 15, 16,
E: lines 17, 18, 19
F: lines 20, 21, 22

There is a structural parallel between A, C, and F (repeating the phrase "master of still waters"), and also between B and E. This leaves lines 10 and 11 as a kind of pivot. The lines are part of the central core of the song, and they combine both the name of the animal and the mastery of the still waters. The lines thus represent a synthesis of AB/DEF.[10]

There can be no doubt that parallel structures are essential parts of the *sangére*. In discussions with me, however, the Suyá never specifically talked about parallelism. The parallelism above, however, does intersect with another structure, about which the Suyá are quite specific, the structure of songs. The essential feature of songs is that they have two halves, in each of which there is a progress from an initial part "without meaning" through a phrase involving an action, to naming a particular animal which is responsible for the action or attribute. After the second half, in which a different animal is named from that of the first half, the song ends with a clear coda.[11]   Applying the general song structure to this example, the line divisions are as follows:

KRADI

kwā kaikaw:	1
sinti sulu:	2,3,4,5,
sinti iaren:	7, 8, 9, 10, 11, 12

SINDAW

sinti sulu:	12, 13, 14, 15, 16,
sinti iaren:	17, 18, 19,
kuré:	20, 21, 22.

Curing songs do not follow song structures exactly. One difference is that there is only one place that is entirely "without meaning" (*kwā kaikawkumeni*). Another is that most of the curing songs name the same animal in both halves, while songs virtually always name different animals in the *kradi* and in the *sindaw*. The similarity appears in an error, however. The same performer who recorded the curing song under analysis (which names the white cayman) followed it with one naming the black cayman. That one had virtually the same overall structure. In the repetition of the animal's name, however, he named the white cayman (as would be characteristic of a song) instead of repeating the words "black cayman." It was an error, but it was one that reinforces the argument that song structure and the structure of *sangére* are very similar.

Heard melodies are sweet.....

I have described the *sangére* briefly in *Nature and Society in Central Brazil* (pp. 212-219). Since then I have desultorily been pursuing information about them. These investigations indicate (1) that the Upper Xingu Indians have a similar form, but the curing songs seem to be addressed to someone or something (usually a spirit) in the Upper Xingu, while Suya curing songs invoke neither spirits nor other intermediaries; (2) the structure of *sangére* is similar in its overall form to Suyá musical forms; (3) the key to understanding the efficacy of the *sangére* is in the metaphors used in them; and (4) badly performed *sangére* are considered to be dangerous - one must be careful of inexact or inexpert applications of these metaphors which can harm the patient. Adults rarely hear each other's performances, however, so there is hardly ever a direct confrontation over whether a particular person performs "correctly." I never heard a performance criticized during my entire stay in the field.

What, then, accounts for the anomalous position of the *sangére* as a genre? I believe it has to do with the intended audience. The intended target of a *sangére* is not so much a person's (or group's) ear(s) - as with all of the other vocal genres - but the patient's body. As the *sangére* is recited, the skin or body part may be lightly stroked as well as blown on. The rapid, quiet, speech/song is directed at the affected part of the patient's body. Some *sangére* may even be effective from a distance, beyond the hearing of the patient. The only ones of this type, however, were malevolent ones, which were sung in retaliation against a woman who refused a suitor. Unlike other genres of Suyá vocal art, *sangére* may be effective even when they are not heard. I have observed the word "sangére" used humorously to describe people who are whispering. One man asked two others who were talking very quietly to each other in the men's circle at night "what curing song are you singing?" He later described this usage as "joking" or metaphoric.

There is some justification for considering the curing song to be a kind of song (*ngére*). It has the dual structure of most song: a "nothing" section (line 11), an "approaching the naming" (lines 2-6), a "naming" - where an animal is named - (line 7), and then a repeat of the whole process in line 12. Yet the *sangére* is neither song (the rhythm does not determine the words), nor speech (the structure of the whole piece is like song, not like any piece of *kapérni* I heard). It is closest to a kind of *iarén*: the text forms the melody, rather than being fitted into the musical pattern; it uses glissando; and it has a relatively fixed text (the Suyá say one has to be very careful not to make a mistake or it will harm the patient). But it is not *iarén*. No form of *iarén* has the song-structured text, and the Suyá distinguish them.

Comparative information on curing songs in the Xingu region might be of some assistance in resolving the anomalousness of the Suya curing chants. The *sangére* is probably a form of curing learned from the Indians of the Upper Xingu. Something quite similar in performance style has been reported for the Mehinaku, the Kalapalo, and the Kamayura. I do not know whether they rely on metaphors, however, and the examples described to me seem to structure text quite differently.

What sets the *sangére* apart from all of the other vocal genres (with the exception of "bad speech," which I never witnessed during my fieldwork) is that it is specifically not intended as a public form of address. The principles of the *sangére* are known to the entire community, but the actual performances are heard by very few, most of whom are patients. As a form of discourse its performance is usually restricted. While some restricted forms rely on special ritual language, the *sangére* uses everyday language (with sometimes esoteric metaphors) but is characterized by virtual inaudibility.

While they may be virtually inaudible, the *sangére* are structured as if for an audience. Their parallel structures and the insistence on the "correctness" of the performance indicate that while the objective is not to reach the ear of the public, the *sangére* is a public and verifiable genre.

The *sangére* indicate that we might do well to be sensitive to certain forms of discourse whose object is less to be heard and understood than to be performed and seen. Their efficacy is in the fact of the performance, and to some degree in their success at relieving symptoms, rather than in the aural reception of the sounds and their direct evaluation. The *sangére* themselves are not faked: they are really performed and they have a very elaborate system of metaphors which are employed in a highly structured way. But they are not performed to be heard by more than a very few people, one of whom may be quite sick. This kind of performance has been suggested by John Keats in "Ode on a Grecian Urn." If one simply replaced the word "spirit" in the last line that follows with "body," it gets close to the heart of the *sangére*:

Heard melodies are sweet, but those unheard
  Are sweeter; therefore, ye soft pipes, play on;
Not to the sensual ear, but, more endeared,
  Pipe to the spirit [body] ditties of no tone;

This study has important implications for work on Suyá music. First, since all Suyá music is song, it is impossible to separate music from forms that are usually called "speech forms." Discourse, oratory, and song all structure time, tone, and timbre. The relationship of the text to these structures (whether inserted into them or creative of them) varies among the genres, and can only be understood when examining the whole gamut of music and discourse. Second, Suyá song texts, as represented by the curing song analyzed in the second part of the paper, reveal clear parallel structures. These may be examined in a purely formal way, which produces structures with some parallels with the Suyá divisions of song texts as parts of a performance. This formal analysis can be compared to the Suyá divisions of song into sections according to the referential meaning of the text.

There is a tremendous variety of forms of discourse among the Native South Americans. Rather than studying them singly, in the supreme isolation of different scholarly disciplines, we would be far better off considering them as interrelated systems of genres which employ phonetics, text, time, tone, and timbre in different but possibly systematic ways. By showing how the genres are interrelated, and illustrating their use in social contexts, we will be able to better analyze each of these forms. We will also help our respective disciplines break out of the isolation which has hampered our treatment of the complexity of actual performances.[12]

Notes

1. The reason for concentrating on this genre in an earlier version of this paper, presented at the Austin Native South American Discourse Conference, was to take advantage of the presence of Dr. Ellen Basso, who has worked among the Kalapalo of the Upper Xingu. The Suyá curing songs may have been learned from the Upper Xingu Indians, and I thought the occasion particularly opportune for the discussion of a Suyá text which may have borrowed some of its key features from the Upper Xingu groups, among them the Kalapalo.

2. All the recordings of the Suyá are deposited in the Indiana University Archives of Traditional Music, where they are available for further study. Other examples of Suyá verbal art, especially song, are to be found on Seeger (1982).

3. For an ethnography of the Suyá, see Seeger 1981. Earlier short papers have addressed body ornamentation (Seeger 1975), and the relationship of two genres of Suyá song to selected features of Suyá social organization and cosmology (Seeger 1979, 1980).

4. The Suyá consider themselves to be the only ones who now perform the Jawari - originally a Trumai ceremony - correctly, since the Upper Xingu groups, they argue, have altered the songs to conform to their own singing style.

5. By this I mean that the relationships are very similar to those of quarter/half/full beats within fairly fixed larger units of time. This is quite distinct from the formal speech (*kapérni*), although both have structured phrasing and *fermata*.

6. Charles Boilés (ms), although agreeing that many genres have musical features, maintains that song should be distinguished from speech by the existence of a fixed fundamental. We were still debating this point at the time of his death in 1984.

7. There are a few pioneering attempts to put the "music" back into the performances (for example, Sherzer and Wicks 1982), but these are recent and very rare. Discussions of song are also relatively rare; with the exception of an article by George List (1963) and one by Charles Boilés (ms.) there have been few systematic attempts by ethnomusicologists to deal with the relationships of song and speech.

8. In an earlier publication I referred to *sangére* as "curing chants" in order to stress their difference from songs (Seeger 1981: 212-219). I used the word "chant" there because the tonal features of the *sangére* are quite different from those of the musical genre *ngére*. At the time I was not aware of the structural similarities between the curing songs and the *ngére*. Here I have chosen to call them "curing songs" as that now seems to best characterize their form and performance.

9. In a similar fashion, the Suyá would go to the post to consult shamans from other groups, and simultaneously to make use of the post's western medical facilities.

10. Greg Urban pointed out the formal parallelism in the form I have given it, rather than in terms of the Suyá song structure that I had been using.

He also suggested that there was possibly a structurally important implication in the use of the words "*iasu* and "*su*" (which I have translated as "still"), which he suggested may have something to do with aspect. This possibility remains to be explored.

11. The structure of Suyá songs is presented in some detail in Seeger (1980).

12. I would like to thank the participants in the Austin Native South American Discourse Conference for their comments on an earlier version of this paper. I am indebted to the performers of the examples who permitted me to use them: Mbeni, Peti, Robndo, Uetagu, and the adult men of the Suyá community. The same individuals provided me with many of the ethnographic details interpreted in this analysis. The total time spent among the Suyá was twenty-two months between 1970 and 1982. The research was funded by the National Institutes of General Medical Sciences, the Ford Foundation of Brazil, the Wenner-Gren Foundation, the Financiadora de Estudos e Projetos (FINEP), and the Federal University of Rio de Janeiro. I gratefully acknowlege the support of these institutions.

References

Boilés, Charles L.
  ms.   "Canto." Mimeographed translation of a published encyclopedia entry in an Italian encyclopedia which is not cited in the paper itself.

List, George
  1963   The boundaries of speech and song. *Ethnomusicology* 7: 1-16.

Seeger, Anthony
  1975   The meaning of body ornaments: a Suyá example. *Ethnology* 14: 211-224.

  1979   What can we learn when they sing? vocal genres of the Suyá Indians of central Brazil. *Ethnomusicology* 23: 373-394.

  1980   Sing for your sister: the structure and performance of Suyá akia. In *The ethnography of musical performance*, N. McLeod and M. Herndon (eds.), pp. 7-43. Norwood, Pennsylvania: Norwood.

  1981   *Nature and society in central Brazil: the Suyá Indians of Mato Grosso*. Cambridge: Harvard University Press.

in press   Thieves, myths and history: Karl von den Steinen among the
           Suyá, 3-6 September 1884. To appear in a volume edited by
           Vera Penteado Coelho, commemorating the centenary year of the
           voyage of Karl von den Steinen.

Sherzer, Joel and Sammie Ann Wicks
   1982   The intersection of music and language in Kuna discourse. *Latin
           American Music Review* 3: 147-164.

Steinen, Karl von den
   1942 [1886]. *O Brasil central,* C. B. Cannabrava (trans.).   São Paulo:
           Companhia Editorial Nacional.

Three Modes of Shavante Vocal Expression: Wailing, Collective Singing, and Political Oratory

Laura Graham

The interrelations of three vocal styles in Shavante (Portuguese orthography: Xavante) society can be understood by contrasting them according to three parameters: (1) the degree to which each makes use of the phonology, morphology, and syntactics of the Shavante language, (2) the degree of melodic complexity exhibited, and (3) their correlations with Shavante cosmology and ideology of social space. A comparison of ceremonial wailing, collective singing, and political oratory illuminates how the performance of these vocal forms acoustically and physically represents a fundamental notion of Shavante ideology, the dialectic between nature and culture. While the nature/culture dichotomy is by no means unique to Gê societies, its elaborate formal manifestations have captured the attention of many Gê specialists (see Lévi-Strauss 1967: 145; Maybury-Lewis 1979; Turner 1979; Seeger 1981). In Shavante society this dichotomy is both vocally and physically represented in these three expressive styles. It is depicted in the elaboration of the linguistic code and melodic composition, as well as in the prescribed performance locations of each one. However, rather than supporting the clear-cut binary nature/culture division, the contrasts between these three expressive forms indicate a gradual transition from "more natural" to "more cultural." In this paper I describe the salient features of the three styles to illustrate how, using language, melodic organization, and space, instances of ceremonial wailing, collective singing, and political oratory instantiate a more general set of meaningful relations in Shavante society.

Characteristics of Shavante Society

The Shavante belong to the central branch of the Gê linguistic family. They currently live on six indigenous reserves in the state of Mato Grosso, Brazil. Principles of binary opposition in social organization as well as in cosmology characterize their society, and indeed Gê societies in general, hence the label "dialectical societies" (Maybury-Lewis 1979). At the level of ideology, Shavante oppose nature to culture. They conceive of the dichotomy between nature and culture as the division between an arena in which human actors have control over events (culture) and one in which events take place in a sphere that is beyond their control (nature). Shavante thought concerning the organization of social space directly reflects this distinction and is well documented for other Gê societies (Da Matta 1976: 61-68, 1979: 97; Lévi-Strauss 1967: 144-147; Maybury-Lewis 1979: 9, 234, 305; Seeger 1981: 66-79; Turner 1980; Vidal 1977: 65). The actual layout of the village, as conceptualized by members of Shavante society, physically represents this division between nature and culture.

All Shavante villages correspond to an ideal form, a horseshoe-shaped semi-circle opening toward a river. The horseshoe shaped ring of huts represents a boundary between social and nonsocial space. The village center plaza, *warã*, is conceived of as the epitome of social space. It is the male sphere and, in particular, the exclusive domain of adult men during the morning and evening men's council reunions. The women's domain is the domestic sphere. Shavante tend to associate women and their activities, both biological and social, with the household and nature. The nature/culture dichotomy is thus perceived as existing between men and women and is physically represented in notions of social space: the village center is associated with maleness and society, contrasting with the periphery, or femaleness and nature.

As in all Gê societies, Shavante social organization involves multiple and complex oppositions. It consists of a set of intersecting exogamous and agamous moieties. Moiety affiliation influences politics, marriage, and ceremonial activity. The patrilineally determined exogamous moieties, *poridzaʔono* and *öwawẽ*, form the basis for political factionalism and influence mature males especially. The age-set system (Maybury-Lewis 1967: 105-154) forms a second bilateral complex which effectively crosscuts the fundamental moiety division and creates a further set of ties and oppositions. Formal recognition of age-set membership is established at the time of collective indoctrination into the bachelors' hut (Maybury-Lewis 1967: 105).

Relations of solidarity characterize members of the same age-set and members of the same age-set moiety. Age-set ties exert maximum influence during the period of collective residence in the bachelors' hut and during the *ʔritaʔwa* (novice) period. During these social phases especially, ceremonial and ritual activities constantly remind participants of their age-set associations. Later, factional ties and individual political aspirations take precedence over age-set loyalties.

In addition to the exogamous and agamous moiety divisions, Shavante divide male society into a number of hierarchically ranked age grades. Age grade divisions correlate with the Shavante ontological division between nature and culture. As men mature, they progress from the domestic sphere, associated with nature, to men's society linked to the village center and locus of social activity.[1]

The movement from the domestic to the social sphere in the male life cycle is mediated by a period of collective residence in the bachelors' hut, *hö*. From the time of indoctrination into the *hö* until initiation, boys in this phase are considered part of the *wapte* age grade. During their residence in the *hö*, approximately four years, they undergo a series of ceremonies in which music plays an important role (see *dañoʔre* below). These activities serve as preparation for the initiates' reintegration into adult society. They are also subject to the teachings of their sponsoring age-set (*danimñohu* - first ascending alternate age-set, *simñohu* 3s, 3p) which belongs to the same age-set moiety.

Having completed the series of initiation-focused ceremonies, the *wapte* undergo an elaborate ceremony in which their ears are pierced. Pierced ears mark the termination of the *wapte* phase and their new status as *ʔritaʔwa* novices. Following one last ceremony (*saʔuriʔwa*) they officially pass into the *ʔritaʔwa* age grade. During the period of *ʔritaʔwa* status the group continues to be the focus of ceremonial activities in which the adolescent boys demonstrate their maturity. They are, however, not yet considered full adults. *ʔritaʔwa* do not have license to attend the men's council in the *warā*.

After the birth of the first child, men are considered young adults, *ipredupte*. This event entitles a man to participate in the men's council reunions, which take place in the central plaza and social center of the village. After the birth of several children, men are classified as fully mature, *ipredu*, and are considered to be fully socialized individuals. Men with many children and grandchildren, are said to be "elders," *ihire*.

Having sketched the ethnographic context in which the three vocal styles are situated, we can focus more specifically on the details of each mode. In particular, I shall stress the relationship between linguistic features, melodic content, and performance locations for each style, and their correlation with Shavante ideology and the nature/culture dichotomy. In discussing them individually I shall point out: (1) who has license to perform them; (2) situations in which performance is appropriate or requisite; (3) how a particular genre is learned; (4) the prescribed performance location and its relation to notions of social space; and (5) the linguistic and musical features of the style.[2]   This analysis is limited to a discussion of only three of the expressive vocal styles used by Shavante males: *dawawa* - ritual wailing, *dañozre* - singing, and political oratory. I shall devote more attention to male use of these forms of vocal expression; their performance by women can only be mentioned briefly here, although it merits equal attention and further analysis. Other forms of vocal expression not considered here include a musical genre (*resa*) associated with the Christian religion,[3] forms of speaking used in myth telling, political verbal dueling, and other marked styles of conversational exchange used in the political arena, as well as that employed in unmarked verbal interactions.

dawawa - Ritual Wailing

dawawa [4] in Shavante denotes a highly musical form of ritual wailing, or, as Seeger puts it "songlike keening" (Seeger 1981: 172).[5] Shavante do not consider *dawawa* a form of singing but classify it as a distinct expressive type. Individuals receive and learn *dawawa* through dreams. Only fully matured individuals who have at least one child have the capability to dream wailing. An individual must have the proper means to receive *dawawa* through dreams; that is, he must wear the earplugs that not only mark his status as a mature male, but also enable him to receive *dawawa*.

Women also dream *dawawa*.[6] Since women do not wear earplugs they receive *dawawa* through a fiber cord (*sorebzu*) tied by their husband around the neck. Without it, women do not receive *dawawa*. Wailing is thus accessible to both men and women who possess the proper means to receive it through dreams.

As a form of expressive communication that is equally available to both sexes, it cannot be considered a predominantly female genre as is the case in many societies (see Caraveli-Chaves 1980, 1982; Danforth 1982; Feld 1982; Honko 1974; Huxley 1956; Klymasz 1975; Sherzer 1986; Titiev 1949; and Tiwary 1975). On the basis of the Shavante data and that from other native South American societies, I suggest a possible implicational universal: that in societies where ceremonial keening is a male form of expression, it is also a mode of expression available to women (see Henry 1941: 65-66; Seeger 1981: 160, 165; Urban 1985).

Any instance of wailing indexes a special relationship between two individuals. Wailing focuses attention on a strong bond between close kin or individuals united through ceremonial affiliation (e.g., *aʔãma*[7]). An individual expresses profound emotion toward the other through wailing. The strength of the bond and the emotional intensity are indicated by the duration of the wailing period, both by the length of each instance of wailing, and by the period of general mourning marked by wailing.

Shavante express intensely felt emotions associated with profound feelings of loss, separation, abandonment, and death through wailing. Wailing is also used to indicate sympathy for persons experiencing difficult transitions in the life cycle. Thus, for instance, elderly women wail for their grandsons during rituals such as the *waiʔa* in which *ʔritaʔwa* are considered vulnerable to external spiritual forces (see Maybury-Lewis 1967: 255-269).

Wailing is also performed in contexts other than those associated with profound feelings of loss or abandonment. Individuals employ *dawawa* to express extreme joy, at the return of a departed kinsmen for instance (see also Wagley 1977), or to emphasize pride. The former of these uses is traditional, separation being related to death, transition, growing up, and so on. The latter use appears to be creative and is less frequent. Wailing thus appears to be a form of emotional expression that is socially prescribed in certain situations but that can also be manipulated for individuals to spontaneously express deeply felt sentiments in other contexts.

Wailing is employed to express sentiments experienced by a single individual. It is a form of emotional expression associated with the domestic sphere. Normally individuals wail in isolation, from the sleeping mat or bed. It is not a device used to provoke others to similar expression or evoke other expressive responses, as is wailing among the Kaluli (Feld 1982). Rather, *dawawa* are messages sent out to all members of the community, who interpret the signal as the expression of one individual's experience of intense emotion. *dawawa* convey the actual experience. The lamenting individual sends his message of grief from the sphere most closely associated with the natural world, far from the social center of the village. Thus, the prescribed location for *dawawa* expression reinforces the solitude and antisocial sentiments of the weeping individual.

Normally wailing occurs at the transitional periods of the day; thus, ritual laments are most often heard at dawn and dusk. *dawawa* may be performed immediately following death at any hour; grief however, is not expressed through stylized wailing until the body has been laid out in a hut. In situations where wailing takes place in the presence of others it is not a coordinated group expression. Individuals retain their separate forms and seemingly lose themselves, as if entranced, in their individual expressions of grief. Close kin weep at interment while others remain silent. Individuals may wail at any time when reminded of the deceased, such as when seeing a photograph or visiting the grave.

Wailing texts use a minimum of sounds from Shavante phonology. Vocalizations are restricted to combinations of three vowel sounds: [a], [e], and [i]. The linguistic elements of wailing thus involve oppositions between a low central vowel and higher vowels from either the mid or front range with [i] the highest of the three. In the example given (see appendix), the sequence of vowels is the same for each phrase: / i a e i e /. The wailer thus articulates a phonetic progression from a high onset glide to low to mid to high and back to mid range. Vocalic utterances are sometimes preceded by glottal stops or occasionally slight aspiration, these being the only consonants to appear in Shavante keening. Similar linguistic restrictions are reported by Salmond for Maori women's wailing (1974: 205), and Feld for Kaluli men's lament (1982).

Of the three vocal styles considered here, wailing texts involve the most restricted set of linguistic elements from the Shavante language. Based on its limited use of language, wailing resembles signal systems of nature more than the socio-cultural system of human language (see Benveniste 1971). In this respect Shavante wailing is similar to the most spontaneous forms of wailing found among the Kaluli (Feld 1982). According to Feld, Kaluli men's wailing (gana-yɛlɛma, iligi-yɛlɛma, and gana-gili-yɛlɛma) is a direct response to feelings of profound emotion (Feld 1982: 32-33, 91-94). It is explicitly iconic of the muni bird song, an important figure in Kaluli ideology, and Kaluli men imitate the muni bird song when weeping. To mirror the bird song they sing melodies of three or four descending pitches with the vowel [e]. Unlike Kaluli women's weeping, men's wailing does not incorporate semantico-referential text.

> The major point about Kaluli weeping ... is that the three- or four-note melody is used as a sound metaphor for sadness, expressing the sorrow of loss and abandonment. The reduction to a state of loss becomes equivalent to the state of being a bird [Feld 1982: 331].

Neither Shavante wailing nor Kaluli men's weeping employs linguistic text beyond the level of vowel sounds. The lack of semantico-referential content associates wailing, as a form of human expression, with modes of communication in the realm of nature. Distinct voice quality features further intensify the iconic image between Shavante wailing, as a conventional form of expression, and natural, universal signals of human emotion, for instance the frequent use of creaky voice and wavering pitch. These voice quality features are intrinsically linked to natural expressions of human emotion (see Urban 1985).

In contrast to the limited inventory of linguistic elements, the melodic composition of *dawawa* is the most elaborate of the three expressive styles considered here. The instances of wailing I recorded consist of a variable number of repetitions of two phrases. These are noted as A and B in the instance transcribed (see appendix). Each phrase is composed of four to five discrete pitches, with falsetto considered as a constituent tone.[8] The voice quality used in *dawawa* is analogous to singing voice considered from the Western perspective. Pitches are clearly audible and identifiable. For each phrase, or tone progression with the exception of the low glide [i] onset, the relative pitch associations are consistent with the vowel quality of the corresponding linguistic utterance. Thus in each phrase [a] is linked with the lowest tone, [e] to the mid-range tones, and [i] to the highest tone and falsetto pitch. From a phonetic point of view higher vowels have a higher intrinsic pitch than lower vowels. This association is mirrored in the *dawawa* melody and is typical of all *dawawa* I heard. [9]

Although A and B phrases are rhythmically identical, each alternating between either of two motifs, A/B (/__ -- _ _ _/) or A'/B' (_ -- _),[10] they can be distinguished on the basis of their different relative pitch levels. B phrases consistently commence between a third and a fourth higher than A phrases. In the *dawawa* examined, two B phrase repetitions punctuate a series of between five and eleven A phrase repetitions, typically. An A' phrase initiates the performance and regularly occurs after each repetition of two B phrases, (e.g., A' A A A A B B A' A A...).

The most salient musical characteristic of *dawawa* is the gradual pitch ascension which takes place throughout the entire performance. This melodic movement is achieved through upward microtonal changes or intervals approximating Western semitones. These changes occur in different "paradigmatic slots" of the A phrase. Phrases, viewed as syntagmatic wholes, maintain a consistent melodic integrity while continually adjusting to the upward microtonal or semitonal changes that take place in variable paradigmatic slots.[11] The pitch of B phrases moves upward in similar fashion, following changes in A phrases; however, there is less initiation of pitch-level changes in B phrases, in contrast to the continuous upward rising of A phrases. In the instance of *dawawa* transcribed, for example, the initial pitch of phrase A has moved up a fourth, from middle C to the F above, between the first and last repetitions of the phrase in this performance if plotted on the Western music staff (see Graham 1984). This is achieved by the cumulative effect of the microtonal or semitonal rising that takes place throughout the entire performance (compare pitch of initial phrase (A-1) with that of the final phrase (A-14) in *dawawa*, appendix). This range of pitches is best conceived of as a continuum.

We can thus conclude that the pitch inventory of *dawawa* is quite extensive and that the mechanism of upward motion is extremely complex.

Indeed, the musical action and expressive communication in wailing occur through the manipulation of tones and the melodic structure, rather than through rhythmic motifs, as in the case of *daño?re*. The microtonal rising in *dawawa* may possibly be interpreted as a mechanism of emotional intensification in Shavante vocal expression. (Indeed, microtonal rising may be a more widespread means of emotional intensification among the forms of vocal expression in traditional cultures generally).

daño?re - Collective Singing

daño?re, in Shavante, refers to a collectively performed combination of song and dance. Participants sing and move in unison forming a circle with clasped hands. Shavante classify three distinct performance types under the generic term *daño?re*. *dapraba*, *dasi?rene*, and *dahipopo* are differentiated on the basis of the accompanying physical movements of the dance steps and the time of day suitable for their performance.

dapraba are performed in the morning. The singing dancers mark time by stepping one foot to the side on one beat and bringing the other to join it on the next stressed beat. In this fashion the entire circle rotates in one direction. At transitional pauses in the song, the movements are reversed and the circle doubles back in the opposite direction. Shavante call songs sung at noon *dasi?rene* or *dazarono*. Dancers performing *dasi?rene* remain in a fixed spot while stomping one foot slightly forward and to the side. *dahipopo* are performed at night. When dancing *dahipopo*, men stand in one place bending their knees outward in time with the metric pulse of the music. The deep knee bends cause the dancers' feet to shuffle back and forth.

Like *dawawa*, individuals receive *daño?re* through dreams. Shavante explain that when dreaming *daño?re*, one first perceives the movements of the dance (i.e., the *daño?re* type), then the melody and text. *daño?re* are transmitted to receiving individuals through the earplugs worn by all initiated males. Hence, initiate status and its concomitant indexical sign, the ear plugs, are prerequisites to receiving *daño?re*. Moreover, dreaming and subsequently recalling a *daño?re* definitively mark the completion of the *wapte* phase and signal a successful transition to *ʔritaiʔwa* status. In short, earplugs and *dañoʔre* together index adult-male status in Shavante society.

    dañoʔre singing is especially important for young males, particularly for *ʔritaiʔwa* novices. They associate the performance of *dañoʔre* with male prowess and virility. Shavante consider both *ʔritaiʔwa* and young men (*īpredupte*) prolific dreamers of *dañoʔre*. *ʔritaiʔwa*, deemed especially vital, are expected to demonstrate their prowess by singing their *dañoʔre* around the village at night. These performances highlight their exceptional strength and their ability to stay up while others sleep (Maybury-Lewis 1967: 140).

    In addition to these nocturnal performances, *dañoʔre* are performed in connection with many ceremonial events: in conjunction with the *wapte* festival (collective indoctrination of *airepudu* into the bachelor's hut), after log races, and during the *waiʔa*.[12] *dañoʔre* can also be performed prior to the departure of hunting groups embarking to collect meat for ceremonial exchange at the *adaba* wedding ceremony. They may also be performed collectively by all males as part of the expressive complex of mourning behavior after the death of important persons.

    dañoʔre are expressions both of individuality and collective solidarity. They mark an individual's social maturity and also his membership in an age-set. The process by which *dañoʔre* become part of an age-set's expressive repertoire underscores the relationship between individual expression and collective solidarity. *dañoʔre* evolve through four distinct phases, progressing from comprehension of *dañoʔre* structure to actual public performance. Each stage directly reflects the processes of the other stages. Thus, similar processes operate in the ways that : (1) the actual pattern of *dañoʔre* singing is learned by the *wapte*; (2) a given individual receives *dañoʔre* through dreams and commits them to memory; (3) an age-set learns the *dañoʔre* of its constituent members; and (4) *dañoʔre* are publicly presented in singing performances around the village.

    wapte learn the pattern of *dañoʔre* singing by imitating and learning the daño're of their age-set sponsor (*simñohu*). They are taught *dañoʔre* by the *simñohu* in a fashion that primes them for the process of receiving personal *dañoʔre* through dreams, for the technique of incorporating individual *dañoʔre* into the age-set repertoire, and finally for the correct method of performing *daño?re* publicly. The process begins the very day the boys are formally indoctrinated into the bachelor's hut, after the *wapte* ceremony. It is the first activity the *wapte* engage in collectively as an official age-set.

Learning the *daño?re* of the *simñohu* continues throughout the period of collective residence in the *hö*. The teaching process proceeds as follows. Immediately after the ceremonial induction of the *wapte* into the bachelor's hut, the *simñohu* visit them and begin teaching one of their own *daño?re*. The *simñohu* sing one song twice through. First they sing softly, then repeat the performance at full volume. The *wapte* join in as they begin to perceive the pattern. After singing the song through twice in this fashion, the boys file out of the *hö* and make their way to the patio of the first house where they will sing in public. The *simñohu* join them shortly and together they perform the song in front of predetermined huts around the village.

The same song is sung once in front of each hut. The *wapte* and their *simñohu* then make their way back to the bachelor's hut where they learn another song. This process is repeated all day, and periodically during the *wapte* phase. Thus the *wapte* learn the pattern of *daño?re*. They imitate those of their sponsor group, sung softly at first, then loudly; and finally they perform around the village. This is the basic two step pattern by which individuals and groups learn *daño?re*. Actual public performance marks a third step in the acquisition of *daño?re* communicative competence (Hymes 1974).

Once the boy's ears have been pierced and they have been reintegrated into society, they are eligible (in fact, obliged) to receive their own *daño?re* through dreams. While dreaming, an individual hears the *daño?re*, wakes, and sings the song through softly one time. Shavante say a man "sings quietly so as not to forget (*te tiño?re sirudi tete waihu?u da*)." He then repeats the song loudly to etch it indelibly in his memory. At this point Shavante consider the dreamer the owner of the song. That night he calls the members of his age-set together and teaches them the song.

The process of imparting the individual's song to the group mirrors the individual's reception of the song and the process by which *wapte* learn those of their *simñohu*. Members of the *?ritai?wa* age grade assemble in the *warã* at night, after the elders have returned to their huts, to learn the new song. The individual sings his new song through once quietly, then loudly a second time. Others join as they pick up the pattern. At this point the song becomes the property of the age-set; it no longer belongs exclusively to the individual who dreamed it. Having thus incorporated the song into its repertoire, the age-set is able to perform it publicly around the village in front of the huts. The singing binds the adolescent boys together as a group. It also signals their maturity and group identity to those listening in the huts.

The pattern for performing *daño?re* around the village again resembles the earlier phases of learning, receiving, and transmitting individual *daño?re* to the group. Prior to singing in front of the huts the *?ritai?wa* meet in the *wará* to rehearse. They sing a song through one time softly, then again at full volume. Having thus "practiced" the song they sing in front of the designated houses beginning with the last hut of the village arc opposite the location of their *hö*. After singing around the village the *?ritai?wa* return to the central plaza to converse into the wee hours of the morning before slipping into the huts of their new brides.

?ritai?wa, who perform *daño?re* in this manner, are at an intermediate stage in the Shavante life cycle. They are no longer children, linked with the domestic sphere, yet they are not considered fully socialized adults associated with the mature men's social sphere, the *wará*. The locations for *?ritai?wa daño?re* performance represent the intersection of these two spheres. *?ritai?wa* sing *daño?re* both in the village center and close to the domestic sphere. They assemble in the *wará* prior to performances around the village that are "for the elders" as they say.

daño?re melodies are accompanied by vocables, either syllables or words from the Shavante language. These syllables and words are not arranged systematically into organized syntagmatic relations; hence, they do not combine in any meaningful way to produce higher levels of signification. *daño?re* texts do not carry any propositional content or semantico-referential meaning. The vocables do, however, make use of the full complement of sounds in the Shavante linguistic inventory. Furthermore, the sounds combine according to the phonological rules of the language. Thus, *daño?re* texts employ "linguistic structure" in greater measure than do *dawawa* texts. Yet the texts do not take the next step of combining and contrasting groups of sounds into meaningful semantico-referential units or utterances which convey propositional messages.

Although *daño?re* texts do not communicate any semantico-referential meaning, they do evidence the beginnings of language structure by conforming to elementary phonological rules. They represent the initial stage in the social manipulation of sounds.

The linguistic structures of *daño?re*, like the group associated with them, are half way between the domains of nature and socialization. *?ritai?wa* who sing *daño?re*, like the texts, are in a transitional phase between childhood, residing in the domestic sphere associated with nature, and the social world of adult men. *daño?re* texts, through language, metaphorically represent the transitional nature of the *?ritai?wa* phase. Both the linguistic organization of the texts and those who sing them are half way between natural and social domains.

daño?re group performances conform to a leader/chorus ensemble organization. The leader initiates new phrases and is joined by the chorus after a single or partial repetition of the introduced phrase. Marked pharyngeal constriction together with loud, forced voice characterize *daño?re* delivery. The acoustic timbre thus produced lies somewhere between singing voice, as we conceive it, and shouting-chanting. This style of delivery often effectively obscures the identity of well defined musical pitches. Indeed, a continuum seems to exist between song and speech voice in *daño?re* singing; at some points all semblance of identifiable musical pitch seems to disappear. The ambiguous nature of *daño?re* pitch is thus notated accordingly in the transcription. Where approximate pitch is identifiable, it is notated by (---) above the pitch-range baseline; greater ambiguity in musical pitch (i.e., beyond the point where I and several colleagues were able to identify acoustic pitch) is correspondingly indicated by (---) located below the baseline.

In contrast to *dawawa*, the melodic pitch inventory of *daño?re* is extremely limited. Within the performance transcribed here, we identified three tones -- G - A - A# -- as the entire melodic content (this does not include changes in intonation in the speech-like sections). Thus the melodic range lies within an augmented second and the pitch level remains constant throughout the entire performance. In *daño?re* the manipulation of rhythmic motifs, rather than melodic variation, is the salient variable. This occurs within a strict binary metric structure. *daño?re* are performed with a fast driving tempo, which offers further contrast to the slower and essentially non-metered *dawawa*.

Political Oratory or Plaza Speech

Elderly Shavante males have the ability to speak in a formally structured, stylized manner that is not part of the verbal repertoire of other Shavante, either male or female. This style is used in political oratory, which, as a style of speaking, has no special metalinguistic gloss in Shavante. Not all elders develop oratorical skills. Only those who have accumulated a large amount of prestige, authority, and respect as factional leaders speak in this fashion. Political oratory thereby differs from *dañoʔre* in that the *dañoʔre* verbal expression ceases to be the property of the individual. Plaza speech, in contrast, continues to be the orator's own while members of the men's council assume the role of audience. Speeches delivered in this rhetorical style take place exclusively in the men's council -- the most social arena of the Shavante domain -- and only in evening reunions, never in the morning gatherings.[13] Speakers use the oratorical style to attract the attention of those attending the council meeting. By manipulating his speech, the orator manipulates the audience as well, causing it to focus on the message delivery itself as well as the content (Jakobson 1960).

Messages delivered by means of political oratory in the men's council often extend beyond the boundaries of the men's domain. Any messages relevant to female members of the community are transmitted by the male members of each household to the periphery and women's sphere. Thus a speaker's message is directed first to the men in the *warã* and then, in a mediated fashion, to the women.

Unlike the other expressive styles, political oratory uses the complete system of language, which is distinct due to the presence of syntagmatic relations. Phonological and morphological units are systematically combined to form higher levels of meaning according to syntactic principles of the Shavante language. Texts actually combine strings of propositions into a coherent argument. Political oratory is therefore distinct from the other two forms of vocal behavior considered here in that it alone involves the transmission of true propositional content.

In plaza speech orators manipulate linguistic texts to achieve systematic, indeed music-like, sound patterns. Speech in this style is marked by explicit repetition of phrases and semantic parallelism (see appendix). The unique combination of words in each phrase produces a distinct intonation pattern for each utterance. A music-like quality thus results from the repetition of phrases and clauses with parallel intonation contours. Although it is impossible to identify acoustic pitch in rhetorical speech, the parallel structure of intonation contours in adjacent phrases produces an aural quality that is indeed "music-like" (see List 1963).

Other paralinguistic devices further underscore the acoustic effect of parallel intonation contours in rhetorical speech. In plaza speech each phrase is marked by a slight rise rather than decline in pitch phrase finally. Additionally, phrase final glottal stops and distinct pharyngeal constriction, especially in phrase final syllables, effectively establish phrase boundaries. These features produce a regular staccato rhythmical effect, which frames the music-like intonation patterns and highlights the variation between juxtaposed parallel sets. Orators speak relatively softly forcing members of the audience to focus directly on the speaker, his style of delivery, and the message.

Phrases can be grouped together based upon two organizational principles: first, they fit together in terms of thematic or message content; second, they are formally marked by the speaker into segments that are separated by exaggerated glottal stops (noted 'ʌ' in the transcription). This sound, accompanied by a brief pause, marks transitions in semantico-referential message content. The poetic structure of the narrative is thus based upon formal grammatical features as well as expressive features of the presentation itself (see Hymes 1977, also Tedlock 1977, 1978). These two combine to define the underlying rhetorical and music-like structure of the discourse as it is marked into verses through the use of pauses and exaggerated glottal stops.

As recent work in discourse analysis has pointed out, transcription itself is a form of analysis (see Hymes 1977; Sherzer 1982; Tedlock, 1977, 1978). Indeed the same text may be justifiably represented in a variety of ways to underscore different dimensions of rhetorical structure (see Woodbury 1985). The following transcription of Shavante political oratory (appendix) is designed to highlight the poetic structure based on the juxtaposition of semantically parallel utterances. Phrases having identical semantic content are aligned thereby setting them off from the introduction of new material. Interlineal spaces do not indicate pause length, as in the transcription system advocated by Tedlock (1977, 1978), but are intended to visually define the recurrence of semantic content. Similarly, indentations are intended to mark the introduction of new material rather than to distinguish between lines and verses (see Hymes 1977).

The first two phrase groups in the transcribed excerpt suggest that propositional statements in Shavante oratory are constructed through the combination of smaller propositional units. By combining such segments the oratory gradually builds up to completing a propositional statement. Sally McLendon (personal communication) noted that oratory among the Eastern Pomo is characterized by a similar rhetorical technique whereby the orator builds to a climax at which time the most important information is given. Following this peak the same parallel structures are repeated in reverse order, thus gradually easing down from the informational peak of the speech. At the present time analysis of the rhetorical structure of Shavante oratory is not complete. However, it may be the case that a more complex pattern of macro-parallelism such as the one described by Urban (this volume) is in place.

Ideology, Social Space, Language, and Melody

The three modes of expression I have discussed here can be juxtaposed against the Shavante divisions of social space to illustrate the relationship between social space and expressive forms. Wailing, the expression of individually experienced emotions, takes place in the domestic sphere, in isolation and far from the social center of the Shavante village. *dañoᴣre,* performed by groups in transition from childhood and the domestic sphere to mature male society and the village center, are practiced both in the village center and close to, but not inside of, the domestic huts. The prescribed performance locations for *dañoᴣre,* midway between the social center and village periphery, underscore the transitional nature of the group. Oratory, the form of expression linked with the most "socialized" group of Shavante males, occurs in the most "socialized" area of Shavante space, the *warā.*

The three expressive forms make differential use of the components of the Shavante language. The linguistic texts, that is, make differential use of phonology, morphology, and syntax.[14] Indeed, the three forms of vocal expression can be ordered hierarchically to illustrate how each builds upon the linguistic elements present in preceding ones.

dawawa texts contain only vowel sounds. They are used to express directly the emotion experienced by grieving individuals. Repeated sound patterns together with the absence of linguistic organization enable the individual to suspend thoughts and focus on emotion. Stripped of any semantic content, *dawawa* represents pure emotional expression.

dañoʔre texts augment the sounds of *dawawa* with the full complement of consonants and vowels of the Shavante language. They also apply the first rule of linguistic combination by forming phonologically correct syllables and words. These sound groups do not combine further to form higher levels of meaning or communicate propositional content.

Finally, political oratory stands at the highest hierarchical level and utilizes the full inventory of Shavante phonology, morphology, and syntax. Political oratory thus employs the linguistic elements present in the other two expressive forms and combines them into systematic syntagmatic relations that communicate propositional meaning. It can therefore be said to occupy the most elevated position in the linguistic hierarchy of expressive forms.

If position in social space and degree of linguisticality are seen as the first two axes of comparison, a third comparative axis is that of melodic content. The melodic relationships between the three expressive styles are exactly the inverse of their linguistic relationships. Whereas *dawawa* texts employ few linguistic elements, as musical structures they involve the most elaborate pitch inventory and complex principles of melodic organization. Further, melodic action in *dawawa* is not constrained by the linguistic text; microtonal pitch changes can occur in any paradigmatic slot of a given phrase. Melody thus moves independently of the text. Despite this, relative pitch continues to be correlated with vowel height.

As melodic entities, *dañoʔre* occupy an intermediate position between wailing and oratory: in terms of melodic complexity, they are relatively unsophisticated; however they are melodically more complex than speech in the oratorical style. Furthermore, the vocal style used to perform *dañoʔre* falls between what we might consider "speaking-voice" and "singing-voice." They are distinctly unlike speech, however, in that the melodic contour moves independent of the linguistic text. For example, in the transcribed piece, the phrase "*höi wa nem hö za*" can be accompanied by a variety of melodic contours (see appendix).

Political oratory, although most sophisticated with regard to semantic content, lies at the lowest end of the melodic hierarchy. Indeed, the "music-like" quality of political oratory derives from the repetition of linguistically similar (or identical) phrases. Consequently there is no melody independent of linguistically produced intonation patterns. The intonation patterns that render speech in this style "music-like" depend totally on the voice modulations of spoken utterances and the repetition of linguistic text. Thus, in plaza speech the musical effects of language use are directly tied to propositional parallelism.[15]

The present analysis has focused on three parameters relevant to three expressive forms of communication from the Shavante vocal repertoire: (1) linguisticality, (2) melodic complexity, and (3) performance location and social space ideology. I have attempted to show that *dawawa* wailing, *daño?re* singing, and political oratory, can be ranged along a continuum. The poles of this continuum are, to use structuralist terminology, "nature" and "culture." On the side of nature is language-less wailing, highly melodic (in terms of pitch manipulation) and localized in the domestic sphere. On the side of culture is political oratory, linguistically sophisticated and localized in the village center, yet melodically impoverished. Mediating between the two is *daño?re* singing, less melodic (in terms of pitch content) yet more linguistic than wailing, less linguistic yet more melodic than oratory. Fittingly, it is localized between village center and periphery.[16]

Appendix 1: *dawawa* -Wailing

Key: F = falsetto of indistinct pitch;   ' . . . ' denotes short pauses of indefinite length between phrases, varying up to two seconds.

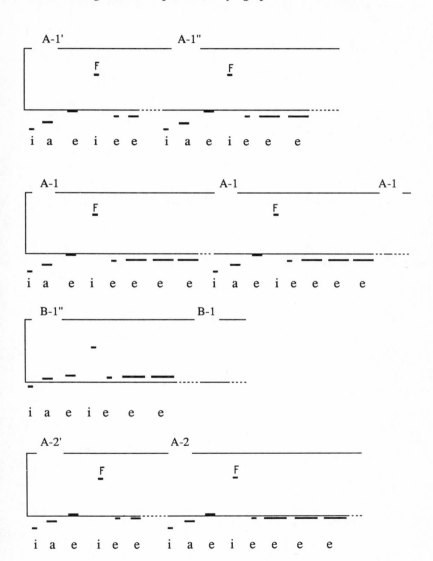

i e   e   i   e   e   e   e

i a e i   e   e   e

i a   e i e e

i e e i   e   e   e

i a e i e e   i a e i e e

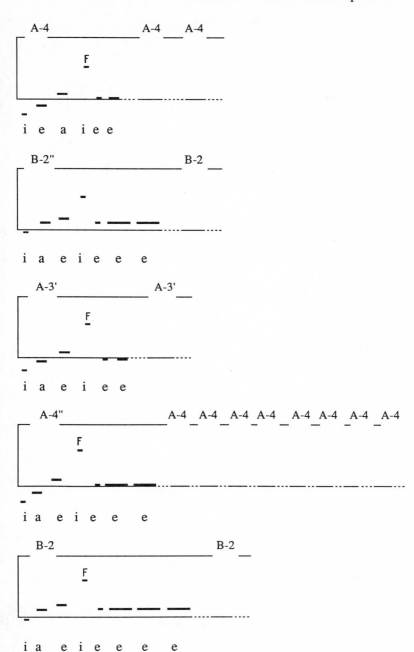

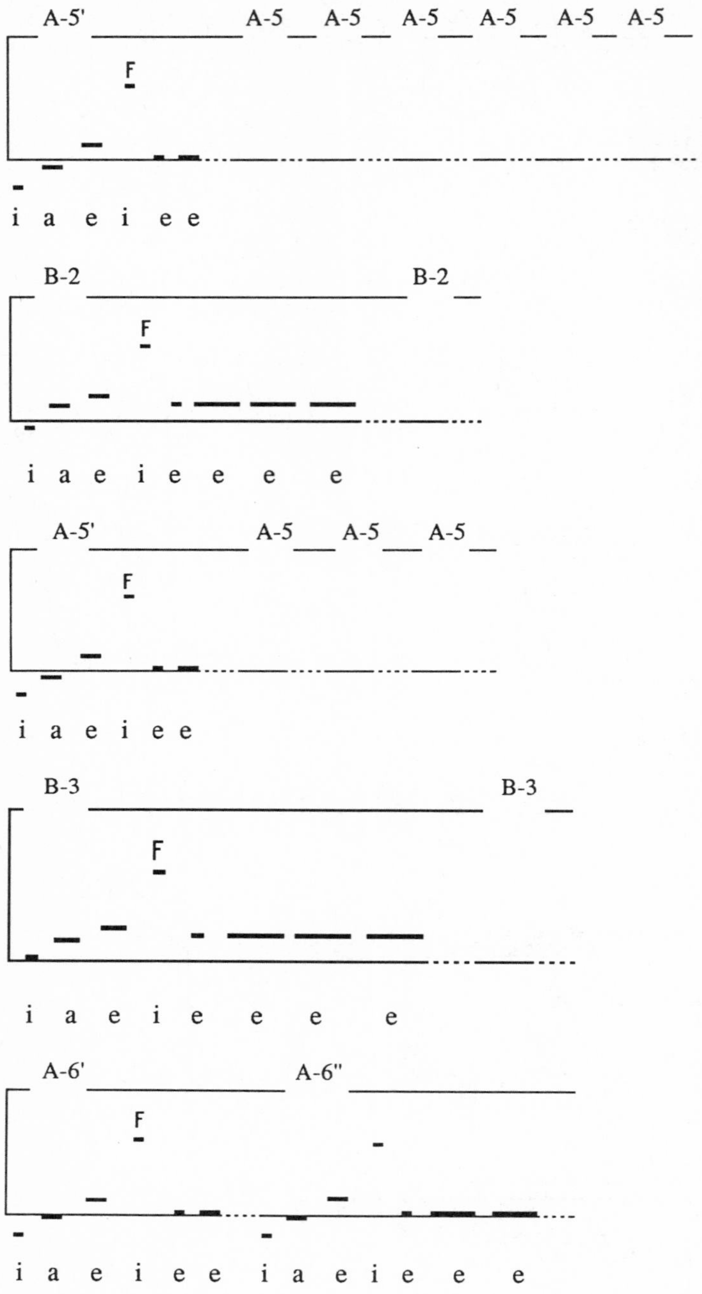

A-5'   A-5   A-5   A-5   A-5   A-5   A-5

F

i a e i e e

B-2   B-2

F

i a e i e e e

A-5'   A-5   A-5   A-5

F

i a e i e e

B-3   B-3

F

i a e i e e e

A-6'   A-6"

F

i a e i e e i a e i e e e

A-5   A-5   A-5   A-5   A-5

i a e i e   e   e

A-5   A-5   A-5   A-5 A-5   A-5

i a e i e   e   e

B-3   B-3

F

i a e i e   e   e

A-7'   A-8'   A-9

F   F   F

i a e   i e e   i a e i e e   i a e i e e   e   e

A-10   A-11

F   F

i a e i e e   e   e   i a e   i   e   e   e   e

A-12   A-12   A-12   A-12

F

i   a   e   i   e   e   e

B-4   B-4

F   F

i   a   e   i   e   e   e   i   a   e   i   e   e   e

A-13'   A-12

F   F

i   a   e   i   e   e   i   a   e   i   e   e   e

A-13   A-13   A-13

F

i   a   e   i   e   e   e

B-5   B-5

F

i   a   e   i   e   e   e

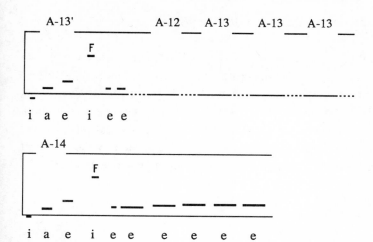

Appendix 2:   *daño?re*   - Collective Singing

As suggested in the text, *daño?re* voice quality ranges along a continuum between singing voice and shouting-chanting. To indicate the ambiguity ' . . . ' is used in the transcription. Where musical pitch is identifiable ' . . . ' appears above the pitch reference line. ' . . . ' marked below the pitch reference line indicates the absence of identifiable musical pitch, in my judgment. Differences in utterance length are indicated by the length of dashed lines. The pitch reference line corresponds to E above middle C.

Leader

hoi   wa   nem hö za   hoi   wa   nem hö za

Chorus

hoi   wa   nem hö za   hoi   wa nem   hö za

Chorus

hoi   wa   nem   hö za   hoi   wa   nem   hö za

Leader   Chorus

hoi   wa   nem   hö za   hoi   wa   nem hö za

Chorus

···· ···· ···· ·· ···   ···· ···· ···· ·· ···

hoi wa nem hö za   hoi wa nem hö za

Chorus

····   ···· ·· ···   ···· ···· ·· ···
····   ····
hoi wa nem hö za   hoi wa nem hö za

Chorus

···· ···· ·· ···
····
hoi wa nem hö za

Chorus

···· ···· ···· ···· ···· ····

hö   hö   wē   wē   wē   wē

Chorus

··   ··   ···· ····   ···· ····

a   zɛ na   he   he   he

Leader   Chorus

···· ···· ····   ···· ····

····   ····   ···· ···· ···· ···· ···· ····

hi   he   he   he   hi   hi   hi   hi   hi   hi   hi   hi   hi

Chorus

··   ··   ····   ····   ···· ····   ···· ···· ····

····

a   zɛ   na   he   he   he   hi   he   he   he

Chorus

···· ····

····   ···· ···· ···· ···· ···· ····

hi   hi   hi   hi   hi   hi   hi   hi   hi

Chorus

···· ····

···· ···· ···· ···· ···· ···· ····

hi   hi   hi   hi   hi   hi   hi   hi   hi

Chorus

···· ····   ···· ····

···· ····   ···· ·· ··

hi   hi   hi   hi   hi hi   hi   wa ma

Chorus

....

....

hi   hi   hi   hi   wɛ̄   ɛ̄   ɛ̄   ɛ̄   nem hö za

Chorus

....

.. ..

hoi wa nem hö za   hoi wa nem hö za

Chorus

....

hoi   wa   nem hö   za   hoi wa   nem hö   za

Chorus

....

hoi   wa   nem   hö   za   hoi   wa nem hö   za

Chorus

....

hoi wa nem hö za hoi wa nem   hö za hoi wa nem hö za

Appendix 3:   Political   Oratory

te mari
te mari ma ĩno höiwi
    ma ĩno höiwi
            mato uprosi te
te mari ma ĩno höiwi mato uprosi te
        'ʌ'
ʔrowɛna
ʔrowɛna
ʔrowɛena tama
    tama hösu ba mono ne za hã
    tama ĩʔa hã
        ĩʔa waʔrori hã
        ĩʔa waʔrori hã
tete riba upse ba mono pari
ʔrowɛna tama hösu ba mono ne za hã
        'ʌ'
mari te poto uprosi wamha
mari te poto uprosi wamha
    tama waihuʔu aba
    tama waihuʔu aba
        to nɛme
        to nɛme
            anɛ mato
            anɛ mato
            amɛ te toibö
            amɛ te toibö ma
                sorõ ha
                sorõ ha
        tiwi ma hö õ
        tiwi ma hö õ
        'ʌ'

A detailed translation of this text is not available at the present time; the text can be paraphrased as follows:

> what filled the child
> what caused its death
> he was sick with fever in his throat
> what caused him to die
> you all shall know
> it died from a serum

Notes

1. In order of seniority, the age grade classifications are: *airepudu* (young boys), *wapte* (pre-initiates, residents of the bachelor's hut), *ʔritaiʔwa* (novices), *ĩpredu* (mature men). Shavante further divide the mature men's age grade into the categories of *ĩpredupte* (young men; those with one child), *ĩpredu* (mature men with many children), *ĩpredu uptabi* or *ihire* (very old men).
2. Musical transcriptions are located in the appendix. Numerous performances of *daño?re* were recorded, a representative composition is transcribed for the purpose of illustrating the argument presented here (but see Aytai 1976 for further musical description). Wailing understandably proved more difficult to record. The instance transcribed and analyzed offers a representative sample of numerous expressions I heard by the same individual. A second individual's wailing, which was also recorded and examined, conforms to the same melodic principles discussed below. I also heard, but did not record, at least five other wailing laments from other individuals. It should be noted, however, that all statements regarding musical organization made here are based upon etic criteria.
3. The extent to which this genre corresponds to traditional musical patterns has not been established at this time.
4. The prefix "da-" is a collective genitive which, when combined with the verb root "*wawa*" -- to wail, results in the nominalized form "*dawawa*." It is not a morpheme related to the organization of sound or sound articulation.
5. Others describe similar forms of melodic laments as "weeping" (Feld 1982) or "tuneful weeping" (Sherzer 1986, and Tiwary 1975) however, I shall refer to such expressive behavior as ritual wailing, or keening, in

keeping with the terminology established in the South American literature concerning ritual lament where both women and men wail (see Carneiro da Cunha 1978: 24; Henry 1941: 65-66, 188; Maybury-Lewis 1967: 279-280; Seeger 1981: 172; Urban 1985; Wagley 1977).

6. Women in the eastern Shavante village of Pimentel Barbosa, the most traditional of all Shavante communities, dream both *dawawa* and *dañoʔre*. Those of the western Shavante villages in the Kuluene Reserve claim they do not. They explain that their husbands or fathers dream and give *dawawa* to them. It is possible that this difference is the result of missionary influences on the Shavante of Kuluene, or perhaps an expressive difference between the eastern and western Shavante generally. However, at the present time, this hypothesis remains at a purely conjectural level.

7. *aʔãma* are chosen from the mature mens' age-grade to represent the boys residing in the bachelor's hut. Ideally there should be at least two, one from each patrilineal moiety. They should also be from the opposite age-set moiety relative to the sponsored set. The role is analagous to that of a ceremonial father associated with the boys during the liminal phase of residency in the bachelor's hut. *aʔãma* have rights to favors and labor services from the *wapte*. They wail for the *wapte* when the boys render their services.

8. The term "pitch" is not intended to describe an emic category pertaining to the social organization of tones. However, more extensive analysis of Shavante music and sounds may suggest a range of "pitches" that are selected as the emic sound/vocal inventory. I would like to thank Steven Feld for pointing out the potential importance of this distinction.

9. My thanks to John Kingston for observing this correlation.

10. A third rhythmical motif, A"/B" /_ _ . . __ __/, appears irregularly, perhaps as a varient of the A/B motif.

11. In the *dawawa* transcription phrases are marked with numbers to indicate pitch changes, e.g., phrase A-1 goes to A-2 according to a corresponding rise in pitch.

12. For a description of the *waiʔa* see Maybury-Lewis 1967: 255-269.

13. Incumbents of the ceremonial role *wamarĩ tedeʔwa* (owner of the *wamarĩ* - a "dreaming stick" similar in shape to Shavante earplugs but much larger) give counsel to the entire village after dreaming using the

wamarī. wamarī tede?wa receive messages in the same way individuals dream *daño?re* and *dawawa*. However, counsel is transmitted through the "more powerful *wamarī* stick" rather than through the earplugs. I did not observe *wamarī tede?wa* haranguing Shavante communities in either village I visited and am therefore unable to comment on the speech style used in this situation.

14. Suyá song texts perform the same operation, isolating the principles of linguistic organization such that songs evolve from a natural state to a social state through language (see Seeger 1979).

15. I would like to thank Greg Urban for suggesting the differential correlation between text and tune in the three vocal forms.

16. An earlier version of this paper appeared in *Latin American Music Review* 5: 161-185, 1984. Research in two Shavante villages (October, 1981 - May, 1982) was supported by grants from the Inter-American Foundation and the University of Texas at Austin. I wish to express my appreciation to Greg Urban, Richard Bauman, Gerard Béhague, Steven Feld, John Kingston and Joel Sherzer for their comments on earlier drafts of this paper. To Tom Turino I extend special thanks for his assistance with musical analysis and transcriptions.

References Cited

Aytai, Desidério
 1976 O mundo sonoro Xavante. M.A. thesis. Universidade Católica de Campinas, Brazil.
Benveniste, Émile
 1971 Animal communication and human language. In *Problems in general linguistics*, M.E. Meek (trans.), pp. 49-54. Coral Gables: University of Miami Press.
Caraveli-Chaves, Anna
 1980 Bridge between worlds: the Greek women's lament as communicative event. *Journal of American Folklore* 93: 129-157.
 1982 The song beyond the song: aesthetics and social interaction in Greek folksong. *Journal of American Folklore* 95: 129-158.

Cunha, Manuela Carneiro da
   1978   *Os mortos e os otros: uma análise do sistema funerário e da noção de pessoa entre os índios Kraho*. São Paulo: Editora Hucitec.

Da Matta, Roberto
   1976   *Um mundo dividido: a estrutura social dos Indios Apinayé*. Petrópolis: Editora Vozes.
   1979   The Apinayé relationship system: terminology and ideology. In *Dialectical societies*, D. Maybury-Lewis (ed.), pp. 83-127. Cambridge, Mass: Harvard University Press.

Danforth, Loring M.
   1982   *The death rituals of rural Greece*. Princeton: Princeton University Press.

Feld, Steven
   1982   *Sound and sentiment: birds, weeping, poetics, and song in Kaluli expression*. Philadelphia: University of Pennsylvania Press.

Graham, Laura
   1984   Semanticity and melody: parameters of contrast in Shavante vocal expression. *Latin American Music Review* 5: 161-185.

Henry, Jules
   1941   *Jungle people: a Kaingáng tribe of the highlands of Brazil*. New York: Vintage.

Honko, Lauri
   1974   Balto-Finnic lament poetry. *Studia Fennica* 17: 143-202.

Huxley, Francis
   1956   *Affable savages: an anthropologist among the Urubu Indians of Brazil*. New York: Capricorn Books.

Hymes, Dell
   1974   *Foundations in sociolinguistics: an ethnographic approach*. Philadelphia: University of Pennsylvania Press.
   1977   Discovering oral performance and measured verse in American Indian narrative. *New Literary History* 8: 431-457.

Jakobson, Roman
   1960   Closing statement: linguistics and poetics. In *Style in language*, T.A. Sebeok (ed.), pp.. 350-377. Cambridge, Mass.: MIT Press.

Klymasz, Robert
1975 Speaking at/about/with the dead: funerary rhetoric among Ukranians in western Canada. *Canadian Ethnic Studies* 7: 50-56.
Lévi-Strauss, Claude
1967 *Structural anthropology*, C. Jacobson and B. G. Schoepf (trans). Garden City, New York: Anchor.
List, George
1963 The boundaries of speech and song. *Ethnomusicology* 7: 1-16.
Maybury-Lewis, David
1967 *Akwē-Shavante society*. New York: Oxford University Press.
Maybury-Lewis, David, ed.
1979 *Dialectical societies: the Gê and Bororo of central Brazil*. Cambridge: Harvard University Press.
Salmond, Anne
1974 Rituals of encounter among the Maori: sociolinguistic study of a scene. In *Explorations in the ethnography of speaking*, R. Bauman and J. Sherzer (ed.), pp. 192-212. Cambridge, England: Cambridge University Press.
Seeger, Anthony
1979 What can we learn when they sing? vocal genres of the Suyá Indians of central Brazil. *Ethnomusicology* 23: 373-394.
1981 *Nature and society in central Brazil: the Suyá Indians of Mato Grosso*. Cambridge: Harvard University Press.
Sherzer, Joel
1982 Poetic structuring of Kuna discourse: the line. *Language in Society* 11: 371-390.
1986 A diversity of voices: men's and women's speech in ethnographic perspective. In *Language, gender, and sex in comparative perspective*, S. Philips, S. Steele, and C. Tanz (eds.). Cambridge: Cambridge University Press. To appear.
Silverstein, Michael
1976 Shifters, linguistic categories, and cutural description. In *Meaning in anthropology*, K. Basso and H. Selby (eds.), pp. 11-55. Albuquerque: University of New Mexico Press.
Tedlock, Dennis
1977 Toward oral poetics. *New Literary History* 8: 507-519.

1978   *Finding the center: narrative poetry of the Zuni Indians.*
       Lincoln: University of Nebraska Press.

Titiev, Mischa

1949   Social singing among the Mapuche. In *Anthropological Papers
       of the Museum of Anthropology of the University of Michigan* ,
       no. 2.

Tiwary, K. M.

1975   Tuneful weeping: a mode of communication. *Working Papers
       in Sociolinguistics*, no. 27.   Austin, Texas: Southwest
       Educational Development Lab.

Turner, Terence

1979   The Gê and Bororo societies as dialectical systems: a general
       model. In *Dialectical societies: the Gê and Bororo of Central
       Brazil*, D. Maybury-Lewis (ed.), pp. 147-178.   Cambridge:
       Harvard University Press.

1980   Le dénicheur d'oiseaux en contexte. *Anthropologie et Sociétés*
       4(3): 85-115.

Urban, Greg

1985   The semiotics of two speech styles in Shokleng. In *Semiotic
       mediation: sociocultural and psychological perspectives*, E.
       Mertz and R. J. Parmentier (eds.), pp. 311-329. New York:
       Academic Press.

Vidal, Lux

1977   *Morte e vida de uma sociedade indígena Brasileira.* São Paulo:
       Hucitec EDUSP.

Wagley, Charles

1977   *Welcome of tears: the Tapirapé Indians of central Brazil* . New
       York: Oxford University Press.

Woodbury, Anthony

1985   The functions of rhetorical structure: a study of central Alaskan
       Yupik Eskimo discourse. *Language in Society* 14: 153-190.

Quoted Dialogues in Kalapalo Narrative Discourse

Ellen Basso

This paper is one outgrowth of a project I began in 1978, involving the ethnographic study of the forms of explanation in a native Amazonian community, the Carib-speaking Kalapalo. My original intention was to discover how such forms might be created and used among a fully non-literate people so as to preserve and communicate knowledge and understanding. To this end, I was especially concerned with learning what sorts of things were considered problematic by the Kalapalo and in need of clarification, how inferences were organized and linguistically coordinated in the construction of explanations, and the ways of speaking used for conveying explanations of different kinds.

As it turned out, the Kalapalo make especially elaborate use of narrative speech to preserve knowledge and to communicate insight and understanding in a process that involves the complex and subtle interplay of didactic, poetic, and psychodynamic functions. The manner in which these functions emerge during the telling of any particular Kalapalo story can only be fully understood in context, that is, with respect to a particular instance of performance involving a specific narrator and a specific listener. This is because Kalapalo narratives are performed dialogically, with a pair of participants (one the narrator, the other a "what-sayer" or responder-ratifier) together constructing the text of a story. While the explanatory content of narratives is quite substantial, narrative functions occur very subtly, almost imperceptibly, since the occasions for story-telling are usually relaxed and enjoyable situations, with people sitting around in the plaza or lying in their hammocks, hoping to hear something detailed and titillating. Narrative performances flow in and out of many ordinary conversations, and while often solemn in tone and sober in content, are a source of entertainment and interest for listeners. The Kalapalo seem to be nearly always seeking information about something, to be trying to figure out why and how something happened, to probe their sources of information. They are apparently deeply concerned with their own place in the world and the meanings of their experiences in it. Little seems to be taken for granted, or dogmatic. Much is questioned and alternative points of view receive willing - though often sceptical - listeners. And yet, there is a sense of persistent solidarity that accompanies the notion of *kuge* , "we people" - the term Kalapalo use to contrast themselves with outsiders and to thereby assert their unique identity. One very important way in which this solidarity is achieved is through persistent attempts by individuals to achieve (through conversational dialogue) validation of goals. This is an important process among the Kalapalo, being at the root of personal and social cooperation and often resulting in substantial and powerful community consensus. In this paper, I examine this process of dialogical validation indirectly, or rather, as the Kalapalo themselves represent it in mythological narrative discourse.

The Kalapalo narrative (*akiña*) is a way of speaking that includes both personal and traditional stories. Personal narratives are told in conversational contexts but also in public, somewhat formal situations when a person narrates in the central plaza, a setting representing community interests and therefore implicating the truth-value of what is said. Examples of these situations include a hereditary leader-messenger who has returned home from inviting a neighboring settlement to a ceremony, or a person who has come to visit after a long absence, when meticulously detailed events of journeys are expected. Hunters, fishermen, traders, and shamans all narrate their experiences in public places - in the central plaza where men congregate, and in front of the house, a gathering spot for women - especially when these are unusual and therefore worthy of being shared for the common good. Less formal, gossipy narratives (which are considered somewhat dubious by listeners) are heard embedded in conversations of all kinds held in more private settings, being whispered inside a house, for example, or told more openly to a party of travelers canoeing along a stream, or even in the plaza during informal gatherings of men.

The distinguishing feature of a Kalapalo narrative is the presence of a "what-sayer" (*tiitsofo*) who responds (*etiitsa*) in several conventional ways following the narrator's pauses. These responses fall into several types. The most common are monosyllabic expletives that indicate various feelings about the story (awe, excitement, interest, boredom, or simply, that the listener is paying attention). Second are repetitions of significant words from the preceding utterance, which signal the listener's understanding that they are significant; these tend to be repeated once more by the narrator (to validate the listener's comprehension of their importance) which results in pervasive repetition and parallelism in the text (an important emergent feature of narrative performances). Finally, at certain major breaks in the story, the what-sayer can   (and probably, should, since those who don't are prompted to do so by the speaker) ask questions and thereby gain clarification or further detail. Thus, the what-sayer contributes substantially to the construction of the text: by marking line segments, by politely signalling to the speaker that the images he or she is constructing are understood, appreciated, and agreed with, and by diverting the speaker into new channels of detail and explication which might not be strictly pertinent to the story but enhance the listener's understanding while confirming the expertise of the narrator.

Kalapalo narratives are performed to varying degrees, depending upon the context. The more public the context and the more traditional the content, the more performed the narrative tends to be, and the more authoritative the text is considered. This authority is in part based upon who is doing the telling (hereditary officials called *anetau* usually are the public narrators, expected to narrate myths in the ceremonial house, for example). But also, authority is related to the fact that traditional narratives are considered to be knowledge that has been deliberately preserved for the succeeding generations of listeners. Hence, the public nature of the telling tends to implicate a truth-value to these stories, even when they are personal narratives of recent vintage.

A Kalapalo performed narrative is one that is evaluated basically in terms of the success of conveying content; a good story-teller, the Kalapalo say, is one who keeps repetition to a minimum, and does not bore or embarrass the listener with excessive personal opinions or digressions. But a Kalapalo performance also necessarily involves the what-sayer, who is being evaluated (especially by the narrator, but also anyone else who might be interested in hearing the narrative) according to how alert the responses are and how much they are in keeping with the rhythms of the narrator's telling. These rhythms are created by the patterns of intonational contouring that are the results of pausing after lines for the what-sayer's response, repetition of significant lines, and modulation of the voice in keeping with the segmenting processes.[1]

Quoted Speech

One of the more striking aspects of a Kalapalo narrative - be it personal or traditional - is the amount and variety of quoted speech embedded in the story. In many narratives, quoted speech constitutes as much as eighty percent or even more of a text so that we must consider strongly the possibility that those narratives are "about" dialogues. Given this possibility, it is worth looking closely at how what is quoted contributes to the significance of a Kalapalo story.[2] Indeed, the functions of quoted speech are complex and multilayered, including *metapragmatic* functions having to do with the ideas Kalapalo have concerning speech, its functions and consequences (the "means"), *semantic* functions deriving from the content of what is being said (the "what"), and *pragmatic* discourse coherence functions, emerging from narrative segmentation and the resultant structural features of a story (the "how"). All these parallel functions direct us to an understanding of the "who" - how particular characters are conceived and how these conceptions suggest a broader framework of propositions about language, personhood, and society. In traditional Kalapalo narratives or *myths*, quoted speech is clearly the most important way of developing characters and of giving meaning to their activities, because quoted speech constructs socially dynamic differences in the characters' attitudes towards one another's action. As important characters shift ground from one dynamic posture to another, their quoted speech forms a coherent narrative progression that involves the ordered integration of statements about feelings, goals, enactments, and accomplishments. Through speech, feelings - the emotional quality of experiences - are shown to motivate the formulation of goals, or (to put it somewhat differently) goals are qualified and given shape through what are presented as motivating feelings.

To illustrate this and the various interconnected functions of quoted speech in Kalapalo narrative discourse, I will refer to the story of

"Cuckoo" as it was told to me by the cheerful, musically skilled Kudyu, a man in late middle age, father of six and a notorious joker. Kudyu's story exemplifies the Kalapalo concern with the illusory nature and consequent unpredictability of human action, and with how what is said may conceal another reality. It is one of a large number of stories in which the trickster Taugi appears, although here the story is told not from Taugi's point of view but from that of the people who must deal with his tricks. The tone in which Kudyu told it to me was far from solemn and didactic. He delighted in illustrating the different ways of speaking central to the story by taking on the characters' voices very freely and (as you will see from reading the story) was concerned to draw out the implications of what he said when my bemusement became clear as I struggled with my inner simultaneous translation of the Kalapalo. The complete text and a free translation of this story is found at the end of the paper; the reader should perhaps read it through first, then refer to it from time to time while following my analysis of specific features of the narrative. This is the best way to appreciate the story as an example of Kalapalo verbal art, in which poetic and rhetorical processes are superbly combined by a master storyteller.

Narrative Structures in "Cuckoo"

There are several ways to describe the narrative discourse structure of "Cuckoo". The first draws attention to an important segmentation device ubiquitous in Kalapalo narrative art, which is *reference to the experiencing of time*. Such references are in general allusions to the planning or persistence of a character's goal-oriented action. In the story of Cuckoo, Kudyu makes five explicit references of this sort, which seem to signal shifts in theme of one magnitude or another. There are (counting an opening segment) six resulting units. These, together with the temporal references that introduce each of them as apparently discrete narrative units, are listed in Table 1.

Table I: Major Segmentation in "Cuckoo"
by Temporal Reference

I.   lines 1 -31: begins with the opener,
     Tsakefa, which separates the
     performed narrative from ordinary
     conversation

II. lines 32-137: begins with line "Now, the
     next day at dawn,"

III. lines 138-259: begins with lines "That
     was all that happened until,
             it grew dark."

IV. lines 260-268: begins with line "After
     he had slept three days,"

V.   lines 269-310: begins with line "There
     he slept he slept,"

VI. lines 311-end: begins with lines
     "Listen.
             Then after they had slept a long
             time they went to look at it."

Within all six segments are references to sleeping, which
seem to mark continuity in Cuckoo's psychological orientation to some
existing state of affairs: from creating a plan to carrying it through. First,
Cuckoo expresses his desire to marry and tells his mother he will depart the
next day (I). After sleeping, he carries out this plan (II). Next, Cuckoo
ponders his relatives' need for a real house. He tells his wife he must leave
the next day to visit his mother. After sleeping, he goes to his mother for
ratification of his plan for accomplishing his goal of making their house
possible (III), and then (after saying he will depart the next day and sleeping
once again) he decisively carries out the plan (IV). Along the way,

reference is made to sleeping several more times, which suggests the plan is working (the grass keeps growing until it is mature enough to use, and this takes time) (V).

The last segment (VI) poses something of a problem, because in line 353 Kudyu again uses the expression *tsakefa*, suggesting another narrative break. And indeed, although there is no reference to time following this line (as there is at the beginning of segment VI, in lines 311-12), there is such a major shift in narrative content that I feel justified in creating a seventh segment incorporating lines 353 through 475 (the conclusion). Segment IV and V are clearly less substantial than are the other segments, but I prefer to keep them separate as integral units of the same order as I, II, III, VI, and now VII; references to time and the introductory *tsakefa* are now used as joint markers of major segment breaks. By doing so, segment VII not only introduces a new character, it reinforces the narrative progression of Cuckoo's goal-oriented action. Segment VII in fact involves action that modifies or transforms Cuckoo's expected goal into something different than but nonetheless logically following from certain features of the earlier action, namely, Cuckoo's attitudes toward what he is trying to do. But before examining this point further, I continue with the narrative segmenting process.

Within three of the seven major segmental divisions are smaller ones which I have marked by capital letters (see Table II). These divisions are suggested by Kudyu's references to *travelling*, another important technique in Kalapalo narrative discourse. When a character travels in these stories, there is a sense that imaginative boundaries are being crossed. Travelling emphasizes the differences in the character's experiences occurring in discrete locales, made clear by the distinctive linguistic styles used in each place. Cuckoo, for example, moves back and forth between his mother (with whom he speaks casually and informally) and his in-laws, where conversations follow the very different patterns of "affinal" speech. The segments that result from references to Cuckoo's travels connect Cuckoo's statements of goals with his activities leading toward achieving his plan to give his in-laws a new kind of dwelling. And similarly, Taugi's travelling in segment VII does the same with respect to what he had decided to do about such a dwelling. But these units are even more interesting because they key the shifts in "footing" (to use Erving

Goffman's expression) that mark some distinctive changes in the character's contextually-based point of view.[3] (In other stories, travel-marked segments also underscore contrasts between the points of view between different characters).

Table II: Segmentation in "Cuckoo" by
Features of Narrative Discourse

(In this table, I indicate references to time, to travelling, and to the onset and completion of activities, as well as exhortations to a listener-responder to pay attention).

I. The plan described by Cuckoo and ratified by his mother
        (lines 1-31):

Starts line 1:   Now, listen
                        ah tsakefa

Ends line 31:   That's just what I'll do.
                        isagagey

II. Goal-oriented action initiated and completed (lines 32-137):

    A. Action toward goal initiated:

Starts line 32:   Now, the next day at dawn,
                        ah, mitote kogetsi

                        he went on.
                        etelulefa

Ends line 47:   and he arrived that day.
                        ande timbelu

B. Action toward goal completed:

Starts line 48:   "Kao! Mbuh!
kao! mbuh!

Ends line 137:   she put the bread on top of his
drinking bowl.
tïokugu ugupoŋa

III. New problem described and solution proposed (lines 138-258):

A. Wife describes problem and Cuckoo verifies it:

Starts line 138:   They say that was all that
happened until,
uletsïgïtsedyetifa,

it grew dark.
afugutilï

Ends line 172:   That was all.
aifa.

B. Cuckoo's new plan begins:

Starts line 173:   "Tomorrow I must go to see
Mother and the others.
kogetsifetsaŋe
utelïŋofofo amañuko iña.

Ends line 200:   He had gone to do service for
his parents-in-law.
fatuwïifegey teta.

C. Cuckoo seeks and receives verification of problem and
    ratification of plan by mother:

Starts line 201:   He arrived home.
                          etimbelu

Ends line 239:   "Very well", she said.
                          eh he nïgifeke

D. Goal-directed action begins:

Starts line 240:   So he left.
                          etelïlefa.

Ends line 258:   When he was done,
                          aifa.

                          he came back.
                          sinïgïlefa.

IV. Persistence of goal-directed action (lines 260-8):

Starts line 260:   After he had slept three days,
                          tilako sïŋïpïgï,

Ends line 268:   That was over.
                          aifa.

V. The house-building motive is proposed (269-310):

Starts line 269:   Then he slept, he slept,
                          lepe sïŋïlï, sïŋïlï,

Ends line 310:   He intended to create that very thing.
                          igey fegey iŋïitanïmi.

VI. The house-building is proposed and ratified; new goal-oriented actions begin, and are nearly completed (lines 311-352):

Starts line 311: Listen.
etsakefa.

Then after they had slept
a long time they went to
look at it.
lepe akïŋi sïŋïpïgï
atani iŋiluliña tuteko.

Ends line 352: They were finished.
etïkilïko.

VII. Modification of final goal (lines 353-475):

A. Cukoo's premature declaration of accomplishment:

Starts line 353: Now listen!
ah tsakefa!

Ends line 361-2: I mean we'll soon be inside of this thing here,
igeatsehale tiñanïgï,

this thing here."
igea.

B. Taugi's unratified plan declared:

Starts line 363: Then, well, someone told Taugi about it.
lepe, ah Taugi iña tikagi.

Ends line 376:   Mm, mm, mmmm! Now, they came as wind after that,
mm mm mmm! ah fitembe...

C. Action toward goal begins:

Starts line 377:   "Look at how these stems are growing out!"
ikefa ifigikundïgïfa ah sinïgï,

Ends line 444:   He went on after that.
etelumbe.

D. Completion of goal:

Starts line 445 :   Then after that happened, even so he went back to where they were pulling it up.
lepetalelegey, lepembe togopisi, ñokitofona

Ends line 453:   This time it came up the way it does now.
laŋope fegey.

E. Realization that goals have been modified:

Starts line 454:   Then the others went to their clearing to pull some out.
lepe tsupofoŋo ōkiluiña tuteko.

Ends line 474:   That's how it happened.
alaŋo fegey.

End of story (performance closure achieved):

Ends line 475:   That's really all there is to that.
apïgïaketsaŋe.

These contextually-located (and dialogically constructed) points of view are suggested by the grammatical marking (through verb inflections such as tense, aspect, mode, and mood, and through evidential deixis) of dynamic relations between characters. Generally, these relations are indicated through the (usually) grammaticalized typification of different "ways of speaking" (oratory, affinal conversation, "normal" conversation, joking, the quiet modesty of pubescent youths) but more specific and narrow "ways of thinking" (such as assertion, negotiation, doubt, dissimulation, defiance, and validation) are also suggested. Although the latter are made apparent by semantic content, evidential and validation suffixes and words in particular serve to indicate the values surrounding what is being said, ideas about procedure, and the perceived consequences of a decision to act in a certain way. These grammatical forms assist markedly in giving Cuckoo and his relatives substance, and in contrasting them one with another, and with Taugi himself. This is, in fact, how we come to understand the psychological process of doubt, assertion, dissimilation, domination, and humility which underlie their various speech acts. These and other feelings - marked and unmarked - contribute to the formulation of propositional statements, questions, and directives of various kinds.

It is especially worthwhile to examine statements of motive with regard to evidentials. Ideas about a character's motives are expressed through that character's own statement of feelings concerning a situation or another character, through responses to past or anticipated actions of others (as causes or effects of their own actions) and through references to authority (be it political, traditional, common sense, or even their own in the case of hereditary leaders). What makes Cuckoo especially attractive as a character is that Kudyu portrays him in this story as an active, conscious person faced with necessities and purposes that force him to be ever mindful of choice and consequence, with the result that he expresses various feelings of uncertainty, commitment, self-assurance, and necessity or even duty. The latter develop from his successful affinal relations, established early in the story, which commits him to completing the exchange begun when he was allowed to marry his cousin. His decision to make a new house is as much a consequence of his new son-in-law status as it has to do with his eyes. And these feelings of Cuckoo are made most explicitly meaningful in social contexts which bring them to the surface, contextualize them, and allow them to be commented upon and responded to favorably by others because they constitute the substance of action. Such supportive acquiescence seems needed initially because Cuckoo's proposals are couched in terms of uncertainty and emphatic modesty. But even later on, Cuckoo (having been confirmed by his relatives all along) becomes much too sure of himself, even though his support seems to follow naturally because the relationship is proceeding well.

Shifts in Footing

The first kind of shift in footing involves Cuckoo moving between the environment of his mother and the environment of his affines. There are three instances of this: the first described in lines 33-47, when Cuckoo leaves home to seek a bride; the second (line 210), when Cuckoo returns home to seek confirmation of his desire to give his in-laws a new house; the third (line 240), when Cuckoo returns to his wife's family in order to accomplish his new goal of making thatch for them to use.

The different environments are of course made clear by what Kudyu tells us about where Cuckoo happens to be at any moment, and shifts in footing are suggested by the different ways of speaking he and his relations use in each place. Among his affines, Cuckoo's speech is metaphoric and self-abnegating - that is, allusive and indirect. When Cuckoo and his hoped-for father-in-law are speaking to each other, for example, inversions figure prominently (lines 54-137); when Cuckoo later needs to convey some information to his (now established) father-in-law, the affinal avoidance taboo necessitates his wife serving as intermediary for Cuckoo and her father.[4]

Contrasting with this highly marked affinal speech is Cuckoo's conversations with his mother and his wife. These are entirely open, being non-metaphorical and direct.[5] But there is more than a simple contrast here between affinal and "familiar" or "informal" speech. Cuckoo experiences another interesting change during the progress of the story, which is a reinforcement in his point of view. Despite the several shifts in footing this reinforcement is achieved because of the pragmatic function (rather than style or register) of the dialogues, which is, in a word, *validation*. In the specific context of this story, validation involves the assertion of a generally accepted authority, that of the community of relatives, perpetuates exchange within the context of marriage relations, and in the end acts convincingly to overcome doubt and hesitation.

Validation in "Cuckoo"

In line 14 Cuckoo informs his mother of his desire to marry, but he is anxious and uncertain about being able to accomplish this. Cuckoo's modest doubt about his own worth as a husband (however stereotyped and expected it might be of a young man) is conveyed by his use of the expression *talokimukaketsaŋe* (structurally, "without reason" + devalued mode + emphatic action mode, that is "the worthless, fruitless action that I must follow"). This statement is coupled with the continuous aspect/conditional mood marker *fota* ("might"). (The narrator's paraphrase, however, makes use of the intentional mode ("wanted to") in line 18). Despite this uncertainty, Cuckoo's mother validates his plan by the agreement phrase, "Very well" (*eh he*). By contrast, Cuckoo is very assertive in line 30, when, in response to his Mother's advice that he return immediately if his relatives don't accept him (a plausible expectation for Kalapalo suitors), he uses the punctate aspect/potential mood form *iŋo* ("will"). He is even more assured when (in lines 173ff.) he tells his new wife that he needs to visit his mother: this time Cuckoo uses the emphatic declarative + punctate aspect/ potential mood form *ketsaŋe* + *iŋo* ("must"). And finally, Cuckoo confirms his own good judgement in lines 265-6 and 273-4, using the positive confirmation through first-hand experience (recent past tense evidential marker *-maki*). There is, in other words, a clear progression from Cuckoo's hesitation, modesty, and slight anxiety to an attitude of smooth confidence and self-assured anticipation of success. Towards the end, there is even an excess of confidence when, as the final segment begins, he assures his relatives (lines 359-62), "As you see we're all ready here, once and for all ... we're all ready. And we'll soon be inside here, here." The progression from doubt to self-confidence seems to be a consequence of the continuous validation that Cuckoo receives (by the statement *eh he*) virtually every time he speaks to someone.

Why do I sense that Cuckoo's assurance about the future good life of his family is inappropriate? This is because of how, somewhat later, Taugi speaks in lines 398-400. There, reference to the future by means of the continuous aspect/ potential mood marker *ni* sets up this character as dominant, in the sense of controlling transformative power (*itseketu*) over the others. As exemplified by this particular usage of the curse *lafa itsani*, transformative power can involve the reshaping of goals, and the resultant unanticipated conclusion of action directed by some earlier plans whose success seemed certain.

Lies about Himself;   Taugi's Invalid Action

I turn now to what must have struck the reader as an obvious (and neglected) topic, the strange disconformity between events involving Cuckoo and his family (segments I-VI) and those involving the trickster Taugi and his brother Aulukuma (VII). Taugi's speech and action all seem to invert the formula laid out in Cuckoo's actions. His speech is (in Mikhail Bakhtin's sense) *dialogical*, representing a point of view that is resisted, even irreconcilable with those around him. His actions are unratified and invalid, or even, incapable of receiving validation. Although his brother Aulukuma apparently validates his plans, there is a muttered aside (lines 406-8) that tells us of his disapproval. Taugi's actions are therefore not developed through dialogue but monologically in his mind - or the trickster's *itseketu*. Rather than being convinced or even coerced through speech, people are enchanted by Taugi. At best, they can only ineffectually protest to one another. (At worst, they are destroyed outright.) Taugi (whose name means, "lies about himself") is the trickster who created human beings and who established much of the conditions (usually the unfortunate conditions) that presently govern human life. In "Cuckoo" Taugi's character is particularly clear regarding his non-validated, unratified monological speech and actions.

Related to the contrast between validation and non-validation is a social distinction. In the segments concerned primarily with Cuckoo's activities, there is a continuous chain of interactions in which one of the participants in each of the constituent segments also participates in the dialogue that follows that segment. But there is a disjunction between these segments and the last one, when the chain of interaction is broken. At the beginning of VII, an unidentified "someone" tells Taugi about the grass. There is no evidence that this person was a participant in the previous action involving Cuckoo and his relatives, and, to judge from other stories, most likely this "someone" spied upon human existence as an outside accidental observer (an *agouti*, perhaps, digging in the trash mounds around the house). In other words, Taugi does not actively participate in Cuckoo's social network, but stands apart. This is much more than a "geographic" distance; it is more truly ecological in that Taugi's speech and actions can't actually be validated at all because he exists outside the sphere of human social life. More cosmological than personal, there are implications in how Taugi is portrayed for all human beings "now and forever". Whereas the validation of Cuckoo's actions perpetuate a situation of solidarity that is characterized by exchange, Taugi's action is not invalid action, but the opposite of exchange: one-sided, senseless destruction that doesn't even benefit the destroyer. And yet, we have to remember that Taugi is a trickster. While his actions can't be validated, there is an ambiguity to them which we see in the consequences he attributes to them. Thatching grass is no longer easy to work with, but the very fact that it is now an unpleasant and difficult material to work with makes human beings stronger, since they are forced by necessity to work harder. It is in such hidden consequences that Taugi's trickster character most certainly achieves its most morally significant expression

Conclusion

As we have seen in the story of Cuckoo, most quoted speech in Kalapalo narratives is dialogue discourse, involving two people talking to each other.[6] Indeed (like many people), the Kalapalo understand speech in general to be preeminently dialogical in *that* sense. But within this dialogue discourse there is often emergent monologicality, in which the power and authority of a collective whole is gladly contributed to by the participants, most notably through ratification, validation, and reference to traditional or commonly agreed-upon authority. There is replication in mythological quoted speech of what occurs in real life, the quoted speech content of a narrative functioning metalinguistically as a replica of the functions of "real speech". Dialogicality is in the service, in other words, of creating a monological understanding or perspective on the content, of effecting a shared understanding and explicit acceptance of explanatory or didactic messages in a narrative and of particular points of view. I now have some basis for suggesting that the quotative frame (indicated by the use of one or another of the speech act verbs) provides a special interpretive focus upon the efforts of characters - whether they assert solidarity, try to establish a common ground within contexts of social action by negotiating different points of view, or emphasize their differences of feeling and of identity. As I noted earlier, the emotional quality of these efforts always involves a point of view about *action*.   Deception, defiance, and estrangement, as well as validation or ratification, confirmation or verification of evidence, and acquiescence or agreement with a plan, are dominant feelings that emerge in Kalapalo dialogues concerning plans about activites. Characters are fleshed out both through what they say and how they say something but more significantly their acts are made meaningful in terms of the emotional flavor of cause or motive as well as some anticipated potential effects.

With this in mind, and turning once more to the story of Cuckoo, the dialogicality there now seems to be most basically functioning to ratify or validate goals, and to suggest the social and personal implications and consequences of that validation. In "Cuckoo", solidarity, achieved through dialogical validation of goals, effects successful exchange, which expands the domain and increases the force of generational ties, and ultimately, the perpetuation of a particular way of life.

Fitsagu the Cuckoo. Told by Kudyu to Ellen Basso at the Kalapalo
Settlement of Aifa. July 4, 1982

I   Now, listen.
    ah tsakefa.
        He was Cuckoo.
        fitsagu eley.
            Cuckoo, you know who I'm talking about, don't you?
            fitsagu, tufutisanafa ekefe
            The one with the long tail.
            igokogo igeyfunu itumitsugu
                He was Cuckoo.   5
                fitsagu eley.
Well, he sat down.
um! isakandïfïgï atani,
        He sat down.
        isakandïfïgï.
      "Mother," he said,
      ama nïgifeke,
          "Mother."
          ama.
"Yes?", she answered,   10
ai nïgifeke,
        "Yes?"
        ai.
"Listen now to what I am saying.
tsakefofo ukilï,
        Listen now to what I'm saying.
        tsakefofo ukilï.
I want to go try for Uncle's daughter, even though it
probably won't work out.
eŋufetsaŋe talokimukaketsaŋe awadyu
indisïna utefota.
        At the Igifagafïtu settlement."   15
        eŋufa Igifagafïtuna.[7]

He was going there to be the husband of the
daughter of the Igifagafïtu leader.
  Igifagafïtu anetugu endisï iŋisoi ege teta.
    He was asking his mother about her.
    igia ikatafa legey tïtina.
      He wanted to go there.
      etetomi.
Because Cuckoo wanted to go do service for
his parents-in-law.
eŋïfa fitsagu tetomifa afatuwïi.
    At Igifagafïtu.   20
    Igifagafïtuna.
"All right, go ahead," his mother said.
en he kiŋi nïgifeke
    "That's all right with me.
    eh he kiŋi
Go if you wish,
etekepapa,
    go then.
    eketefa.
If your sister doesn't want you,   25
ñafetsïfa iñandsufeke etifuñetote,
    you'll come back to me right away."
    enïmiŋo
"All right," he answered.
eh he nïgifeke
"that's just how I'll be,
sagagey witsani,
    Just that way.
    isagagey.
I'll come back if that's what she does,   30
Mother
sagageydyetafa wenïmiŋo ama.
    That's just how I'll be."
    isagagey.

II A   Now, the next day at dawn,
    ah mitote kogetsi,
        he went on.
        etelulefa.
  Then,
  lepene,
      "I'm going right now Mother.   35
      utelakigey ama.
      I'm going right now."
      utelakigey.
      "All right, go then."
      eh he teketsïfa.
         All right, go then,
         eh he teketsïfa.
            go then.
            teketsïfa.
         If your uncle wants you to give up your
         sister,   40
         ñafefa isogofekefa iñandsu etifunetote,
            you will come right back."
            enïmiŋo.
    "All right," he said,
    eh he nïgifeke.
      "That's just what I'll do if he feels that way,
      sagageyfetsaŋe witsani,
         That's just what I'll do if he feels
         that way," he said.
         sagageyfetsaŋe witsani nïgifeke.
He went on after that.   45
etelumbe.
  So he went on,
  telïlefa,
      and he arrived that day.
      ande timbelu.

B   "Kao !" *Mbuh* !
    kao ! mbuh !
        all the people of Igifagafïtu called out to him!
        ah Igifagafïtu otomo etukwenïgï.
            The people of Igifagafïtu Community.   50
            Igifagafïtu otomo.
        He was going there to do service for his
        parents-in-law,
        segatifa etetofo fatuwïi,
            to do service for his parents-in-law.
            fatuwïi.
    "Why are you here?", they asked,
    uwameitsa nïgifeke,
        as Cuckoo stood beside his uncle.
        ah tïdyogokaiŋa.
    "Uncle," he went.   55
    awa, nïgifeke.
    "Yes?", the other answered.
    ai, nïgifeke.
    "Now, as you see I am here.
    ah, andeaka uwanïgï.
            I am certainly here.
            andeaka uwanïgï.
        I have certainly come here to you because,
        even though it might not work out,
        I want to try to be lazy,
        wetaketsaŋe igey talokimukefa eŋïñei
        witsomi,
            to be lazy."   60
            eŋïnei.
    "Well yes, I agree," he answered.
    eh he kiŋi, nïgifeke.
    That was Cuckoo.
    fitsagu feley.
    He was going there to do service for his
    parents-in-law.
    fatuwïi eteta,

     to do service for his parents-in-law.

     fatuwïi.

"Well, yes, I agree," his uncle said,   . 65

um ! eh he kiŋi nïgifeke,

     "That's all right with me."

     eh he kiŋi.

  "Look, your younger brother is here for you,"

  he said.

     eŋï, ŋikefa, efisu enïgï eiña, nïgifeke

     To you alone,

     wegeykutsufa,

     to you alone.

     wegeykutsufa.

"Look what's happening to our daughter," he said

to his wife.   70

ŋikefofo ukindisï, nïgifeke tufitsufeke.

     "Look what's happening to our daughter."

     ŋikefofo ukindisï

"That's just the way it should be, that's just

the way it should be.

alatsï alatsï.

     Let him come do service for you if he

     wishes to be with our daughter.

     lapapa efatuwï etanitsïfa ukindisïña

          Let him do that."

          la.

"All right."   75

eh he.

"All right, as you wish."

ohsipapa

     Her father tied Cuckoo's hammock about

     her.

     idyatelïlefa isupoŋa isuwïfeke.

Above his daughter.

indisï ahtupoŋa.

There,

inafa.

there.   80

ina.

So his wife slept beneath him then.

ofiñelefa ifitsu nïgï.

"All right, go ahead,

ogiña ogi,

all right, go ahead.

ogiña ogi.

Say, make something to drink for your
younger brother.

ah efisï imbake,

Make something to drink for your younger
brother."   85

efisï imbake.

"All right," she answered.

eh he nïgifeke

Well, then she made some cold manioc
drink.

ah tïlisiñe enïgïfaifekelefa.

She made some cold manioc drink.

tïlisiñe enïgï.

Kukuku, heh ! Cuckoo drank it all up while he
sat there.

ku ku ku heh ! tuakandimbele fitsagu itsalefa.

While he sat there.   90

tuakandilefa.

On a seat.

tuakandi.

That was all.

aifa.

"Here, drink some more."

ande timbake.

"All right," he said.

eh he nïgifeke.

"My young relative, drink this stuff that your
sister just washed her hands in.   95
untsi, ah iñandsu etiñatitsïgï iñambake.
    This stuff your sister washed her hands in."
    iñandsu etiñatitsïgï.
"All right," he said.
eh he nigifeke.
Kuku so he drank it up.
kuku elidyulefaifeke.
    He drank it up,
    elidyulefaifeke.
        a big gourdful.   100
        igeyfuna.
"All right, go ahead, make some of that cheap
solo for your younger brother.
ogiña ogi, ah efïsïña solo eŋukitse,
    Some *solo*."
    solo.
He was talking about manioc bread.
kinefeke.
That's what a kind of manioc bread is
called.
kine ititï aketsigey.
If it's poorly made--poorly made manioc
bread--   105
fesiñïfa, fesiñïfa kine ikidyumbedya
    made from crudely made manioc starch,
    fesiñïfa timbuku,
        it's called *solo*.
        solo ititï.
That's what the Kanugidyafïtï people call it,
igatafoifa kanugidyafïtïfeke.
    I mean the Kalapalo people.
    kalapalofekedyetsa.
Solo.   110
solo.

solo.

solo.

It's just like a dove's nest

when it's made that way

tafafotofïŋï ekugumbedya.

   That's what it's called.

   ititïfegey.

Solo is it's name,

solotsïfa itï.

    solo.   115

    solo.

When we have a lot of good starchy food,

ikinealefale igeyfuŋutalefale, tuiñaŋgi,

ukwatani kine,

   we prepare *kine*, *kine*.

   ekinetsale, ekine.

      But *solo* is made from that other stuff.

      solotsalehale igeyfale,

         Solo.

         solo.

            That's just what's done.   120

            laŋoaketsigey.

"All right, go ahead. Make some *solo*."

ogi ñafe solo eŋukitse.

Now, that meant his mother-in-law was preparing

something good for him,

ah, eŋïfa ifotisofofekefa ugu ikidyu,

     his mother-in-law.

     ifotisofofeke.

   That was special food for Cuckoo,

   fitsagu ugu igey.

      Cuckoo's special food.   125

      fitsagu ugu.

      He was going about there as their

      son-in-law,

         fatuwïifegey etepïgï,

their son-in-law.
fatuwï.
It was ready.
aifa.
"Mother," she said,
ama nïgï,
    "Here it is."   130
    andefa nïgï.
        "Here it is."
        andefa nïgï.
"All right," she replied,
eh he nïgifeke.
"Say, you might as well make him some
cheap *solo*."
ah, talokitofoi solomuke iñambake.
    "All right," she said.
    eh he nïgifeke.
        Now, that's how he continued to speak
        to her about what she was making.   135
        ah nïgimbelefaifeke.
Tuk, she put the bread on top of his drinking bowl.
tuk, tïokugu ugupoŋa,
        she put the bread on top of his drinking
        bowl.
        tïokugu ugupoŋa.

IIIA They say that was all that happened until,
uletsïgïtsedyetifa,
        it grew dark.
        afugutilïi.
    In the darkness, when it was about the way it
    is now, he felt sort of hot.   140
    ñambetï, igeyfuŋufudya, itotuŋufuŋufudya.
    "I never feel very well here,"
    afïtïmbedyale anïgïla,
        that's what she said to him, I'm told.
        ah nïgïtifeke.

"I never feel very well here.
afïtïmbedyale.
Because since it's like this, the smoke drifts
back down
ulegotedyalefalegey gitsitse teta
    and it reddens our eyes,"   145
    tiŋundufisugisifeke,
        that's what she said to him.
        nïgïfegifeke.
It hurt their eyes
iŋuŋu afukenïgï ifeke,
    it hurt their eyes.
    iŋuŋu afukenigi.
Because of that Cuckoo' eyes turned red.
ulepefa fitsagu iŋundu fitsugui.
    While he was at Igifagafïtu,   150
    igifagafïtï atani,
        the smoke irritated their
        son-in-law's eyes.
        fatuwïi iŋundutsipïgï gitsitsefeke.
Before his eyes turned red, they were
veryclear,
iŋundu fitsugu fegey, *teh* iŋugu anïmi.
        he was clear-eyed.
        tuatufisi.
    That's what happened to Cuckoo's eyes.
    fitsagu iŋugu anïmi.
    Because of that.   155
    ulepefa.
While he was there doing service for his
parents-in-law,
fatuwïi fatani,
        he lost the whites of his eyes,
        iŋundutsipïgï,
        he lost the whites of his eyes.
        iŋundutsipïgï.

Her cousin,
itsahenefeke,
her cousin.   160
itsahenefeke.
The wife's brother.
ifitsï fisuagïfekefa.
    Because of the smoke his eyes
    became irritated.
    iŋundutsipïgï igitsitseki.
He addressed her,
tifai,
    "Is this what made you all this way?"
    umaligey igeanikalefigey eiñalïko.
    "Yes, look at us,   165
    eh. ŋikefa tisugey,
      look at us.
      ŋikefa tisugey.
As you see, this is how we are,
igeyfuŋuaka tisugey.
      like this."
      igeyfuŋu.
    "Yes, you are.
    eh he kiŋi.
      Yes you are.   170
      eh he kiŋi.
      Like this."
      igeyfuŋu.
That was all.
aifa.

B   "Tomorrow I must go to see Mother and the others.
kogetsifetsaŋe utelïiŋofofo amañuko iña.
    I'll tell her we're doing well together.
    atëtëi utsatigi.
      I'll tell her we're doing well together."   175
      atëtëi utsatigi.

He wanted to relieve himself.
isikitomi fegey.
> He wanted to relieve himself.
> isikitomifa.
> At his wife's settlement
> tufitsu etute.
He went because of what had happened to
them, since he wanted to make thatching
grass come out of himself.
uletitifegey eteta, isikitomifegey iñefa.
That's how our houses came to be the way
they are.   180
ulepefegey tiñïŋa.
Thatch, thatch, thatch, this thing they tell
about that covers our houses.
iñe, iñe, iñe igeytifa tiñïŋa.
> That stuff of his.
> ulepefa.
> Cuckoo's feces.
> fitsagu itëpefa.
> That's just what it was.
> egeyaketsaŋe.
Now look, as you know when we cut down all the
manioc stalks,   185
iŋkepa, andenahila kwigi figey tiñiketa atïfïgï,
> > the place we cut it down where there once
> > was some forest,
> > tiñiketa atïfïgï itsunipe,
> > that's where Cuckoo would relieve
> > himself, he would relieve himself.
> > isikiŋalïfa fitsagu ikiŋalï,
> > > And from it thatching grass would grow.
> > > iñelefa atiŋalïlefa.
That's what it was.
laŋo eley.

The grass was his droppings.   190
iñe isitui.
But anyway, because he wanted to do that he
went to his mother,
uletomifalegey eteta tutiña alefale.
    to discuss it with her.
    tegikatigi.
    He wanted to relieve himself.
    isikitomifa.
He wanted to make a house.
uŋu fitsomi.
    He wanted them to be able to build
    houses.   195
    iñuŋukoi itsomi
    That was because the smoke kept
    hurting their eyes.
    ulefinefa gitsitsefekefa, inugu
    afukenïgïfiñe.
That's how he was,
laŋofeley,
    that's how he was.
    laŋofeley.
      He was Cuckoo.
      fitsagu feley.
    He had gone to do service for his
    parents-in-law.   200
    fatuwïifegey teta.

C He arrived home.
etimbelï.
    "Look, my son's here.
    iŋketi umukugu.
      He's here.
      ati.
    My dear son is here.
    atiti umukugu.

Why think of it, his sister didn't like him,"
she said,   205
ah, iŋkefa iñandsufeke etifunenïgï, nïgifeke,
   "His sister."
   iñandsufeke.
Tiki, he came inside.
tiki wenïgï.
   "Mother," he said,
   ama nïgifeke.
   "As you can see, I am here to see you."
   andeaka uge eŋiluiña.
   "Yes you are after all," she answered.   210
   eh he kiŋale.
   "Nothing happened to you, did it?
   uwafogima wegey,
       Nothing happened to you, did it?
       uwafogima wegey.
   You were happy there, weren't you?
   aŋifogikafa fekite wegey?
   "I was Mother!
   eh ama!
       "Yes," he answered.   215
       eh nïgifeke.
       "Your niece treats me very well,
       ah atutudyalefa afatifeke witëidyi,
           very well."
           atutui.
   "All right," she said.
   eh he nïgifeke.
"But Mother,
eŋï ama,
       Uncle and the others don't live the
       way you do,   220
       egeyfuŋumakina awadyukoi,
           the way you do.
           egeyfuŋu.

You see how I look."
iŋkenifa ukiŋike.
His mother looked at him.
ïti tiŋifeke.
His eyes were all red!
tiŋundekeneki.
It was the smoke that had made
his eyes red.   225
iŋugu atufisugitsïgïlefa
gitsitsefeke.
"Did something strange happen to you then?"
um! uwakumale igey atïfïgï?
"Yes," he said.
eh nïgifeke.
"Yes, I found out what Uncle's settlement
is like.
igeyfuŋmakina awadyukoi etui.
Like this.
igeyfuŋu.
That's why I must relieve myself,   230
enïaketsaŋe wikilïiŋo,
I'm going to relieve myself."
wikilïiŋo.
"All right," she said.
eh he nïgifeke.
"As you see, I've come to you. Because of
what's happened to them,
uleatiti aka weta,
that's the reason why.
uleatiti.
To let you know about Uncle.
awadyu ifatigi.
To let you know about Uncle   235
awadyu ifatigi.

Yes, I found out what Uncle's settlement
is like.
igeyfuŋutsïmakina awadyukoi.
   Like this."
   igeyfuŋu.
  "Very well," she said.
  eh he nïgifeke.

D So he left.   240
  etelïlefa.
    He went away.
    etelïlefa.
  To a cleared place,
  atïtïgitagelefa,
    where he lay down with his wife,
    tïfitsï iŋati.
    where he lay down with his wife.
    tïfitsï iŋati.
  "Let's go take care of our needs,   245
  faiŋa ukige,
    Let's go take care of our needs."
    faiŋa ukige.
  "All right," she answered.
  eh he nïgifeke.
  He looked around him.
  iŋipïgï itsaifeke.
    He was looking for a clearing.
    tigitafoliñi uifitsaifeke.
  Well, because he needed a beautiful place, 250
  ah eŋïfo atani *teh* !
    he needed a sizeable place,
    etsekegï ekugumbe,
    a place that had been well-cleared.
    atïtï tepïgï tïgitafoliñï tepïgï,
  "I'll put it here.
  ina fitsani.

I'll put it here."
ina fitsani.
He was standing right in the   255
middle of it when he said that,
igitati ekugumbe igifíkïgïna,
  so, that's where he relieved himself.
  ah sikilï.
When he was done,
aifa.
  he came back.
  sinïgïlefa.
He slept, he slept.
sïŋïlï, sïŋïlï,

IV After he had slept three days,   260
  tilako sïŋïpïgï,
    he went back there to see.
    tïte iŋiluiña,
  Over here, over here, over here, over here,
  egefunde, egefunde, egefunde, egefunde,
  there were shoots all over the place,
  laikugu,
    so many of them they were all over.
    tsïgifoti, laikugumbe,
  Thatching grass grew there.
  iñe atani.
"Yes, I was right to do that.   265
hedyemaki,
    Yes, I was right to do that."
    hedyemaki.
  So he came back.
  isinïgïlefa.
    That was over.
    aifa.

V Then he slept, he slept,
  lepe sïŋïlï, sïŋïlï,

and when he went to look it was this
high,   270
igefunde iɲiluiña tïte,
> *bah* it had already started to grow,
> *bah* igeyfunde atïpïgï atani,
> it was almost three feet high, and it was
> still growing.
> igefunde, igefunde atilïfatalefa.
"Yes, I was right to do that," he said.
hedyemaki, nïgifeke.
> "Yes, I was right to do that."
> hedyemaki.
> That's just the way it was.   275
> laŋoaketsigey.
"Yes, I was right to do that."
hedyemaki.
"Now listen to what I say," he said to his wife.
tsakefofo ukilï, tufïtsufeke.
> "I have just the thing we can use to protect
> our poor parents."
> aɲiaketsaŋe ukwotofekemukefa
> ukwetuwandetofoiŋo,
>> There's something here.
>> aɲi.
With that we will be living in a good
place,   280
igeyfiñe atïtïte ukwaniŋofiñe,
>> with that.
>> igeyfiñe.
> We will be living in a good place.
> atïtïte ukwaniŋofiñe.
Where we are now isn't anything like that at
all.
tamigia kunalïko.
There's no reason why we have to keep living
in this place of ours, is there?
afïtïtaka igeyfuŋu toŋofïɲïtifa tisuge,

no.   285
  afïtï.
We are sheltered.
uŋalï tisugey.
  Sheltered."
  uŋalï.
That's what he said to his wife.
nïgïfifeke tufitsufeke.
Then she told her father about it.
lepe tifatifeke tuwïiña.
  "Father," she said,   290
apa nïgifeke,
   "Father."
   apa.
"Yes?", he answered.
ai nïgifeke.
"We have our house."
aŋiaketsaŋe kukïŋï.
"What do you mean, 'We have our house'?"
tïmale kukïŋï aŋi?
" 'A house,' he just told me.   295
une tanaifeke.
Your father will be the one to make it,'
owïfeketsïfa tufanïmiŋo,
   he just told me.
   tanaifeke.
    He just told me."
    tanaifeke.
"Very well," her father said.
eh eh nïgifeke.
Then he went to see.   300
lepe iŋiluiña tute.
  It was all over, wherever he happened to
  walk,
   ege aimbele etelufata,

and there were no spiny parts on it at all,
it was beautiful,
teh ! *he he* ! ñalïma egey ifïgipitsu
    there was nothing spiny on it.
    ñalï.
      Teh ! *heh heh* ! It was magnificent !
      teh ! *he he* ! ñalï ekugu.
That was what Cuckoo had done for him.   305
    fitsagu atsatepïgï fegey.
That was the origin of what became thatching
grass.
igeniŋo figeyiŋo, ulepe fegey iñefa.
    The very first, we've been told.
    iñïŋo tifa.
      That.
      igeyfa.
        That was the origin of it.
        igeniŋo fegey.
He intended to create that very thing.   310
    igey fegey iŋïitanïmi.

VI   Listen.
    etsakefa.
Then after they had slept a long time they went to
look at it.
lepe akïŋi sïŋïpïgï atani iŋiluiña tuteko.
    It was fully grown.
    apïpïgï atanilefa.
Buh, every bit of the cleared space was
covered
buh ! utukufifiti ekugumbekudya !
    by the thatching grass!   315
    iñembefa.
"Uncle," he went.
awa nïgifeke.
      "Uncle.
      awa.

Here is just the thing for you to use to
cover your enclosure."
aŋiaketsaŋe euwa iputegofoiŋo efeke.
"Very well," he said.
eh he nïgifeke.
    "Very well."   320
    eh he.
"This is the thing to use.
igeyfiñefa.
    This is the thing to use.
    igeyfiñe.
        This is the thing to use."
        igeyfiñe.
But anyway, soon afterwards
lepe apaŋaŋufïŋïtalefale egey,
    they cut their foundation posts, I'm told.   325
ñeŋikondotelïletïifeke.
He went to get them.
igey tuilulefaifeke.
    He went to get them.
    igey tuilulefa.
And he cut the rafters.
sikitsu tuilulefaifeke.
And he cut the rafter supports.
afundelïlefaifeke.
The house was ready!   330
aifa!
    "It's all ready, Uncle," he said.
    aifa nïgï awa nïgifeke,
        "It's all ready."
        aifa nïgï.
"All right, then!"
ohsifa!
    "I want our parent to go pull it up.
    ukwoto tetomi iñokiluiña.
        I want our parent to go pull it up."   335
        ukwoto tetomi.

"Very well," she said.

eh he nïgifeke.

"Father," she said.

apa nïgifeke.

"Go pull it up, do you hear!

omokitatïfa!

Go pull it up!"

omokita!

"All right,"   340

eh he.

So he went to pull it up,

ah, tïokifeke.

and he pulled it up.

iñokilïlefa.

Tugu, tugu, tugu,

Tugu, tugu, tugu,

how beautiful !

teh he he !

There weren't any spiny stems at all.   345

ñalïma egey fïgifidyo.

None.

ñalï.

Then they put it on the house,

lepe tufatifekeni,

Teh, there weren't *any* of those things I was

talking about,

teh ! ñalïmaŋu egeyfuŋu tsei,

there weren't any spiny stems on it,

taŋope ñalïma fïgifidyo.

it didn't have any on itself.   350

taŋopena.

Teh, it was magnificent.

teh ! he he, ñalï ekugu.

They were finished.

etïkilïko.

VIIA Now listen !
    ah tsakefa !
           It wasn't like that other place of
           theirs.
           taŋope.
        "Well, " I'm told he said.   355
        um ! a nïgïtifeke.
           "It's all done!
           aifa atïkilï!
    Look at our house," he went.
    iŋkefa, nï
        Look at it.
        iŋkefa.
    As you see we're all ready here, once and
    for all
    kuapuŋukoaka igey,
        we're all ready.   360
        kuapuŋu.
    I mean we'll soon be inside of this thing here,
    igeatsehale tiñanïgï,
        this thing here."
        igea.

B   Then, well someone told Taugi about it.
    lepe, ah Taugi ina tikagi.
        Taugi.
        Taugina.
        He told Sun about it.   365
        Gitinambedya.
        Sun.
        Gitina.
    "Say, I've just heard the leader of
    Igifagafïtu has a house." They said
    something like that to him.

ah, Igifagafïtï anetugu uŋu
nïgïtataifeke.
"Little brother," Taugi said to Aulukuma,
"Ufi" nïgifeke.
    "Now, let's go right away to see this
    thing our grandmother's made,
    ah, kuñitafofo kunitsu atsatepïgï,
        that our grandfather's made.   370
        kutaupïgï atsatepïgï.
            Let's go see."
            kuñita.
        "All right."
        eh he.
Mm mm mmmm ! Now, they came as
wind after that,
um um mmm !, ah fitembe
    they came there,
    sinïŋgo,
    Taugi came.   375
    Taugi enïgï.
        Taugi.
        Taugi.

C   "Look at how these stems are growing
        out !"
inkefa ifïgikundigifa ah sinïgï,
        They saw there wasn't anything
        on them, they were beautiful.
        teh he he, la anïmbiñe !
        They were perfectly bare.
        teh ! he he ! anïmbiñe.
        They came closer.   380
        tuendi.
            They peered down the length of
            the stems.
            timïkaifiko.

Teh heh, there weren't any spiny stems
at all.
teh he ñalimbe ifigifidyoi.
Teh ! *heh heh* ! They were perfectly
made !
teh ! heh heh ! kugumbekudye !
"Well, look at our grandfather's house,
Little Brother,
um ! iŋkefofo kutaüpïgï ïŋï ufi,
    look at it.   385
    iŋkefofo.
It can't stay this way,
afïtïdyale anïgïla.
    no.
    afïtï.
Our grandfather won't stay this way.
tama igia taüpïgï inalï.
      He won't stay this way.
      tamigia inalï.
      And the Mortals won't be this way,
      even though they would want to be, 390
      igeya eykuapalefafigey afako
      if they went to protect themselves.
      etuandefotalefa.
      Like this.
      igeya agage.
        This.
        igeya.
It won't stay like this any longer.
afïtïaketsaŋe igeya nïgïla.
    No.   395
    afïtï.
It's too nice.
etefa igeya nalï.

If if should be like this, then the
Mortal's houses would be too beautiful.
igeyakeñi afakofiliñïgï, atakofolï
kuleŋapalefa.
Let our grandfather's house be that way.
lafa taūpïgï ïŋï itsani.
    Let it be that way.   400
    lafa itsani.
        Let it be that way.
        lafa itsani.
Why does our grandfather's house have to
be like this?
taikuma igia kutaūpïgï ïŋï inalï.
For them to be well made, the Mortals
should have to be strong when they want
to thatch their houses.
tapogi ule, afako filinïgïfeke, tugiga
atani, tifekefa.
        When they want to do that.
        tifeke.
    "Very well," Aulukuma answered.
    eh he nïgifeke.
        "Very well."   405
        eh he.
"Why is he always like that?", his younger
brother said.
fidyumbekufale ! ifisï kilï.
    His younger brother spoke, Aulukuma
    spoke.
    ifisï kilï, Aulukuma kilï.
    "I wish he wasn't like that all the
    time," I'm told he said.
    fidyumbekufale !, nïgïtifeke.
        "I wish he wasn't like that all the time!"
        fidyumbekufale!
"Let's go," Taugi said.   410
kigefa, nïgi,

"*Moh*, let's go see our grandfather's
clearing.
moh taūpïgï ifatigofo kuñita.
        our grandfather's clearing."
        kutaūpïgï ifatigofo.
        He went to see the place where the
        others were pulling out the grass.
        ulefekefa iñokilïña tetofofeke.
MM MM MMM, he travelled as wind.
mm mm mmm, etelï fite.
        The others didn't know,   415
        ñalïma funïmi,
                they didn't know.
                ñalïma funïmi.
Now, *mm mm mmmm*,
ah, *mm mm mm*.
                They were there.
                segati.
What they were pulling out still grew
there.
igeŋa iñokipïgï itïpofoŋo atiga fegey.
Teh heh heh ! There was more of it,
even cleaner than before.   420
teh heh heh ! agetsïkï wate.
Because afterwards when he wanted to
pull it out, *tïdï, tïdï*,
ule atehe iñokilïtifeke, tïdï, tïdï
                he slept, he slept, *bah* !
                isïŋïlï sïŋïlï, *bah* !
                        and it grew up.
                        atilïlefa.
That stuff of his.
ulepefegey.
The new sprouts kept growing up, and so
there was new growth.   425
itïpofoŋo atilïfatalefa, itïpofoŋo atanilefa.

Teh heh heh !

teh heh heh !

It was magnificent !

añalï ekugu !

There weren't any spiny stems at all.

ñalïma ifigifidyoi.

There weren't any yet at that place.

taŋope ñalïmafofo.

"Let's do that to them.   430

etege inalï.

Let our grandfather's enclosure be
that way."

latsa kutaūpïgï ïwa itsani.

"Let's go," he went.

kigefa nïgifeke.

Mm mm mm, they circled around and
came back,

mm mm mm, itsetinefegey ogopidyï.

as wind, to destroy it.

fite feke tuelïina.

To pull off the sheaths.   435

ipulïina.

To pull the sheaths off the thatching
grass stalks.

ipulïina, inepe ipulïina.

Because he thought it was too
beautiful to use as it was.

ulefiñe teh heh anïmbiñe.

MM MM MMM,

mm mm mm,

ku ku ku ku tsu tsu tsu tsu,

ku ku ku ku tsu tsu tsu tsu,

so, they destroyed it all.   440

ah tuelumbelefaifeke.

"Well, Taugi must have done that.

um ! Taugifïnambe.

No one but Taugi.
Taugi tuiñalïma.
Only Taugi could have done that."
Taugimbakegey.
He went on after that.
etelumbe.

D Then after that had happened, even so he went
back to where they were pulling it up.   445
lepetalelegey, lepembe togopisi, ñokitofona.
There he made the stems weak and soft.
tsegati ifïgikamolïiñe,
Then he threw the remains all around,
lepe tufutsikundi ifeke,
buuk,
buuk
and so the stems became very spiny.
lepefiñe fïgipidyoi.
Teh heh ! It had been beautiful.   450
teh heh ! lafa atani.
That's how it had been.
lafa atani.
But this time it came up the way it does now,
laŋope fegey,
this time it came up the way it does now.
laŋope fegey.

E Then the others went to their clearing to pull
some out.
lepe tsupofoŋo ōkiluiña tuteko.
"Look !", the grass was all covered with spiny
stems.   455
ïike ! ah, fugifidyo atanilefa.
"Well !" I'm told he said,
um ! anïgïtifeke,
I mean the owner spoke.
oto kilïtsïfa.

"Well ! Taugi must have done this.

um ! Taugifïnambe.

    Surely Taugi did this.

    Taugi mbakigey.

But why did he have to do that to us?   460

tïmemale igea kwïigate.

    Why did he have to do that to us?"

    tïemigia ukwïite.

"All right," they pulled it up.

ohsi iñokilï.

    Tuguk ! *Tsiuk* ! *Tsiuk* !

    tuguk ! tsiuk ! tsiuk !

And so, look,

aimbefa iŋke,

    before when they pulled on it it came out

    fast,   465

    inokigatïgïpeŋe,

        but now *tsiuk, pok, tsiuk, pok.*

        tsiuk, pok, tsiuk, pok.'

            That's how it was this time.

            laŋopeŋine.

They had to wipe off the spines, we've heard.

ifïdyipitsilïletifa ifekeni.

        Well, that's the way it was.

        ah laŋope fegey.

From that time on the stems grew spiny the

way they are now, when we poor people go

there,   470

ulepeiñe fïgifidyoi ikutifigey,

mukekutitseŋatofoi,

        when we go there.

        titseŋatofoi.

Since then.

ulepefa.

It was Taugi who put the spines on.

Taugifekefa ifïgikundïfïgï.

That's how it happened.

alaŋo fegey.
That's really all there is to that.   475
apïgïaketsaŋe.[8]

Notes

1. See Basso, 1985, Chapter 4 for a more extended discussion of this
    process. In the text of "Cuckoo" which I analyze in this paper, these
    rhythms are represented by my placement of lines, using several tab
    spaces to indicate a) the movement of relatively loud voice, at the
    beginning of a major segment, towards lower voice (often with a return
    to loud voice at its conclusion) and b) segmenting itself, according to
    the narrator's use of various discourse devices I describe below.

2. Some dialogues exhibit a marked stereotypicality to the extent that the
    substance of the stereotype is the very subject of the story. This is
    especially true of "stories of disgusting Dawn People" in which
    narrative clichés occur that seem to arise from the sense that there are
    perpetual occurences of certain feelings, which in turn generate
    perpetual and predictable predicaments.   In comparison with
    conversations, quoted speech in Kalapalo narratives is far more formal
    (no false starts, interruptions, or other "errors" of speech), far more
    stereotyped (both as to substance and to intonational contour patterning)
    and of course thoroughly metalinguistic. However, in terms of how it
    represents functional sociolinguistic consequences (as this paper
    suggests) it can be quite similar to "ordinary" (*taloki*) speech.

3. I am using this term following the suggestions of Erving Goffman in
    Forms of Talk. In segment VII, travelling by Taugi as well as by
    Cuckoo and his relatives underscores the contrasts between those
    characters' points of view.

4. On one special occasion (line 82ff), speech between very close relatives
    sounds very "affinal" because the entire context is charged with affinity.
    In speaking to his daughter, Cuckoo's father-in-law uses a quasi-
    oratorical style signalled by the form *ogiña ogi*, ordinarily used by
    hereditary leaders to initiate collective action that derives from
    community consensus.   Here what is indicated is that the young

woman should perform an activity already deemed appropriate by virtue of something her family has agreed on.

5. Except when, in line 230, Cuckoo declares that he "must relieve himself". With this remark, Cuckoo asserts his obligation to complete the affinal exchage by creating something important and valuable. The fact that thatching grass grows up from his excrement makes it an especially "affinal" gift. Just as Cuckoo's affines refer to precious gifts to him as if they were disgusting or of no value, so (by a kind of inversion of the metaphor) even the waste of the son-in-law is treasured for its exchange value.

6. There are of course particular segments where more than one person is addressed by a speaker (when oratory is quoted, for example), or other contexts in which several persons are addressed in turn. However, there is always a dialogical process, exhibited in these passages by the fact that some kind of response to a statement - even silence - is indicated.

7. I omit a few lines in which I ask for (and receive from Kudyu) clarification that these are human beings.

8. This paper has profited greatly from the perceptive suggestions of the volume editors, who must also be acknowledged for their superb sense of collegiality. My research among the Kalapalo has been supported at various times by the National Science Foundation, the Wenner-Gren Foundation for Anthropological Research, Inc., and the University of Arizona. I am also greatful to Professor Roque de Barros Laraia of the University of Brasilia and officials of the Conselho Nacional de Pesquisas and Fundação Nacional do Indio for making Brazilian research possible.

References

Basso, Ellen B.
  1985   *A musical view of the universe: Kalapalo myth and ritual performances.* Philadelphia: University of Pennsylvania Press.
Goffman, Erving
  1974   *Frame analysis.* Philadelphia: University of Pennsylvania Press.
  1981   *Forms of talk.* Philadelphia: University of Pennsylvania Press.

The Report of a Kuna Curing Specialist: The Poetics and Rhetoric of an Oral Performance

Joel Sherzer

In 1970, the village of Mulatuppu in eastern San Blas awarded a scholarship to Olowitinappi, one of its foremost curing specialists, to study snakebite medicine with a teacher in the Bayano region of Kuna territory who was well known for such medicine. In awarding this scholarship, the village paid tribute to the ability of Olowitinappi and at the same time contributed to the medical protection of their community and the continuity of Kuna tradition. On the evening of June 16, 1970, several days after his return from the Bayano, Olowitinappi delivered a speech reporting on his experience in the Mulatuppu gathering house. (Kuna public meetings are called 'gatherings' in Kuna and the large, centrally located structure in which they are held is called the 'gathering house.')

As an ethnographic document, Olowitinappi's speech is most informative. It conveys a great deal about Kuna medicine and curing as the Kuna themselves view it, and it illustrates the ways in which medicines and associated forms of discourse are learned. It is also an excellent example of Kuna speechmaking and the sorts of rhetorical and poetic devices used by effective speakers.

For both Olowitinappi and his audience, this report is very significant. In this essentially nonliterate community, it is through oral discourse that knowledge and information is conceived, perceived, learned, taught, and transmitted. Olowitinappi's speech is the official, public actualization of his experiences.

For Olowitinappi, his report is a way of informing his community about what he has learned, providing testimony about his achievements. Olowitinappi explains that he has learned the medicines and curing practices appropriate to several types of illness -- not only for snakebites, but also for various complications that sometimes follow snakebites. In addition, he announces that he has learned some medicine and curing practices concerned with childbirth, including chants and verbal secret charms. The speech itself, then, brings Olowitinappi prestige because in it he is able to show that he has added to his already formidable knowledge of Kuna medicine and curing.

For the audience, Olowitinappi's report is equally significant. The community learns from the report that its money has not been wasted because Olowitinappi has learned cures previously unknown in Mulatuppu. It also finds out in advance how he will go about his work and how much he will charge, and since Olowitinappi not only discusses medicine, but also reports in a colorful way on his experiences and observations while traveling, he provides them with information and entertainment.

Olowitinappi's report is a polished and sophisticated example of Kuna speechmaking, including, as is characteristic of both Kuna oratory and Kuna chanting, attention to narrative detail, mixing humor with seriousness, metaphor and other allusive devices, counsel, considerable metacommunication, and extensive quotation and quotation within quotation.

This report then both exemplifies one variety of Kuna formal speechmaking and illustrates the learning of Kuna medicine and curing. It also shows how personal and private pursuits like the learning of medicine and curing are related to the public and political system centered in the gathering house.

Social and Cultural Context and Assumptions

Olowitinappi's speech is one of many forms of discourse performed in Kuna gatherings. There are two major types of Kuna gathering. One, attended by men and women together, is the setting for the public and ritual chanting of Kuna chiefs. This gathering occurs approximately every other evening and at times in the morning. The other type of gathering is exclusively for men and occurs on evenings when chiefs do not chant. A variety of matters are dealt with at these men's gatherings, including legal, political, and economic affairs and disputes of all kinds. Humorous discussions and storytelling also occur here. And this is the setting for public reports, of unusual personal experiences, trips, and learning sessions of the type Olowitinappi was involved in.

Reporting one's experience is a significant verbal activity among the Kuna. It is the only way that individuals can let others know of their experiences and it is expected and required of everyone. Chiefs who have travelled to other villages in order to attend inter-island ritual meetings report on their trips in the form of a gathering house chant. Anyone who has travelled, for politics, work, pleasure, or education (traditional or modern) reports, both privately and publicly, after their return. Olowitinappi no doubt reported on his trip many times -- privately to friends and family in many settings and in many ways. His speech in the evening gathering is the public, official version of his experience.

The purpose of Olowitinappi's trip to the Bayano region was to learn medicinal and curing practices, with a focus on snakebites. It is useful to place this trip and the report of it within the total configuration of Kuna curing practices. Kuna curing involves a combination of herbal medicines and verbal discourse, the latter being communication between humans and spirits in a special, esoteric language, that of the spirit world. When an individual is sick, members of her/his family call on a prognosticator to determine the cause of the disease and the needed cure. This prognosticator is either a *nele* (seer) or medicinal specialist. The cure itself involves the use of herbal medicines gathered by the medicinal specialist who also verbally counsels the medicine (its spirit) in a short chant in order to activate it. In addition, the appropriate curing chant is also performed by a chant specialist. The relatively long curing chants are addressed to spirits and direct the actions of helpful spirits in their struggle against the hostile spirits that cause disease. A verbal secret charm with highly focused magical power might also be used.

Medicinal specialists and chant knowers learn their practice by apprenticing themselves to well-known specialists, precisely as Olowitinappi describes so nicely in his speech. Traditional Kuna teaching consists largely of a series of wide-ranging conversations between teacher and student. While students and teachers are sometimes from the same village, it is much more common for students to seek out renowned specialists from other, at times distant villages, as teachers. This provides them with more prestige and avoids conflicts between teachers and students.

Students work together with their teachers, helping them especially with agricultural work, which is an important form of repayment while at the same time being a context in which student and teacher can observe local plants of medicinal value and converse about them. As is discussed in Olowitinappi's speech, teachers also charge actual money for what they teach. When a student has successfully learned either a chant or medicinal practice, the teacher acknowledges that his student is now also a specialist. This is done in various ways. If student and teacher are from the same village, the teacher makes a public speech in the gathering house. If the student has traveled to study with the teacher, the teacher writes a letter (or more frequently in this mainly nonliterate society, has a letter written) which is then read in the student's gathering house on his return. In these cases, the student also makes a public speech reporting in detail on his experiences.

Snakes and snakebite medicine occupy a special and most significant place among Kuna curing practices. In this tropical environment in which people walk, hunt, farm, wash clothes, and fetch water daily, actual physical snakes are a real and most dangerous reality. At the same time, snake spirits are among the most dangerous of spirits and can cause serious disease, even if the individual attacked never comes into contact with an actual, physical snake. No wonder then that the Kuna are so preoccupied with snakes and that there exists a complex of herbal medicines, chants, and secret charms, all focused on snakebite cure and prevention and cure and prevention of illnesses caused by snake spirits. In addition, there exists a chant whose purpose is to control the spirit of a snake and thereby enable its performer to raise an actual snake into the air.[1]

Because it is performed publicly in the gathering house, Olowitinappi's speech represents an intersection of the curing and gathering traditions. It makes private, esoteric matters public. And it relates Olowitinappi's abilities and prestige as a curing specialist to his role as an active political leader in the community.

An explanation of certain Kuna practices and beliefs is necessary for an understanding of aspects of this text, in particular, some of its allusions. The inter-island meeting Olowitinappi refers to at the opening of his speech is a frequent event involving representatives of several Kuna villages. Both ritual chanting by chiefs and political discussions occur at such meetings. In his speech in the Tigre gathering Olowitinappi uses the history of Inapakinya, a renowned chief of the village of Mulatuppu and leader of the eastern portion of San Blas, who died in 1938, to represent current Kuna concerns. At the time of Olowitinappi's speech, the Kuna were worried about outside incursions into their territory, by Panamanian settlers as well as mineral prospectors supported by the Panamanian government. In the 1930's, Inapakinya was a supporter of close relations with neighboring Colombia, rather than with Panama. His response to the offer of a new young woman in place of his older wife symbolized his views. The old woman is Colombia; the young woman is Panama. This discussion reflects Kuna concerns about outside encroachments. The food and drink which Olowitinappi receives in the Ipeti gathering house on his arrival (line 123 ff) is an instance of the Kuna custom of bringing beverages and food to the gathering house for distinguished visitors, such as chiefs or medicinal specialists.

The full set of Kuna curing practices is reported on by Olowitinappi. Victims of snakebite live in the house of a curer during their treatment. Olowitinappi is taught not only how to cure but how to prevent disease. Kuna midwives can tell at birth what disease or misfortune is likely to befall a newborn baby (line 258). Preventive medicine is then employed. This involves painting individuals' bodies black with the native dye Genipa Americana (line 259 ff). It also involves planting medicine in the ground at the time fields are burned before planting crops (the Kuna practice slash and burn agriculture), a time when snakes are likely to be observed, in order to keep them from harming people working there. Olowitinappi refers to snakes as *tupa* (rope or vine), a common Kuna euphemism. By means of his constant conversations with his teacher, at home, while walking, and while working in the jungle, Olowitinappi acquired the total gamut of snakebite curing practices -- actual medicines and their names, associated verbal secret charms (called 'secret,' 'soul,' and 'boat' in the text), and appropriate curing chants. The teacher speaks secretly (line 146), that is, he uses esoteric language. The word *ikar* is used to refer to chant, general way or practice, and portion, including line, of chant. In lines 305-312 Olowitinappi directly quotes a few lines of his teacher's recitation of a curing chant. The 'clothes line' in the chant which Olowitinappi quotes his teacher reciting (lines 310, 312) is the rope used in the spirit world to catch evil spirits. *Apsoket ikar* (the way of the mass curer) (line 311) is a chant used in the prevention and cure of diseases and problems of epidemic proportions. Drawings are made with colored pencils in notebooks as mnemonic devices for both medicines and chants (lines 153-154, 175, 285).

Charging practices (for both future patients and future students) are part of the teaching process. Olowitinappi pays considerable attention to financial details in his report, particularly important since it is his village which supplied him with the money for the trip and for the needed notebooks, pencils, and cloth (line 201). The cloth is a gift to the teacher, to be used by his wife in making molas (blouses).

The *nelekana* (prophets) (line 316 ff.) were the first great leaders of the Kuna. Ipelele (line 318) was one of the foremost of the prophets. The Choco (line 315 ff.), neighbors of the Kuna, are traditional enemies, but also, as certain traditions have it, sources of knowledge of medicinal and curing practices. Olowitinappi's teacher knows the chants of the elders (line 363 ff.) because in addition to being a curing specialist, he is also a chief. It is rather common for Kuna traditional leaders to have roles in, that is to be specialists in, distinct domains, for example, both gathering tradition and curing tradition. Olowitinappi himself is both a curing specialist (having knowledge of herbal medicine as well as various chants) and an *arkar* (chiefs' spokesman). The letter discussed in line 440 ff. is the proof that Olowitinappi has actually studied; it is his diploma. He showed it in the gathering house. In line 452, Olowitinappi refers to the fact that he has been sick for one year and was not able to work.

Given that the Kuna are essentially a nonliterate society and that Olowitinappi's report is an excellent illustration of the role of oral discourse within Kuna society, it is interesting to note the significance of writing in relation to Kuna curing practices, as expressed in the speech. Mnemonic drawings are used to aid in the memorization of medicines and chants. The Choco is taught in the spirit world on the basis of a letter he brings with him. And Olowitinappi himself carries a written letter validating his experience. While statistically marginal, writing is clearly highly valued and at times crucial and is put to important use by such nonliterate individuals as Olowitinappi and his teacher.

Structures and Strategies

Olowitinappi's speech is organized into a series of narrative episodes, interspersed with counsel, from the teacher to Olowitinappi, on how to behave in the future.   The narrative episodes are the trip to Panama (including participating in a meeting on the island of Tigre, speaking with the inhabitants of Wicupwala, and purchasing eyeglasses in Panama City); the trip to the Bayano village of Ipeti (passing by both Panamanian and Kuna villages, not being able to get the boat repaired, and being appropriately received in Ipeti); the learning and teaching sessions and processes (difficulties in learning, success at last, learning names for herbal medicines, attention to financial matters, description of how to treat victims as well as prevent snakebites); and an invitation to return to study childbirth medicine (highlighted by the story of the origin of the learning of the chant used to grab the devil, including the report of the Choco's learning of this chant, a nicely microscopic parallel of Olowitinappi's report into which it is embedded, and ending with the tracing of the line of the specialists in the chant to its present knower and teacher). The speech terminates with a focus on counsel -- reminding Olowitinappi to get a student/assistant, how to treat him, and how much to charge him and explaining to Olowitinappi how to behave in the face of the criticism he is sure to receive from other medicinal specialists in his village. This latter counsel is illustrated by a lovely miniature narrative about a sick person the teacher-specialist cured after other specialists had decided he could not be saved from death. The final portion of the speech describes the writing of the diploma-letter. Then there is a coda, Olowitinappi telling his own village of Mulatuppu what he will do for them.

The speech makes use of a number of poetic processes and rhetorical strategies which, while all characteristically Kuna, also reflect Olowitinappi's individual style, because of his particular way of employing them. First, dramatization of the voice. I have in mind here loudness and softness, fast and slow speech, modulations of pitch, pause patterns, and two especially characteristic Kuna expressive devices, stretching out the voice and vibrating the voice. Such dramatizations of the voice constitute an aspect of oral performance particularly challenging for transcription, translation, and representation on the printed page.

With regard to rhetorical strategies, there is first of all the use of narratives. As is expected of Kuna report narratives, Olowitinappi includes considerable phenomenological detail, concerning people he met, places he saw, and things he did. Examples are his speech in the Tigre meeting, his description of the villages along the Bayano river, and, of course, his meticulous reproductions of his conversations with his teacher. He thus demonstrates his experience, his knowledge, and his acknowledged prestige. There is also understatement, irony, and humor. Thus Olowitinappi expresses his shame at being like a little kid in not being able to learn quickly. But of course his learning problems are overcome and he acquires knowledge quite impressively. Olowitinappi quotes his teacher saying that the medicinal specialists were going to *iploe* (literally smash to death) (line 433) a man whom they could not cure. But of course the Kuna would never kill a sick person. Quite the contrary. They try by every means possible to keep patients alive. This is a quite ironic and humorous way for Olowitinappi to say that his teacher is better than other specialists; he can cure patients when others fail. The statement is all the more humorous in that it is expressed through the quoted words of the teacher.

There is a certain amount of parallelism and allusive speech, two important characteristics of Kuna verbal art, especially common in ritual speaking and chanting.

The most striking rhetorical strategy employed in Olowitinappi's speech is the use of quoted or reported speech, a most characteristic Kuna verbal device and one which is also apparently widespread in lowland South America (Sherzer 1983: 201-207). Much of this speech is not to be understood as being in the words of Olowitinappi on that evening in 1970 when he delivered it, but rather as quotes of other, previous times and places, of other speakers and voices, including his own, or of future times, places, and voices. In particular, the learning of the snakebite cure is presented through a series of quotations of Olowitinappi's teacher and conversations between the teacher and Olowitinappi.

Reported, quoted speech is a formal property of the text, which is literally punctuated with *soke* (say) and *takken soke* (see he says). The repetition of these forms, at the ends of lines, typical of the Kuna formal speech-making style, contributes to the cohesion and the rhythm of Olowitinappi's oral performance.

The strategic use of reported, quoted speech is striking for its omnipresence. Olowitinappi himself seems to be saying nothing. Such important matters as the prices he will charge patients and his own student/assistant are not presented in his own words, but in those of his teacher, and are to be followed as strictly as the curing practices he describes, also always in the words of his teacher. Notice that by quoting his teacher, Olowitinappi is able to anticipate particular issues and problems he will face in Mulatuppu -- diseases, financial concerns, and personal criticisms.

Quoting is also a most effective way to demonstrate that knowledge has indeed been acquired. Thus when talking about having heard his teacher perform the chant for grabbing the devil and learned some of it, Olowitinappi quotes his teacher reciting this memorized text (lines 305-312).

Reported speech, multiple tellings, and tellings within tellings acquire baroque proportions in the story of the origin of the chant for grabbing the devil, which constitutes the climax of Olowitinappi's speech (lines 314-351). The extreme point of quotation within quotation is reached toward the end of this passage, when Olowitinappi is quoting his teacher, who is quoting Ipelele, who is quoting a Choco Indian, who is quoting a chief of the spirit world, who is quoting God.

It is important to point out two significant features of embedding quotations within quotations, the first having to do with the structure of the telling of narrative, the second having to do with the grammatical marking of embedded tellings. With regard to the telling of narratives, there is a single story line. What is embedded are not different stories but different tellers. This is what I have tried to represent by making use of the clearly insufficient western writing device of single and double quotation marks. With regard to the grammatical marking of embedded tellings, while Kuna grammar provides a rich potential in metacommunicative words, phrases, and affixes, there is not a necessary and unique formal, overt marking for every embedding. Nor do intonational changes mark more than a single level of embedding, and often they do not go even this shallow distance. Thus in spite of a general rule that the last character introduced into a narrative is most likely to be the next speaker quoted, it becomes very difficult at each moment of the narration (for analysts as well as for native members of the community) to decode exactly who is speaking. Competent listening and understanding involve following the story line, recognizing the process of the embedding of direct quotation, and following this to a certain degree. While I have disambiguated possible ambiguities in just who is speaking at particular moments by my use of quotation marks in the written representation of the text, such ambiguities do exist for the audience and perhaps even for the speaker as well.

Olowitinappi's speech is a superb illustration of the verbal artistry of Kuna speechmaking at its best. A modest man and a quiet speaker, Olowitinappi nevertheless draws on the full gamut of Kuna poetic and rhetorical devices in this most engaging report, a travel narrative in which the speaker's experiences are made relevant to the concerns of the audience. Here we have dramatic narration, understatement, irony, humor, allusion, metaphor, parallelism, broad generalization, minute detail, grammar, and the human voice, all working together in one performance. And this gathering house event, which brings together in a single moment so many basic and crucial aspects of Kuna life -- politics, economics, curing and medicine, learning and teaching, and personal relations -- is focused within a text in which Olowitinappi's personal verbal artistry is expressed to the fullest degree.

The Text

In my transcription of Olowitinappi's speech, the line is the basic minimal unit. Lines are determined by pauses coupled with falling intonation. Long pauses without falling intonation are transcribed as blank spaces between words within lines. Olowitinappi makes extensive use of the rich set of Kuna line-framing words, phrases, and affixes (*teki, takkarku, emi, teysokku, emite, inso, soke, takken soke, pittosursoke, _ye, sunto,* etc.) These tend to intersect with pause and pitch patterning, thus reinforcing the intonationally determined line structure. At times they occur line medially and, like the line-medial pauses, confer a certain contrapuntal rhythm to the poetics of performance. Beyond the line, I find no clearly marked poetic structure, such as verse and stanza, although these units do occur in other Kuna verbal genres. At a more macro and general level, the text is organized into episodes. [2]

Other conventional Kuna expressive devices which are found in this text are loud speech (indicated by capital letters), stretched out speech (indicated by dashes between syllables), rising pitch (indicated in parentheses), vibrating voice (indicated in parentheses), and decreasing volume (indicated in parentheses).

While my transcription reflects conventional Kuna expressive devices as employed by Olowitinappi in the poetics of his particular performance, it does not constitute a concrete or detailed phonetic representation. In fact, I use a relatively abstract phonemic representation, marking words and their boundaries quite clearly. Since I use grammatical and semantic criteria more than phonetic ones in separating words, word boundaries are more sharply and consistently reflected than they would be in a more superficial phonetic transcription.

With regard to reported, quoted speech, a very important structural and rhetorical feature of Olowitinappi's performance, in my transcription and representation, I have used quotation marks (single and double) whenever a speaker quotes another or himself, resulting at times in considerable quotes within quotes.

My relatively literal translation aims at providing a sense of the rhythm and style of Olowitinappi's speech. In particular, the translation preserves the extensive use of line-framing and metacommunicative words and phrases, as well as the continual use of direct quotation and quotation within quotation, features which are characteristic of the actual performance I recorded. Certain allusions are explained within parentheses.

In conclusion I have opted for a transcription and representation which highlights expressive oral devices but in which grammatical and semantic devices emerge as well and a translation which is as close to the Kuna as possible while still being understandable and accessible to English readers. Here is the text.

1. teki emite wey peki pankusmarmoye.
2. takkaliku   Tikirse ante, kapitap.
3. aimal ikal ittoeti an tayle.
4. emi, pemar konkreso imaysat kiarsunto.
5. tek aimar per sunmaysaku, kakkwen an kar soymosunto.
6. 'we Inapakinya soysa' takken an kar soke.
7. "'emi ome seret an kwen iptaypisurve.
8. we ome nucukkwa anka uylenaitti tayleku an wiokoye."
9. soysa' takken an kar soke.
10. 'emite a ikar pemar opparsiitti.
11. we waymal ol amimalatti.
12. wekin malatsurye.
13. yotte Alemania kunai Italia kunai.
14. teysokkuti inso.
15. tayleku Europa waymala.
16. teyop   tatkan wiosmove.
17. emite a ipakan anse tanimarmo' takken an kar soke.
18. 'emite Kolompia an kwen iptaypinana' pe tay soke an kar soke.
19. "Panama aisal am papye" soymaitti.
20. unni e sakuyaka mani   unni   "ani pe attursamama"'
    takken an kar soke.
21. 'ol amimalatkine iki mani mani kama pe insa?' an kar soke.
22. 'mani tummat kama' takken an kar soke 'unni arkatiit   unni
    aminasulit unar' takken an kar soke.
23. 'arpalealirte nekapar ekatparye.
24. anmarti satte' takken an kar soke.
25. 'teysokku wis pe, teki appinmakke wilupmalan' takkenye an kar
    soymosunto.
26. 'inso' soke soke 'napir' soke.
27. 'iy tayle takotipa' soke.
28. emit ati ittocurmosunnat.
29. teki aimarka kaypo wis soysa natmosunto panki.
30. tek osetotpali, wicupwalase.
31. tek kapitpali.
32. 'aimal apsosmar' soka.
33. api wis kakkwen anka soymarpa.

34. 'ai Méndez apsosmar' soke 'sappurpa' soke.
35. a wiskus an natparsunto.
36. tek nakate panto.
37. Kolonse waci irpakke.
38. teki aki kapitpa uryaki.
39. teki   tat apal an kep pankutpali, Panamase.
40. Panama moskua   pankose mani wis otosipa aki,
    mani wis onoappa.
41. tulappaa   an onospa.
42. ante ispe wis yopiparye.
43. 'tulapo kakkanpe, kakka kwensak, kakka mannerkwa' soka.
44. teki anka onospa.
45. 'pe, ipappase suo' soke.
46. ai Adriano anka sokku   'pe ittoleket' soke 'pe napier nao'
    takken soke.
47. 'pe sorpa an sunao' soke.
48. kartati kwaple, an ka uysa   kwaple an pennuysa.
49. teki mani, suitampekit an kal uysa natsunto, 'wese nonikkir
    kinkwa, paynonikko' an kar soke.
50. 'napir' soke.
51. teeki aimarte okus tayle waci ilapakkeki.
52. tek anka apparmaysikuste.
53. taytisursokkutii   ittakkayop pinsale sunnawa.
54. tek inso apparmaysii,   Colon emar pankua.
55. Panamaki pe aipinet.
56. suittonkwen manattarmoka.
57. tek an pennus.
58. tek aimarte ur suap takke.
59. aaii sokkomala, kar mottor akkwesiit.
60. tek per otesku anmarkine, muttikuarpinne. (pitch rises
    at end of line)
61. tek anka wis selet takke.
62. muis seles wek opakkaleki anso.
63. tek selesku kep nakkwitepali, tiwarpa.
64. e walase nakkwitesunto.
65. kwenti anapa anmar seletet.

66. ney taysursunnawa ney muttikkucunnat.
67. kwallupi kapupuk an takke opakkal opakkar.
68. ney pukkwa na-te-ku taylene ekisnatapsunto.
69. 'way pukkwatte' soke.
70. mottor urmaysiparsokku, ney nuk ekicursunnaya.
71. teeki, 'Llanose kammalo' soke.
72. waci irampeki an anso.
73. aase an oarmasmarto.
74. tek anmar kammasunna ulacuyaki.
75. ti pelap wicurmo ney yolamo takke.
76. o-wa-wanmaymai, iy pe parsaosunna?
77. kwi surmosunnat.
78. tek anmal oipos natparsunto.
79. Maenayse.
80. tek peece an kalesmarpala.
81. ulacu aisar onakkoeyop pinsae   aimarte ulacu mattumaypie.
82. wayteka kar mattumaymoka.
83. 'anka urko amisulitte' soke.
84. pinsa kamainai, tat yorukku nait.
85. sapan mata.
86. kopet satte.
87. teekin natmarparsunto, kannar ulacu ekwatte (rising pitch),
    pinsa kalittos. (pitch rises at end of line)
88. kep epippitesunto.
89. kep Maese opetapsunto.
90. 'weki an ettinsunno' soke.
91. aate aimarte aki pukkwat.
92. e kwenatse opecunto.
93. 'e ia' soyye.
94. tek opes natemarpali, mas   wis ittosmar an tayye.
95. 'pia an kapitammarpalotipa?' soke.
96. 'kapitappi Tapartinak' soka.
97. 'wek Taparti ney nuy' soka.
98. tiwar tummat yomokat.
99. tey paneki nakkwitemarpali.
100. 'yorukku neyse.

101. Ipeti' soke.
102. 'wesik pe naoet' takken soke, 'tiwar nakkwitet.'
103. tat nakkwesik kwenti tat arkwanesik natmokat.
104. teeki, Ipetise yorukku.
105. tek kammama, osetotparsunto.
106. 'tey waitarte, kinemarpar' soka.
107. ati 'aitiar nasunno' soke.
108. 'iy tat momalo?' an kar soke.
109. 'anmar tat nate mo' soke.
110. tikka an ittosurwa.
111. ante ipapo kusat.
112. tey natemarpali. (voice vibrating)
113. iinso oarmakkarsun 'weki pe peoet' takken soke.
114. takkarku nek kwanerkwa wis sii.
115. teeki, aite teun sensote mamoye.
116. senso etarpema.
117. tense kottamma.
118. 'peki aimar tani' kar soke.
119. 'pialit?' soke.
120. takkarku, 'tata nakkwepalit' soka.
121. 'napir' soka.
122. 'tay' soke.
123. teki kopet irmakkal an takke. (pitch rises at end of line)
124. teki, 'yannu masi' soka.
125. 'mer naoye' soy tayle.
126. aimarte nasokkalit.
127. 'mer nao' kar soke.
128. 'teek, ampa pe naoku pe immar satapposulitteye.'
129. 'tat pukeoe an' soke.
130. tey waci irpokin an insa.
131. napir mone.
132. tek kapitmarsunna. (pitch rises at end of line)
133. tek aite anka nasitepinne an takke. (pitch rises at end of line)
134. 'sekretto ittokwelo' soke.
135. 'a insa an pe oturtakkwelo' takken soke.
136. 'tulakwen kakkanpeki' an ukko takken soke.

137. 'napir' an kar soke.
138. tek an pennus.
139. teeki, takkarku an kwen ittosula. (pitch rises at end of line)
140. kwen kaet an ittosurwa.
141. yeti a.
142. wiste iy saerkepe.
143. an oakkua.
     (laughter, comments from gathered audience)
144. maka an kwen ittosuli yeti.
     (laughter, comments from gathered audience)
145. teki   'nai nai nai' (decreasing volume) soyye.
146. arpakke wis soysisunna. (pitch rises at end of line)
     (laughter)
147. pinket aparki.
     (comments from gathered audience: purwikan kusiyopi)
148. eye   purwikan nue kusii.
149. immar per wicur pilekeyop natsunto.
     (comments from gathered audience: purwikan pinkerpa)
150. teeki   paneki paloiposto.
151. 'pankuosur' soka.
152. 'ilakwen si osetotmalo' soka.
153. e maci kep anka narmakkarsunto.
154. tipuho imacunto.
155. '"weki weki weki" soko takken, "wea wea kwis"' takken soka.
156. 'sokampe, kakkattar.
157. pait sokampe kakka paapak.
158. teki   nia   okwayet' soka.
159. 'teki a,   per wisi.'
160. tale tale wis katanikustole.
161. tek osetotku   wis kasakwakina, ampa kannal iettapali.
162. teki   tek an mettenattaparsunto, 'an sorpa pe kannar
     kannar soysio' soke.
163. 'soy-si-sun-na-ya.' (pitch rises at end of line)
     (laughter)
164. ipapoki an kalecurpa.
165. wis talemas tayle.

166. 'na yerpa' soka.
167. 'kwen kwen puleke taette' soke a.
168. 'napir' an kar soke.
169. kep parkwaisapar naipesik.
170. 'naipe sekretto sunno' soke.
171. na-si-te-pali.
172. teyoppaliwa.
173. 'napirmo' ankar soka.
174. tey pel an, ilemaysapar tayle.
175. teki   kep ina anka   narmakkarparsunto.
176. 'we epuleko takken sailanaka' takken soke.
177. '"toitar tayleku, ippiypa an arpatisuli" an soke.
178. ippo ippaa ippakke unni arpa' takken soke.
179. 'impakkwa   impakwena   tiwar pannat nonitaette' soke a.
180. 'potto ipapokusatti   ati sun ipapaapak an arpa' soke.
181. 'potto ati   poto   poni   ainakkwistaette' soke.
182. 'kwenti emiskwattina sur' soke 'ati pursur an imay' soka.
183. 'sekretto an pentakkette' soke.
184. inso sokene.
185. ina ittoarkua inso potto, we an pe soysamalata, wis
     an   eppenne ittosye.
186. ampa a epumoka.
187. a epumosokku iki pal an akku ittosunna.
188. pinsa impakwen wis akkar pimosunnata.
189. 'aki wisi   an walik SURYE' an korsisunnaya.
190. 'weti an walik sur' takkenye.
191. sappurpa anse oyoarku takkarsunna. (pitch rises at end of line)
192. al a ekka pimoka.
193. teysokku pursur anka natsunto.
194. tek inso arpanakucunto.
195. teki ipakwen   mas emitimarpali   aaki   sunmaynatappali
     'e purpakat suitnerkwa' soka.
196. kal uytepali.
197. 'pait e ulukat' soke.
198. kal uytepali.
199. pelap tulapo oarmattole.

200. natette anka, immar an wis paysa an natpalit.
201. mor kinnit.
202. lapismala.
203. kwaternomala.
204. teymalat paylepalit.
205. kwaple   kwaple purwi purwi oeletet.
206. mottor   pennuspalit suitnerkwa.
207. teymalatse kwaple, tulakwen oarmaspalit.
208. pelap   tulappakustole.
209. 'aka tanikkitte' an kar soke 'ipika an parsapokone.'
210. teki.
211. teki inso, ipakante, kwen sanarkusula. (pitch rises at end of
      line)
212. yoisku ipampe pina. (pitch rises at end of line)
213. an sapomasurmoka.
214. tey perkwaple anka ilemaysa tayle.
215. pinsa tayleku   emi, kalanukkisik kumaloet   pelakwaple
      narmas.
216. takkarku pilakansik   kwen kwen pilakan
      nikkat   'pilakanse kottoette' soke.'
217. anka ilemaysapar tayle.
218. pel anka ikal ukkenasa. (pitch rises at end of line)
219. 'nue salak' takken soke.
220. 'tayleku pe sorpa emi   pepa akkaetti pe amitappo' takken
      soke.
221. 'apakkar pe   amisurkutaerye.
222. pe amisulile, warkwen unnisur' takken soke.
223. anka   soymosunto.
224. 'teki   teukki nainukanki   ina tiket' takken soke.
225. 'nainu, tayleku pulalet   pe niymartipa' soke.
226. 'pinsa pe tiko'   takken soke.
227. 'manisur' soke.
228. 'nekkwepurkatitte' soke. (pitch rises on first word of line)
229. 'tayleku, aimala   peka soytao' takken soke, '"tayleku
      nue   ainis"' takken soke.
230. '"pali walapo walappaa iplo"' takken soke.

231. 'teysokku pe soko takkenye "pek ina tikkoloye."
232. ina tiysal ipapaapakka pe, tiempo nasikko' takken soke.
233. '"mer se parnanao"' takken soke.
234. 'teki pe tiysatki kep, ipapaapakkine   kep arpatpalo' takken soke.
235. 'nekulup saalir' soysunto a.
236. 'nekulup pe saartipa' soke.
237. 'kepe   akkwio ittolesunto kwis kwise.
238. teysokku, pe kannar emuroku   kummaytoku kwen akkarsulitte' (pitch rises)   soke.
239. 'tey sale' takken soke.
240. tanapakke pe tiko' soke 'nainu tummat' soke.
241. 'tey sale' takken soke.
242. 'nainu warkwenat' soke a.
243. 'ai kwensak warkwen   tiypimotipa' soke.
244. 'ati suittompo' soke.
245. 'ati nekkwepursulitte' soke.
246. 'ati warkwen   ekat' pittosursoke.
247. anka soysunto.
248. 'tuppu paitkinet tipa'   soke.
249. 'ati tayleku,   suitpakke' takken soke.
250. 'tuppu pait, sunna   tekit apepimotipa' soke.
251. 'sun tey pe sao' takken soke.
252. 'inso' soke 'napirmo' an kar soke.
253. 'teukkin' parsoke 'tule nailikkustipa' soke a.
254. 'ina   perkwaple pe, nutas' soke.
255. 'takkarku, pane tayleku onoko' soke.
256. 'onosokkalile pe nek, weki onmakkennekki pe soko' takken soke '"emi an onosokkarye.
257. pan emi an onokoye."
258. teysokku mimmi, koe kisikana   mukan soysa' takken soke '"emi tayle ani tup   mu nai"' takken soke.
259. 'teyso pese maynonimalo' takken soka a.
260. 'mukana   e nankana pese maynonikko' takken soke.
261. 'e nan maymoko' takken soke   'e   pap maymokoye.

262. e mimmi maymoko kwaple ati sicii kwenti yokkorpa malo' soke
'e nan   e pap   tey sale' takken soke.
263. 'ippakke   kar wis tiempo uymoko' soke.
264. 'aynep nanaetti pasur' soke '"kwenti paket" oparsunnat ippakke.
265. ina allietse' soysunto.
266. 'tey sale' takken soke.
267. 'weki an sortapukkwat anti anpe kakkappaa nikkatti   pel ina
makarpi' takken soke.
268. 'teysokku anmala   toitar parkwayetsur' soke.
269. 'ar takketi' tay soke.
270. 'kuska tule, nek ipettimokatte' soke.
271. 'ukak unnila   kin   walik kwici takkartamar' takken soke.
272. 'melle tayleku   pese warmakkekarye' soy takken soke.
273. 'tayleku   pasur pe takkekarye aka ina mayle' takken soke.
274. 'peti nekkwepur tummat sokkuti   iki kwaplemakkar pe
mako?' soke.
275. 'kwen kwen sikki na ittomalatti pe oko' takken soke.
276. 'ati ipapaapak pe oko' takken soke 'ati, nue sikkit' takken soke.
277. 'tayleku   inso kwen kwena, sappin seret tipa, punakwa seret
tipa   ome seret tipa   ati pese oko' soke 'suitpakke' soke.
278. 'mani pippipar' takken soke.
279. 'suitpakke oyle' takken soke.
280. tese ukak aite, anka ikal ukkesunto.
281. 'tayle wese, an arpama' takken soke.
282. 'pe ikar pait apepalirtina   pe turtaypar' takken soke
'punmarkat an kanipar' takken soke.
283. 'ampa ayop ilemakkal an kanipar' takken soke.
284. 'mu sokattulakwen kakka pakke an nikka' takken soke.
285. 'teysokku kwaple narmakkar nait e kartakine, anse kwaple
oyosat,' pe takken soke.
286. 'we a mu a mu a mu kwikwis' takken soke.
287. ai Manisiytinappi a ittonamoka, ipampe kapiapmo anse.
288. anyalaparsunto.
289. teki   teysokku ati, nekapar nasis tayle, 'suitnerkwa an wis
seti' soka.
290. 'turkwen e mani' soka.
291. 'ati punmarkat.'

292. Inso sokene.
293. 'nuekampi' an kar soke.
294. 'nia kaet an wispar' takken soke.
295. 'teysokku   pe namaypipartipa' soke.
296. 'turtaytapar' takken soke.
297. 'nia kaet takkarku kiakkwapal a. (pitch rises at end of line)
298. tule, tupki warmastipa' soke.
299. 'niase kottetaette' soke.
300. 'kal an namay' takken soke.
301. 'kan an sunmayye.
302. tek an sama' takken soke.
303. 'muki, tayleku kwenkwen mukin ailatta' takken soke, 'nia
        impakwen nakustaet.
304. kal an sunmay' takken soke.
305. '"emi we, neka an imas"' takken soke.
306. '"ipa, ipanerkwa an imaysamar"' takken soke.
307. '"emi ina an tiysa"' takken anka soke.
308. 'kwaplen kal an namaysa' takken soke.
309. '"emi we sappi, na kwikwicit, kwipa tummakan ailasat a.
310. kwaple anka mortup, ney pilli pakkese an oupos"' takken soke.
311.   apsoetyop ittolesunna. (pitch rises at end of line)
312. '"kaopikine, an, mortup ote"' takken soke.
313. 'teysokkuti   aiye, teki an ikar kanima' takken soke.
314. 'teysokku we   kwenna kwenna soy' takken soke '"pi-la-kat-
        ye."
315. pilakatsur' soke.
316. 'eppenne tayleku nerkan aitearkua.
317. nerkan tummakan aiteskua.
318. tayle ipeler warkwena   sanale kaluyapa, "kalumattuye" ney
        nukatyapa toysa' takken soke.
319. 'emi aki karta   sappurpa oyokwici taylear' takken soke.
320. '"teki karta anniy susmar" soke.
321. "teki karta apsolearku"'   soy takken
        soke   '"ina   anse turtaytamaloye.
322. tominkoki pe takoye.'
323. teki, aimala   karta amisat yappa naetkine.

324. ai pila   yapa toysa" takken soke.
325. "pila ipa   ipampe kakka attar yokkuap" takken soke.
326. "nekurpa.
327. tey pilase ekislearsun" takken soke.
328. "'emi an wey toytekua.
329. emi tayleku, an toyteku nek sicit' takken soke.
330. 'ipya kasa yopye.
331. tek an toysaku taisik, ne-ka-nu-et' takken soke.
332. 'we naptule pukkwayop' takken soke.
333. 'tule sanakwarpuy' takken soke.
334. 'naipe   suaripet' takken soke.
335. 'tekine akkwaser   a arkar' takken soke.
336. 'aase   akkwaser kep anka, macikwa amis' takken soke.
337. "'sailase an perpeap" soke.
338. tey sailase an perpeapku, saila anka soy' takken soke
     "'ipi pe saye?"
339. an soy' takken soke "' an   an we karta setani takkenye."
340. a soketpa kartate parmitsokkutina   yok an oturtakkar'
     takken soke.
341. 'nuet takken soysunto.
342. "'pap weki anka nek uysamo" takken soke.
343. "'yoo tayleku mimmikan   olo tule wek anpakuoet   mer
     ponikan toitar   appinkaekala   weki   ina uymai pe
     saoye'   anka tios soysa takkenye" soy takken soke.
344. teysokku an mosku kwirri an ku' takken soke.
345. 'uysir pukkitar' takken soke.
346. 'teysokku anka ina imaysa' soke 'kannal uatuk an nukus takken.
347. teysokku emi an kannar noarparku, teyop an kuspar' takken
     soke.
348. 'ina an turtacokku   kannal an nutasparye.
349. asu noyse pakkar kwirri an kus takkenye.
350. teysokkuti emite perkwaple pe an takken' soke 'nuet takkenye.'"
351. nue nappira tayleye pinsaarmosun' takken soke.
352. 'aa kep emi tayle an sayla e sakkamo anso (pitch rises at end of
     line)
353. a turtaysamo' takken soke.

354. 'kep a an sayla   kep e sakkase turtasmo' takken soke.
355. 'a ikal emite an   kanimo' takken soke.
356. 'teysokku an   an peece pankuarpimosokku   teyop pani
     pankutanimo' takken soke.
357. 'teysokku ipika tayleku   icakkwa an pek ukko' soke.
358. 'tayle an nuk nopi an apekette' soke.
359. 'ipika kirmar namay' takken soke.
360. '"kattik immar turtaymarye!
361. kattik immar tiymarye!
362. pap neyse ikar nuetye."
363. kirmar namakket an wismar' takken soke.
364. 'anpalla an namaytimo' takken soke.
365. 'teysokku ipika aiye an pey nailekuo' takken soke.
366. 'teysokku teyop pe tayleku sappinkan nikkusar pe
     oturtaymokoye.'
367. anka soysunto.
368. 'pe sappinkwen amioeti   unnila pe pentakko' takken soke.
369. 'immar wis yaipa pe saalir' takken soke.
370. 'mas emiartipa' soke.
371. 'okkop tipa' soke.
372. 'ipi peka wis sapitipa' soke.
373. 'pelakwa' takken soke.
374. 'tuppu pait tipa' soke.
375. 'pe mani oesacun   ati pe oeko, pese mani   uymoko' takken
     soke.
376. 'teysokku aiye mer toitar onaypalo' takken soke.
377. 'kwenna kwenna mani tayleku karkesaila   uyteta' takken
     soke.
378. 'saila teki eka soysayop takkenye' aite anka ikar ukkarsunto.
379. 'teysokku emi tayleku pe mekoeti   kirmarki
     aypinekarsurye.
380. unni kirmar pentakkekarye.
381. pe meko' takken soke.
382. 'tayleku nappanek okannoekar' takken soke.
383. 'tuppu peka   napir   pe takkekar' pittosursokeye.

384. 'kwenti tayleku, inso "kirmarki aypineka immar
turtaysaye"   pe pitamalar' takken soke.
385. 'pe okakkansatamalarye.'
386. anka soysunto.
387. 'ikal iskana mama' takken soke.
388. 'ati an pentakketsurmar' takken soke.
389. 'ikal iskanati tayleku   "tios an takkoteye"   kwen
soylesur' takkenye.
390. 'ati pinsa turtayle' pittosursoke soke.
391. 'kin nekkwen kannoetsur' takkenye.
392. aite anka soysunto.
393. 'teysokku aimar mesar pe sapier, kwen akkarsurye.
394. pe kwen payokosurye.
395. teysokku   aiye mer keker ittokoye.
396. iki tipa pe nappanekkine   inaturkan serkan
mamapartipaye.
397. tupa ikar wismalat mamatipaye.
398. mamasurpartipaye.'
399. soysunto.
400. 'teysokkuti kirmar itu, pe itu mamaitti   inso, peece an
penkus' takken soke.
401. '"pia wekit ina partanikkoye?
402. sailakkar wekit ina an kwen taytisurye."
403. anki ululear' takken soke.
404. 'a-ni-e-ka-so-ke-yo-pi "an pur kanna ina wisi"   e-ka-
so-ke-yo-pi   aimal anki pinsas' takken soke.
405. 'ani ekar soysulitte' (pitch rises) soke.
406. 'wepa tayleku ai   immar turtaysatpali   an turtasmo'
pittosursoke soke.
407. 'emi tayleku itu ikar wismalat   perkwaple milema' takken
soke.
408. 'pel ankatpikus' anka soysunto.
409. 'pela Ipeti ankat pukkwa   tayle Ikkanti pukkwa   tayleku
Narkanti mai   emi Acutup anse arpipa' takken soke.
410. 'iki taetmotipa?' soke.
411. 'wese arpiku   napir tae tayleke' takken soke.

412. 'e tuppu mosku iki taettipa?' soke.
413. 'an nuk isoettipa?' soke.
414. 'ani eka immal icakkwa soysayopi   ai nanaettipaye' anka soke, wicurmosun pitto pinsan' soy takkenye. (pitch rises at end of line)
415. 'teysokkuti ai akkal akkal an kwen kumasuli.
416. ilakwen an   tayleku weki taniku' takken soke.
417. 'unni tayleku, kirmar sorpali   untar an pentayma' takken soke.
418. 'kwen kwen pirkakwento   nailikkusmalat   an pentayti' takken soke.
419. 'inso tayleku kwen kwen kar noe.
420. kwensak emi   an ipe   tua tetterkwa ti' takken soke.
421. 'an pentas' takken soke.
422. 'emi tayleku, e inatulet sokkar' takken soke '"pe tiynamarsunye.
423. par nukuosulitteye."
424. nunusaila appanma' takken soke.
425. 'teki anse noni' takken soke.
426. 'niwalappakus ottartani   kep anse ninoni' takken soke.
427. 'emi wis pentas' pe pittosursoke soke. (pitch rises in middle of line)
428. 'emi karmayti ampa' takkenye.
429. 'al an taysat Panamaki.
430. suarki nanasunnata.'
431. 'ampalla aswe enay' takken soke.
432. 'ampalla tayleku ua makke ampalla ua soe   sappurpa yannu makke, yannu maysar opestae   kep e pap suaptas' takken soke.
433. 'an ipe tekitte iplopimalanatte' (pitch rises) soke.
434. 'teysokkute emite   teki anti wis pentaymain' takkenye anka soysunto.
435. 'teysokkute emit a ikar pe amitanisokku, ikar nuet' takken soke.
436. 'tayleku napir peka   nekkwepurti pinsas' pittosursoke soke.
437. 'teysokku nue salak' takkenye anka soysunto.

438. 'teysokkuti inso tayleku nekkwepurka   nue pe soytappo'
     takkenye.
439. 'emi teysokku, mer pe penkuekala.
440. emite kartate an peka parmitmo' takken soke.
441. 'emit peti karta wiculi.
442. tukkin narmas anso.
443. pekin pinsatamalarye.'
444. anka soysunto.
445. emi, Maenakki narmaynonikkit Maenakki ate karta tulet maita.
446. e maci, kar soysat   'pe ase narmaytappoye.'
447. aki anmar narmaynonisunto.
448. teysokkut a, emite   na teki arpitte emite kannar an pes
     nonimarpali.
449. wiskat ittolekena.
450. toitar akkal akkar   kus kwen ittolesuli.
451. teysokku inso an arpaetti   iy tayletakotipa.
452. 'inso tiosti   pule ponikante   anse
     oyosurmalar   ar pirkakwen anpa an arpasur' pe
     ittosursokeye.
453. 'inso tayleku   ponikan ittakka tayle
     arpalirti   emis, arpaleket   pinsa pese oyotmalo'
     pittosurokeye an soysunto.
454. 'teysokku tiospi wicun' pittosursokeye.
455. PITTOKUA, tese ukaysunto.

Translation

1.   Well now I left you.
2.   And   at Tigre (an island), I slept.
3.   The friends (inhabitants) were listening to speeches (holding a
     meeting) I saw.
4.   Now, for the congress (inter-island meeting) that you had.
5.   Well when the friends had finished speaking, I said a word to
     them also.

6.   'Inapakinya (famous deceased Mulatuppu chief) once said' see I
        say to them.
7.   '"Now I don't want to leave an old woman.
8.   This young woman you are giving me indeed I cannot care for."
9.   He said' see I say to them.
10. 'Now this matter you are conversing about.
11. These foreigners searching for gold.
12. They are not from here.
13. They are from various places some Germans some Italians.
14. Therefore thus.
15. Indeed the Europeans.
16. In this way   they also mistreated our ancestors.
17. Now these same days are coming to us too' see I say to them.
18. 'Now Colombia does not want to leave us' you see I say I say to
        them.
19. '"Although Panama is our fatherland" it is said.
20. Only for its own bag is the money   only   "We (The
        Panamanians) are robbing us"' see I say to them.
21. 'These people looking for gold how much money how much money
        are they taking from them do you think?' I say to them.
22. 'They are taking a lot of money' see I say to them 'they are only
        prospecting   they are not even yet taking it away' see
        I say to them.
23. 'When the work begins half is for them.
24. But for us nothing' see I say to them.
25. 'Therefore you, well, must push back a bit' see I also said to
        them.
26. 'Thus' they say they say 'it is true' they say.
27. 'Let us see what will happen' they say.
28. Now I did not hear (was not present) at that one (the later
        meeting) also.
29. Well I said some words to the friends and left the next day.
30. Well we passed the whole day again, toward Wicupwala (an
        island at the western end of San Blas).
31. Well there we slept again.
32. 'The friends were conversing' I say.

33.   And they spoke some words to me also.

34.   'We conversed with friend Méndez (a renowned chief from the village of Ustuppu)' they say 'in the mountain (jungle mainland)' they say.

35.   Having learned this I left again.

36.   Well I moved on the next day.

37.   We arrived at Colon at 4 o'clock.

38.   Well there I slept again in the boat.

39.   Well   when the sun was half way up in the sky (mid morning) I then left again, for Panama.

40.   When I arrived in Panama   I went to the bank where I have been putting a little money and there, I took out some money.

41.   I took out thirty dollars.

42.   I want to wear some glasses too.

43.   'Twenty-six dollars and thirty cents (they cost)'   they say.

44.   Well they took it out for me.

45.   'You, in three days come and get them'   they say.

46.   Friend Adriano (an inhabitant of Mulatuppu and a relative of Olowitinappi) said to me   'it's your choice' he says 'if you want to go go' see he says.

47.   'After you leave I will go and get them for you'   he says.

48.   I gave him, all the papers   I paid everything.

49.   Well five, dollars I gave him and I left, 'when I come back here I'll buy, bullets' I say to him.

50.   'It is true' I say.

51.   Well the friends (other Kuna) were ready it seems at 4 o'clock.

52.   Well they came running for me.

53.   Since I had never seen this place   I believed it was close.

54.   Well thus the trip, is as far as Colon.

55.   From Panama you go.

56.   It costs 75 cents also.

57.   Well I paid.

58.   Well the friends went to get the boat see.

59.   Some Choco (neighboring Indian group) friends, were taking care of the motor for them.

60. Well when we had loaded everything, night had begun to fall.
    (pitch rises at end of line)
61. Well we floated along a little see.
62. We floated a bit the distance from here to cross over there (from
    the island of Mulatuppu to the mainland) I think.
63. Well having floated then we went up, along the river.
64. We went up the main branch.
65. Then we floated up a branch (of the river).
66. The villages could not be seen it had become night.
67. Only the lights I saw flickering along the coasts.
68. I asked about the villages we saw as-we-went-a-long.
69. 'They are Panamanians' they say.
70. Since the motor was making a lot of noise, I was not truly able to
    ask the names of the villages.
71. Well 'we will sleep in Llano' they say.
72. It was ten o'clock I think.
73. When we arrived there.
74. Well we slept in the pirogue.
75. There was not any rain the weather was good see.
76. We were shiv-ver-ing, what could we do?
77. But there were not any mosquitos.
78. Well when we woke up we left again.
79. Toward the village of Majé.
80. Well it was there we stayed a while.
81. Hoping to be able to raise up the pirogue (to the bank)   the
    friends wanted to repair the pirogue.
82. And have the Panamanians repair it for them.
83. 'But why didn't you bring us wood?' they say.
84. For no reason we were walking along, it was noon.
85. Stomachs empty.
86. Nothing to drink.
87. Well we continued on again, once again we lowered the pirogue
    (into the water) (rising pitch), for no reason we had made the
    effort. (pitch rises at end of line)
88. Then we had to pull it.
89. Then we left it there in Majé.

90. 'Here we must tie it' they say.
91. There are many friends there.
92. We left it with a relative (of one of the persons who accompanied Olowitinappi).
93. 'His older brother' he says.
94. Well having left it we took off again, we   ate a little I see.
95. 'Wherever will we sleep?' they say.
96. 'We slept at the mouth of Taparti river' they say.
97. 'The name of this place is Taparti' they say.
98. It is also a large river.
99. Well the next day we went up (the river) again.
100. 'At noon we'll get home.
101. To Ipeti' they say.
102. 'Here is your route' see they say, 'where the river goes up."
103. This one (river) leads to where the sun rises and the other to where the sun sets.
104. Well, we got to Ipeti at noon.
105. Well we rested there, in fact we spent the whole day there.
106. 'Well the next day then, we continued on again' I say.
107. 'We must go by paddling' they say.
108. 'Where will the sun be (what time will it be) when we get there?' I say to them.
109. 'We will get there when the sun sets' they say.
110. I felt that I was far.
111. In fact two days had passed.
112. Well we continued on again (voice vibrating).
113. Thus we really arrived 'here is where you will stay' see they say.
114. So there were just six houses.
115. Well, our friend   the census taker was there too.
116. Taking the census.
117. They called out (to Olowitinappi's teacher).
118. 'Friends have come to you' they say to him.
119. 'From where?' he says.
120. Indeed, 'from where the run rises' they say.
121. 'Good' he says.

122. 'Come' he says.
123. Well beverages were passed around I see. (pitch rises at end of
     line)
124. Well, 'there is a meal of wild boar' he says.
125. 'Don't go yet' he says (to the others) see.
126. The friends were about to leave.
127. 'Don't go' he says to them.
128. 'Well if you go   you won't be able to do anything when you get
     there.'
129. 'We'll get there with the setting sun' they say.
130. Well it was 2 o'clock I think.
131. Surely.
132. Well then we slept (pitch rises at end of line)
133. Well the friend (the teacher) began to teach me I see. (pitch
     rises at end of line)
134. 'First we will study the secret (verbal secret charm)'
     he says.
135. 'That is what I will teach you first' see he says.
136. 'Fifteen dollars'   I will have to pay see he says.
137. 'Good' I say to him.
138. Well I paid.
139. Well, in fact I didn't understand. (pitch rises at end of line)
140. I couldn't catch it.
141. No ah.
142. I didn't know what to do.
143. I couldn't do it.
     (laughter, comments from gathered audience)
144. I didn't understand even a single thing.
     (laughter, comments from gathered audience)
145. Well   'continue continue continue' (decreasing volume) he
     says.
146. Secretly he was speaking a little. (pitch rises at end of line)
     (laughter)
147. Surrounded by shame.
     (comments from gathered audience: like little kids.)
148. Yes   just like little kids.

149. As if I didn't know how to pronounce things.
     (comments from gathered audience: little kids full of shame.)
150. Well   next day we woke up again.
151. 'You won't go out' he says.
152. 'All day long we'll stay at home' he says.
153. His son then wrote for me.
154. He made the drawings.
155. '"This this this" you will see, "like that like that"' see he
     says.
156. 'It has, fifteen lines.
157. The other one has eighteen lines.
158. Well   it is to frighten the devil' he says.
159. 'Well, you know it all.'
160. Little by little I was catching on.
161. Well when the day ended   I had caught on a bit, and then I
     would forget again.
162. Well   well he left me alone again, 'after I leave you will sit
     saying the words over and over' he says.
163. 'You-will-sit-say-ing.' (pitch rises at end of line)
     (laughter)
164. I needed two days to learn this.
165. I felt I had learned something it seems.
166. 'It is good' he says.
167. 'There are some who are worse' he says ah.
168. 'It is true' I say to him.
169. Then we changed over to snakes.
170. 'This is truly the secret for snakes' he says.
171. I-be-gan-a-gain.
172. It is just as difficult (as the first one Olowitinappi learned).
173. 'It is good also' he says to me.
174. Well I, got everything in order it seems.
175. Well   then he began to write down the medicine for me again.
176. 'For this you must touch see the origin' see he says.
177. '"Never indeed have I worked many days" I say.
178. Only two three or four days I work' see he says.

179. 'Sometimes   at times   people come from other rivers (villages)' he says ah.
180. 'People who were bitten already two days ago   those I can truly work on (cure) in eight days' he says.
181. 'Already in these (cases) already the evil spirits   have risen everywhere' he says.
182. 'A person bitten the very same day is easy' he says 'this one I handle very easily' he says.
183. 'The secret really helps me' he says.
184. Thus he says.
185. The medicine I studied there thus already, as I told you, a little I   had studied a long time ago.
186. And I had also used it.
187. Since I had also used it how could I not learn it again.
188. But for no reason at times it has a slightly different name.
189. 'This one   we DON'T have at our place' I would shout to him.
190. 'That one we don't have at our place' see.
191. But when he showed it to me in the jungle I saw. (pitch rises at end of line)
192. That we have it too.
193. Therefore it went easy for me.
194. Well thus we were working.
195. Well one day   as we were clearing his plantain plantation again   there   we were talking as we were walking along 'the soul (another secret charm) costs three dollars' he says.
196. I paid him again.
197. 'The other is the boat (another secret charm)' he says.
198. I paid him again.
199. Everything had now reached twenty dollars.
200. When I left, I bought some things as I went.
201. Red cloth.
202. Pencils.
203. Notebooks.
204. These purchases.
205. All   all small small expenses.
206. For the use of the motor   I also paid three dollars.

207. All these things, came to ten dollars.
208. The total of everything was thirty dollars.
209. 'But that is what I came for' I say to him 'Why should I save
     the money.'
210. Well.
211. Well thus, the days, were passing by rapidly. (pitch rises at
     end of line)
212. Already ten days had quickly gone by. (pitch rises at end of
     line)
213. He didn't keep anything from me either.
214. Well he put everything in order for me see.
215. For no reason indeed   now, some people get rheumatism
     (because of the snakebite)   he wrote it all.
216. In fact enemies' disease (gonorrhea)   some (snakebite
     victims) have enemies' disease   'they are called (affected) by
     enemies' disease' he says.
217. He put everything in order again for me it seems.
218. He taught me all these rules. (pitch rises at end of line)
219. 'Carry on well' see he says.
220. Indeed after you leave now   you must get an assistant' see he
     says.
221. 'If by chance you   don't get one.
222. If you don't get one, one person alone can't do this' see he says.
223. He said also   to me.
224. 'Well   with regard to the fields   planting medicine' see he
     says.
225. 'If you, indeed have a communal farm,' he says.
226. 'You must plant for free' see he says.
227. 'No money' he says.
228. 'For it belongs to the village' he says. (pitch rises at beginning
     of line)
229. 'Indeed, the friends   will say to you' see he says, '"indeed
     many (snakes) came out"' see he says.
230. '"It is possible to kill two even three"' see he says.
231. 'Therefore you will say see "I will go and plant medicine for
     you."

232. After having planted the medicine for eight days you, will
     regulate the time (stop people from going there)' see he says.
233. "'Don't go there"' see he says.
234. 'Well there where you planted it then, after eight
     days   then they can work again' see he says.
235. 'Within the earth do it then' he said ah.
236. 'Within the earth you will do it then' he says.
237. 'Then   you must dig did you hear shoveling shoveling.
238. Therefore, when you have covered it over again   when they
     come to burn it (the field) nothing will happen' (pitch rises) he
     says.
239. 'That is how it is done' see he says.
240. 'You must plant in four places' he says 'if the field is big' he
     says.
241. 'That is how it is done' see he says.
242. 'When the field belongs to one person' he says ah.
243. 'If a single friend   wants to plant too' he says.
244. 'You charge him one dollar' he says.
245. 'This one does not belong to the village' he says.
246. 'Rather a single person   is the owner' don't you hear he says.
247. He said to me.
248. 'If there are persons from other islands' he says.
249. 'These indeed, you will charge two dollars' see he says.
250. 'Another island, truly   if they want it too'   he says.
251. 'Truly you will do it this way' see he says.
252. 'Thus' he says 'It is good too' I say to him.
253. 'Well furthermore' he also says 'if a person is bitten' he says
     ah.
254. 'With medicine   you will cure, everything' he says.
255. 'In fact, the next day indeed you will send him out' he says.
256. 'When you are about to send him out of your house, you will
     announce in the gathering house' see he says "'now I am about to
     send him out.
257. Tomorrow I will send him out."

258. Therefore with regard to babies, to newly born infants   the
     midwives said' see he says '"now it seems this one belongs to the
     vine (snake)   has this potential"' see he says.
259. 'Therefore people will come to you to be painted (as protection
     against snakebites)' see he says ah.
260. 'Grandmothers   and their mothers   will come to you to be
     painted' see he says.
261. 'The mother will be painted also' see he says 'and the father will
     be painted too.
262. Their baby itself will be completely painted black but the
     others will be painted only up to the knee' he says 'the
     mother   the father   will be done that way' see he says.
263. 'Four days   you will give them to rest' he says.
264. 'It doesn't make any difference if they walk about' he says 'but
     "they must wait" you will say the four days.
265. Until the medicine goes away' he said.
266. 'That is how it is done' see he says.
267. 'Here I have thirteen of my people   all are painted with
     medicine' see he says.
268. 'Therefore we   are not at all afraid' he says.
269. '(snakes) Are always seen' see he says.
270. 'Because they also are owners of (belong to), our land' he says.
271. So that they are only around   close by   are seen nearby'
     see he says.
272. 'So that indeed   they don't approach you' he says see he
     says.
273. 'Indeed   so that they don't bother you that is why the
     medicine is painted' see he says.
274. 'Since your village is really big   how can you paint
     everyone?' he says.
275. 'You will bathe those who are affected by this disease (have
     potential to be bitten by snakes)' see he says.
276. 'You will bathe these people for eight days' see he says 'these
     people are very affected' see he says.

277. 'Indeed   thus sometimes, a young man, sometimes a young girl   sometimes an older woman   will come to you to bathe' he says 'it costs two dollars' he says.
278. 'It's cheap' see he says.
279. 'Two dollars for bathing' see he says.
280. Up to this the friend, counseled me.
281. 'It seems up to here, is my work' see he says.
282. 'If you want to learn another chant   if you want to study again' see he says 'I also know the one having to do with women (childbirth)' see he says.
283. 'And like the other one I again have it ordered' see he says.
284. 'I have twenty-four parts about childbirth' see he says.
285. 'Indeed it was all written in his notebook, he showed it all to me' you see I say.
286. 'These are for this birth these are for this birth these are for this birth' see he says.
287. Friend Manisiytinappi (another Kuna medicinal specialist, from another village) was also studying it, he also stayed ten days at our place.
288. At my side.
289. Well   indeed as for him he only finished half it seems, 'I only brought three dollars' he says.
290. 'It costs ten dollars' he says.
291. 'The one having to do with women.'
292. Thus he said.
293. 'It is good' I say to him.
294. 'I also know the one to grab the devil' see he says.
295. 'Therefore   if you want to chant again' he says.
296. 'Come study another time' see he says.
297. 'The one to grab the devil in fact is short also ah. (pitch rises at end of line)
298. If a person, encounters a vine (is bitten by a snake)' he says.
299. 'It might happen that he calls the devil (becomes crazy)' he says.
300. 'I chant for him' see he says.
301. 'I speak for him.

302. Well that is what I do' see he says.
303. 'In childbirth, indeed at times, in childbirth they (women)
     faint' see he says, 'the devil sometimes attacks them.
304. I speak for them' see he says.
305. "'Now I prepared the farm"' see he says.
306. "'For six, six days we prepared it"' see he says.
307. "'Now I planted the medicine"' see he says to me.
308. 'All this I chanted for them' see he says.
309. "'Now these trees, standing there, the big kwipa trees,
        fell down ah.
310. I sent the entire clothes line, down to the fourth level under the
        ground"' see he says.
311. It truly sounds like the way (chant) of the mass curer. (pitch
     rises at end of line)
312. "'Within the kaopi tree, I, lowered the clothes line"'
     see he says.
313. 'Well   friend, indeed I have (know) this chant' see
     he says.
314. 'Well   there are those who say' see he says "' it-be-longs-
     to-the-Cho-cos (a neighboring Indian group)."
315. But is does not belong to the Chocos' he says.
316. 'A long time ago indeed when the seers started to come down.
317. When the great seers came down.
318. It seems Ipelele (one of the great seers)   corporally entered
     a stronghold, a place called "Kalumattuye"' see he says.
319. 'Now there in the jungle   he showed a letter it seems' see he
     says.
320. "'Well they took the letter away from me" he says.
321. "Well when they read the letter"'   he says see he says
     ""'come   to my place to learn medicine (the letter says).
322. You should come on Sunday.'
323. Well, the friends   who found the letter did not want to go.
324. Friend Choco   entered inside" see he says.
325. "The Choco stayed there fifteen   fifteen days" see he says.
326. "Under the ground.

327. Well the Choco was asked (when he returned, to report on his experience)" see he says.
328. "'Now when I entered this place.
329. Now indeed, when I entered the place was dark' see he says.
330. 'As if my eyes were held shut.
331. Well when I entered some more, it-was-clear' see he says.
332. 'Like the people on this earth' see he says.
333. 'Are those people corporally' see he says.
334. 'The snake   is policeman (Kuna village official)' see he says.
335. 'Well and the spider   he is spokesman (Kuna village official)' see he says.
336. 'When   I got there the spider then got me, a boy' see he says.
337. "'To take me to the chief" he says.
338. Well when he took me to the chief, the chief says to me' see he says "'What have you come to do?"
339. I say' see he says "'I   I brought this letter see."
340. By order of this letter because it was sent   immediately they taught me' see he says.
341. 'It was good' see he said.
342. "'God gave me this place" see he (the chief) says.
343. "'Before indeed the children   the golden people (the Kuna) lived here   so that they don't encounter   evil spirits   here   you will give medicine'   God said to me see" he says see he says.
344. Well when I arrived there I had my ears all bitten up' see he says.
345. 'There were many bats' see he says.
346. 'Well he administered medicine to me' he says 'he cured my ears again see.
347. Well now when I left once again, the same thing happened to me' see he says.
348. 'Since I had learned this medicine   I cured myself once again.
349. I was all bitten up to my nostrils see.
350. Therefore now you see me' he says 'completely well see."'
351. This seems to be true and I also believe it' see he says.

352. It then now seems the father-in-law of my teacher I think.
        (pitch rises at end of line)
353. He learned too (with the Choco)' see he says.
354. 'Then my teacher   then he also learned with his father-in
        law' see he says.
355. 'I also now   have (know) this chant see he says.
356. 'Therefore I   as I also had to travel far   similarly
        you also have traveled to me from far away' see he says.
357. 'Therefore why indeed   would I give you bad counsel' he says.
358. 'Indeed I want my name to be known many places' he says.
359. 'That is why the elders chant' see he says.
360. '"Learn many things!
361. Plant many things!
362. The road to God's house is good."
363. I know the chants of the elders' see he says.
364. 'I have also chanted the same ones' see he says.
365. 'Therefore why friend would I trip you up' see he says.
366. 'Therefore when you have your student indeed you will teach
        him the same way.'
367. He said it to me.
368. 'The student you will get   he will help you only (will not
        pay you)' see he says.
369. 'When you have some little things to do' see he says.
370. 'When you clear plantain plantations' he says.
371. 'Or coconut plantations' he says.
372. 'Whatever thing you want to do' he says.
373. 'Everything' see he says.
374. 'As for people from other islands' he says.
375. 'The money you spent   that money which, you will
        spend   they will give you too' see he says.
376. 'Therefore friend don't raise the price' see he says.
377. 'There are those indeed who put the price   very high' see he
        says.
378. 'As if their chief (teacher) told them to do so see' the friend
        counseled me.

379. 'Well now indeed you must   not turn around (hurt) the elders.
380. But only help the elders.
381. You must' see he says.
382. Indeed in order to strengthen the earth (your village)' see he says.
383. 'So that your island   recognizes you   truly' don't you hear he says.
384. 'In fact indeed, thus some people will say about you   "you studied things in order to turn around (hurt) the elders"' see he says.
385. 'They will be telling lies about you.'
386. He said to me.
387. 'There are evil ways' see he says.
388. 'These are not helpful to us' see he says.
389. 'It is not said   of these evil ways indeed   "they will lead us to see god"' see.
390. 'These are taught for free' don't you hear it is said he says.
391. 'They do not serve to strengthen' see.
392. The friend said to me.
393. 'Therefore if friends criticize you, it is nothing.
394. You should not pay attention.
395. Therefore   friend do not be bothered.
396. Perhaps in your village   there are elderly medicinal specialists.
397. There are perhaps those who know the way of the vine (snake medicine and chant).
398. And again perhaps there are not.'
399. He said.
400. 'Well the elders, who were before you   thus, they competed against me' see he says.
401. '"Where could this medicine have come from?
402. Before we didn't have this medicine."
403. They criticized me' see he says.

404. 'As-if-I-was-say-ing-to-them   "I know medicine better than
     you"   as-if-I-was-say-ing-that-to-them   the friends
     didn't have confidence in me' see he says.
405. 'But I did not say that to them (pitch rises)' he says.
406. 'The friend (my teacher) indeed   had learned things   and I
     learned them also' don't you hear it is said he says.
407. 'Now indeed those who before used to know chants   all
     of them are disappearing' see he says.
408. 'All are mine (my students)' he said to me.
409. 'All those in Ipeti are mine   indeed in Ikanti there
     are many   indeed in Narkana there are some   now
     someone also came to me from Acutuppu' see he says.
410. 'And how might he behave?' he says.
411. 'When he came here   he behaved well it seems' see he says.
412. 'When he got back to his island how did he behave?' he says.
413. 'Did he slander my name?' he says.
414. 'As if I had said bad things to him   how will the friend go
     about' he says to me, 'I do not know really I think' he says see.
     (pitch rises at end of line)
415. 'Therefore friend I do not behave just any way.
416. I am always   indeed this way' see he says.
417. 'I am only indeed, helping   the elders a lot' see he says.
418. 'Some sick people   for one year   I have been helping' see
     he says.
419. 'Thus indeed some have fractured bones.
420. One now   I have   with a torn thigh muscle' see he says.
421. 'I helped him' see he says.
422. 'Now indeed, his medicinal specialist said to him' see he says
     '"they are surely going to bury you.
423. You will never get better again."
424. He smelled very bad' see he says.
425. 'Well he came to my place' see he says.
426. 'For three months he had been suffering   then they brought
     him to my place' see he says.
427. 'Now I helped him a little' don't you hear it is said he says.
     (pitch rises in middle of line)

428. 'Now he is still walking about' see.
429. (Olowitinappi says to teacher) 'I saw him in Panama.
430. He was going about with a stick.'
431. (The teacher responds) 'he can still climb up after avocados'
    see he says.
432. 'He can still indeed spear fish he can still catch fish   in
    the jungle he can kill wild boar, the wild boar that he killed he
    leaves   then his father goes to get it' see he says.
433. 'And this one (patient) of mine well they wanted to kill him' 3
    (pitch rises) he says.
434. 'So now   well I was helping him a little' see he said to
    me.
435. 'Well now this chant that you came to gather (study),
    it is a good chant' see he says.
436. 'Indeed your village   thought well of you' don't you hear it is
    said he says.
437. 'Therefore do well' see he said to me.
438. 'Therefore thus indeed to your village   you will say well
    there' see.
439. 'Now therefore, so that they don't contest you.
440. Now I will send a letter for you' see he says.
441. 'Now you don't know (how to write) letters.
442. That you yourself wrote it I think.
443. They can't think.'
444. He said to me.
445. Now, when we arrived in Maenak we wrote it in Maenak there is
    a man who knows how to write.
446. He told, his son   'you will write it there.'
447. There we wrote it.
448. So ah, now   well this is how my trip was and now again
    I have returned to you.
449. A little has been learned.
450. Nothing out of the ordinary   happened.
451. Well thus my work   I don't know how it will be.
452. 'Thus if god   does not send   evil spirits to me   so that
    again for one year I am not able to work' don't you hear I say.

453. 'Thus indeed   if evil spirits come near it seems   now, what
I worked (learned)   for free I will show to you' don't you hear
it is said I said.
454. 'Well only god knows well' don't you hear I say.
455. YOU HAVE HEARD, up to here.

Notes

1. See Sherzer (1981).
2. My representation of Kuna discourse draws on and integrates the
approaches of Dell Hymes (1981) and Dennis Tedlock (1983). See
Sherzer (1982) for a discussion of the line as a central feature in the
structuring of Kuna discourse.
3. The Kuna verb used here is *iploe* (literally: to smash to death). This is
ironic humor on Olowitinappi's part, since the Kuna would never let a
sick person die and surely would not kill a patient.

References

Hymes, Dell
   1981   *"In vain I tried to tell you"*: essays in Native American
          ethnopoetics. Philadelphia: University of Pennsylvania Press.
Sherzer, Joel
   1981   The interplay of structure and function in Kuna narrative, or:
          how to grab a snake in the Darien. In *Analyzing discourse: text
          and talk*. Georgetown University Round Table on Languages and
          Linguistics 1981, D. Tannen (ed.), pp. 306-322. Washington,
          D.C.: Georgetown University Press.
   1982   Poetic structuring of Kuna discourse: the line. *Language in
          Society* 11: 371-390.
   1983   *Kuna ways of speaking: an ethnographic perspective*. Austin:
          University of Texas Press.
Tedlock, Dennis
   1983   *The spoken word and the work of interpretation*. Philadelphia:
          University of Pennsylvania Press.

Styles of Toba Discourse

Harriet E. Manelis Klein

1. Introduction

Toba or Namqom is a Guaykuruan language spoken by the Toba Indians in Argentina, Bolivia, and Paraguay. The majority of these speakers, some 15,000, are found in the northeastern Argentine provinces of Chaco and Formosa. About 1,000 more are scattered through the adjacent Gran Chaco region of Bolivia and Paraguay. Aside from this central zone, recent immigration has led to the settlement of about 1,000 speakers in the Gran Buenos Aires area and about the same number in several cities in the province of Santa Fe.

Although they are rapidly becoming acculturated, the Toba linguistic repertory remains large, complex, and diverse. The Toba have a variety of discourse genres in their native language: informal conversation, formal disquisitions, informal storytelling (*relatos*), myth telling, historical narratives, praying and chanting. Additionally, they have adapted some of these styles for similar functions in Spanish.

The purpose of this paper is to add to the literature on Native South American discourse by analyzing data from the oral tradition of the Toba. Native awareness of styles of speaking and, indeed, of the significance of their verbal art, is low; not surprisingly, since centuries of domination by Spanish speakers, who call their language "un dialecto," have convinced them that their language is an inferior dialect of Spanish. Nevertheless, when encouraged to discuss their language, they eagerly point out who can tell a good story and who is a good speaker of Toba, which was of enormous help both in obtaining the data and in the subsequent analysis.

In undertaking this study of discourse, I have been influenced more by the exigencies of my data than by the dictates of any one theoretical position.[1] Through the analysis of both elicited and non-elicited texts, I attempt to establish the relationship between Toba linguistic forms and discourse units.   On another level, this paper exemplifies the functional interconnections between the grammatical and pragmatic features of language.   Encouraged by the recent efforts and advances in discourse analysis, but discouraged by the lack of agreement on a metalanguage, this paper utilizes a syncretism of terminology. In order to avoid the possible confusion that this eclecticism might engender, I prefer to define the terms that I am utilizing.

By discourse I refer to all types of Toba speech. Thus, speech which is either natural or elicited is included in this definition. All speech can be divided into segments. Any piece of speech, whether a one word exclamation or a lengthy narration, can be considered a discourse segment. Every discourse segment is composed of a phonological, morphological, syntactic, semantic, as well as discourse system (McLendon 1981:285).

For Toba, the phonological, morpho-syntactic and semantic systems can be best seen in the works by Klein (1973, 1974, 1979, 1981). A comprehensive vocabulary recently published by Buckwalter (1980) provides much needed lexical material. The discourse system, on the other hand, has received scant attention.   This paper addresses that imbalance by demonstrating that, in a text, there are "relations among sounds, among lexical items, among grammatical patterns, and among discourse units, which structure a discourse and signal its organization and meaning" (McLendon 1981:285).

Discourse units in Toba are units which have their own markers and which I, following Woodbury's example, have arranged hierarchically from minimal to maximal levels (1985). In Toba, there seem to be four levels, from a word to a section or episode. Each of these four units or levels has associated with it specific rhetorical or discourse features which include intonation and prosody (Woodbury 1985). The concatenation of the various features produces different styles or genres of discourse, as well as a range of variation within each style or genre. For example, stylistic distinctions can be recognized in Toba in discourse structures from simple conversations to baby talk, to narrative retellings of life histories or myths, to ecstatic Pentecostal chanting.   Within a genre, discourse features co-occur according to such variables as setting, age and sex of speakers and hearers and the intent of message (see Section 4). These features, which reflect affective meaning, add the dramatic dimension to the flow of speech. In typological classificatory terms, the more formal the style of speech, the less variation there is in discourse features within the genre.

2. Discourse System of Toba

I posit four hierarchical levels of discourse or rhetorical structure in Toba. They are from the smallest unit to the largest: the word; the phonological phrase or minimal intonation unit; the line; and the section or episode. Each of these units can be defined in purely phonological terms: however, since non-phonological features such as modifiers, expletives, hesitation and response phenomena corroborate discourse units and their boundaries, they too must be included in the definition.   In Section 3, a strong argument for the naturalness of these levels for the Toba discourse system is made. Furthermore, this hierarchy of structural units relates to models of other languages demonstrating in a comparative way that these units are the essential components which integrate discourse systems in many Amerindian languages (Hymes 1981, Tedlock 1983).

2.1 Word

A word is the smallest unit to which clear, unequivocal meanings can be attached. All words in Toba have one syllable which is more prominent in loudness and pitch than any other syllable. Primary stress is always placed on the final syllable of the word, which is followed, in slow speech, by the briefest of pauses. This feature of non-phonemic stress can also be used as a further criterion for word borders. *Palabra*, or word, is a unit that my informants could readily comprehend and to which they responded "yes, that's a word," or "no, that's not a word" when asked about a linguistic form. The word, unlike other structural units, also has significance because it is the only unit which reflects the native speakers' overt understanding of the structure of the Toba language. That is, it is the result of their own segmentary analysis as well, and is thereby an empirically tested unit.

2.2 Phonological Phrase or Minimal Intonation Unit

This unit consists of one or more words carrying a single intonation contour. In the examples cited in this paper, the contours are marked above the word. Each contour is bounded by a pause or by the onset of a different intonation contour signaled by a quick breath. Sandhi may occur in rapid speech between words within a phonological phrase or intonation unit. Because this level or unit of discourse structure overlaps regularly with the line (frequently it is also a line), these features of sandhi are covered in more detail in the discussion on lines in Section 3.

2.3 Lines

Lines consist of one or more phonological phrases or minimal intonation units. They are bounded by short breaths or pauses in Toba and are equivalent to a sentence syntactically. Pauses are marked in the examples in this paper by a single vertical stroke near the right hand margin at the end of the line. Since the line is the *basic* unit for Toba discourse structure, its features will be discussed in greater detail in 3.

2.4 Sections or episodes

A section or episode consists of one or more lines, bounded by long, clearly perceived pauses. Sections from more formal speech frequently end with a sentence particle such as *haha* (yes, well then) or a modifier *enawak* (that's all). Sections in informal speech correspond to short paragraphs; while in conversation, they correspond to a single speaker's exchanges. In this paper the ends of sections are marked with a double vertical stroke.

3. Lines: Basic Discourse Units

The discourse system of Toba can best be discussed by analyzing the attributes of the line. The line can consist of either a single word or a single phonological phrase. Even a section can consist of a single line. A line is additionally the discourse unit equivalent to the sentence. It is for Toba the basic unit for describing the formal aspects of discourse.[2]

3.1 Phonological Parameters

The specific identification of a line in Toba is primarily determined by its phonological parameters. These are:

1. One or more minimal intonation units or phonological phrases comprise a line. Such a line, unit or phrase has at least one primary word stress. However, there are instances within rapid discourse when nominal classifiers instead of remaining prefixed to nominal forms float backward and become instead suffixed to the preceding word. The result then is a word which contains two stresses. The new penultimate syllable, which in slow speech is always the final syllable of the word, retains its primary stress and the ultimate syllable takes on the feature of secondary stress.

For example:

Slow	Rapid	Gloss
/nategana sošikayt/	/nateganosò šikayt/	It happened here yesterday.
/hi'otta napapel/	/hi'ottanà papel/	They're moving papers about.

2. The boundaries between lines are marked by pauses which are noticeably longer than between words or phonological phrases or intonation contours.

3. Different intonation contours clearly mark each mode. Pitch is an especially significant feature to express modal distinctions. This is especially the case in sentences in isolation, or conversation. Thus, for example, a rising contour is placed on the final segment of a sentence or line to indicate a question rather than a statement. A statement can be identified by a long level contour or several short contours with falling pitch at the end of each. An imperative on the other hand is indicated by a

long level pitch which ends abruptly with a rapidly rising pitch which drops on the stressed syllable. Since there is such a tight fit between discourse lines and grammatical sentences, it is not surprising that the intonation contours generally reinforce the syntactic structure.

For example:

'awayateteget   Do you understand it clearly?

sa'ar'igalaqčigi   Don't come back soon!

naya nan'ašigak   Is he coming to the party?

naya nan'ašigak   He is coming to the party.

hayem sasayamagaren kamačika   I don't like anything.

Intonation contours, however, can be affected by vocal qualities, such as dramatization of voice, speed of verbal presentation and loudness. Thus within a discourse genre - narratives, for example - countour shape may be transformed according to the affective meaning.[3]

3.2 Syntactic features of the line

In addition to phonological features, there are syntactic features which identify a line and will be described below.

1. Lines are marked grammatically by a set of non-nominal single word modifiers. These are used more in monologues than in conversation.

2. There is a specific type of structure that is used in dialogue which is quite different from monologue discourse. In the former case, there is a regular repetition of certain words, particles or response phenomena, as a sociolinguistic device, indicating continued interest and

participation in the dialogue. Thus, these morphological forms also serve as grammatical markers of the line.

This reiterative pattern of dialogue is found in a number of other South American Indian languages. Arthur Sorensen notes that in Tukanoan languages spoken in the Vaupés, the verb is repeated by the listener (Sorensen 1967); while Sherzer notes for Kuna that the addressee-listener ratifies the narrator by repeating a key word or an "a, mm" (1982:380). Given the geographic spread of this phenomenon, it is quite probable that dialogic ratification is an example of the existence of areal patterns in discourse structure.

For Toba, it is clear that the phonologically defined lines are reinforced by other elements, such as modifiers and particles, both to mark styles of discourse and to distinguish them.[4] Furthermore, this interdependence between the phonology of the line and these syntactic devices is additional evidence for the position taken that the discourse structure of Toba must be viewed as part of Toba grammar.

4.   Toba Texts

Although I first started to work on Toba texts in the early 1970's, it is only recently that I have returned to their study. The enormous gains in discourse analysis of native American languages has been a strong impetus to revise my earlier analyses. In 1971, during my first period of field work among the Toba, I was able to collect a variety of different types of discourse. Some of these were collected from my main informant, a 38 year old man from the central Chaco region of the Toba, who had migrated to Buenos Aires and who was working as a stock handler in a small restaurant. He was an excellent teacher, who provided me with a number of different styles of speaking. When I was better acquainted with the language, I went north to the western Chaco and recorded a variety of texts from several additional speakers in Resistencia, Saenz Peña and Castelli. However since my interest at that time was primarily in a phonological and morphological analysis, I did not explore the world of myths, fables, songs, games or jingles. Although I did record some examples of the ritual chanting as part of the native church ceremonies, the style is radically different from speaking styles, and its analysis would form still another study. Thus, the present study of Toba discourse does not include these genres.

In organizing and elaborating the categories of discourse, I conclude that there are three basic styles of speaking: a formal speaking style, which is equivalent to an oratorical style or that of a disquisition; a storytelling or narrative style, which is less formal; and conversation or informal speech. The formal speaking style is utilized in contexts of seriousness, which can be determined by the age of the speaker or by the intent of the message. This style can be utilized for educative purposes, manipulative purposes, and to show off linguistic abilities and generally is spoken in institutional settings, such as churches, schools, and public spaces. The storytelling style is a much more versatile form. Stories can be told at anytime and by any speaker who has a listener. While this genre can be used for serious purposes as well, it tends to be used in more informal circumstances, and humor frequently plays a role. The location of storytelling is as versatile as its narrators. Conversation or informal speech is even less contextually confined: it occurs anywhere at anytime by anyone.

In the sections which follow, examples of Toba speaking styles will be provided. In the representational system I have decided to utilize in order to capture the nature of the original speech performance, I have marked pauses, interruptions and hesitations, as well as intonation contours.

4.1 Most formal type of speaking style

The primary feature of this style of speech is the tempo, which is considerably slower than in less formal styles or genres. Pauses are short but clearly heard breaks between lines. Slightly longer pauses between sections or episodes are also noted. Intonation contours are more level and less varied than in informal speech.

Forms such as *qaq* (and), *nagi* (now), *qalqa'a* (and then) are frequent markers of the beginning of a line in this style. A common final marker of the line is *haha*. This same form also appears regularly at the end of several consecutive lines, but is then preceded and followed by a longer pause, and is therefore to be considered as the marker of a section or an episode. A marker of the end of the discourse is *nače* (it's over, it's finished).

The following examples of formal speech were elicited from an elderly monolingual speaker of Toba, who only recently had come into contact with the national culture. The context, a school room in a rural tuberculosis center in Casteli, in the northwest corner of the province of Chaco, influenced this man's choice of themes. The excerpts include two long sections (A and B), two one line sections (C and D), one short section (E), and a concluding section consisting of one word (F).[5]

(A)	qalota	rañi'ačik
	qalota	ra-ña-'ačik
	modifier	class.-1s.poss.-nom.root
	many	present-my-thanks

nagi	hayem'olek	maši	iɣayki
nagi	hayem-'olek	maši	iɣay-ki
modifier	ls.pro-attrib.	mod.	nom.root-attrib.
now	I-diminutive	almost	old-man

ko'oĺaɣa	qalqayka	qayka	naroqšik
ko'oĺaɣa	qalqayka	qayka	n-roq-šik
modifier	modifier	neg.	4s.poss-nom.root-attrib.
a long time ago	before	was not	one's-non-Toba-male

qalqa'a	nagi	ñi'ačik'olek	haha
qalqa'a	nagi	ña-'ačik-'olek	haha
modifier	mod.	1s.poss.-n.rt.-attrib.	paragr. part.
and then	now	my-thanks-little	

Thank you very much. Now I am an old man. Before, there were no white people in my life. And now I give them thanks.

(B) Neget   to'okokà
     neget   to'oko-ka
     interr.   adverb-class.
     what   else

sasawana   kamari
sa-sa-wa-n-a   ka-mari
neg-1s.-v.root-punct.   class.-base.3s.pro
    aspect-s.obj.
not-I-know-something   not yet present-it

sañawane'   ka'arina   sañawane'
sa-ña-wane'   ka-arina   sa-ña-wane'
neg-1s.-v.rt. class.-n.rt.   neg.-1s.-v.rt.
not-I-find   absent-flour   not-I-find

               kayirwa
               ka-yirwa
               class.-n.root
               absent-herb tea

ndotrek   namayče   ñiqar'olqay   haha
ndotrek   na-mayče   ñi-qar...i-'olqa   haha
modifier   class.-mod.   clas.-2pl.poss.-n.rt.
only things   approaching- position-your-unculti-
              one's own   vated food products

What else? I didn't know these things. I didn't know about flour, I couldn't find yerba tea. The only thing I ate was food found on the ground.

(C) hayem   ray'enaɣak
     hayem   ra-hi-'e-naɣak
     1s.pro.   class.-1s.poss.-n.root-part.
     I   present-my-name-it is true

Oh yes, I have a name.

(D) negetto   ram   roqšik   l'enaɣak
     neget-to   ram   roq-šik   l-'e-naɣak
     interr.-part. class.   n.rt.-attrib.   3s.poss-n.rt.-part.
     what is it   present-   non-Toba-male   of it-name-it is
                    emphatic   true

What is the name the white man gave me?

(E) hayem   yapi'   kal'enaɣak   megesoqoče
     hayem   hi-pi'   ka-l-'e-naɣak   megesoqoče
     1s.pro. 1s.poss-n.rt. class.-3s.poss-   n.rt.(unknown)
                            n.rt.-part.
     I   my grand- absent-his-name-   megesoqoče
             father   it is true

     hayem   lawal
     hayem   l-wal
     ls.pro.   3s.poss.-n.rt.
     I   his-grandchild

hayem	nesogoǰi	hi'enaǥak	haha
hayem	nesogoǰi	hi-'e-naǥak	haha
ls.pro.	n.rt.(unknown)	1s.poss.-n.rt.-part.	
I	nesogoǰi	my-name-it is true	

My grandfather was named Megesoqoče. I am his grandson. I am named Nesogoǰi.

(F)   qaqnačehaǰi
            qaq-nače-haǰi
            mod.-mod.-class.
            and-it's finished-here

That's it.

4.2 Storytelling

Another style of speaking is that of storytelling or narration. These are told in a less formal way than the oratorical or more formal style just described. Lines in this style frequently begin with the words *wo'o* (there was), *nači* (and then), *qaq* (and), as well as such Spanish forms as *bueno*, *un día*, and *recién*.

In this style, there is greater variety in the various line indicators than in more formal speeches, that is, the endings of lines vary considerably in intonation patterns and grammatical classes. This is illustrated in the following examples, which include four complete sections or episodes, plus one line from a fifth episode. Two of the episodes are single lines. All of these segments of discourse are taken from a very dramatically told story about an intrepid hunter of wild cats, called tigers, in the Chaco.

(A)   wo'o   kam   siɠawa   ne'eptak
      wo'o   kam   siɠawa   n-'ep-tak
      mod.   class.   n. root   3s.pro-v.rt.-prog.
                                          aspect
      there   absent   person   hunting
      was

There once was a man who was hunting.

(B)   ne'epiɠayk
      n-'ep-ɠayk
      3s.-rt.-nominalizer
      he-hunt-person

A hunter.

(C)   qaq   qan   kewo   nači   natenagetto
      qaq   qan   Ø-kewo   nači   n-tena-get-to
      mod.   mod.   3s.-v.rt.   mod.   3s-v.rt.-direct.-
                                                      dual
      and   then   he-go   then &   he-meet-towards-
                              alone   there   both moving

      kam   kiĵok   nači   relogi'
      kam   kiĵok   nači   r-logi'
      class.   n.rt.   mod.   3s-v.rt.
      absent   tiger   then &   he fought
                              there

And afterwards he went alone. And right then and there he encountered the
tiger and did battle with it.

(D)

nači	yalawat	kam	kiĵok
nači	i-lawat	kam	kiĵok
mod.	3s.-v.rt.	class.	n.rt.
then & there	he-kill	non-present	tiger

qaq	qan	yalawat	kam	kiĵok
qaq	qan	i-lawat	kam	kiĵok
mod.	mod.	3s.-v.rt.	class.	n.rt.
and	when	he-kill	non-present	tiger

nači	pelgeko	lkiĵakte	lšinek
nači	Ø-pel-ge-ko	l-kiĵak-te	l-šinek
mod.	3s.-v.rt.-direct.-single	4s-n.rt.-enumer.	4s.-n.rt.
then & there	he-cut-towards-moving	heart	point

načeček
n-ček
3s.-v.rt.
he devoured

And then he killed the tiger. When he killed the tiger he cut out the point of its heart. He ate the whole thing!

(E)	Un dia	natenagetto	kam	puestero
		n-tena-get-to	kam	puestero
		3s.-v.rt.-direc-	class.	n.rt.
		tion-dual		
		he-meet-towards-	non-	ranch foreman
		both moving	present	

One day he meets the foreman....

4.3 Conversation or Informal Speech

Still another style of speaking is everyday conversation, or what we may call informal speech. In some ways, informal speech, in the form of everyday conversation, shows the greatest variation. Here we find discourse segments of considerable length, which appear very similar to the more formal style in terms of contours, but have the faster pace of storytelling or narratives.

For example, the following excerpt is taken from a conversation between two church leaders. The speaker is explaining to the listener the contents of a letter I had brought to them from a relative of the speaker, who at that time was trying to get a job in Buenos Aires.

en Buenos Aires	qalota	naqom
	qalota	na-qom
	mod.	class.-n.rt.
	many	present-Toba

wotaike	rkat	nalaqtak
0-wotaike	r-kat	n-laq-tak
3s.-v.rt.	3s.-v.rt.	3s.-v.rt.-progr. asp.
-want	-lose	-talking

(above three words repeated for emphasis)

qaq	nači	ne'ena	qa'araqtakpi
qaq	nači	ne'ena	qa'a-raqtak-pi
mod.	mod.	demo.pro.	1p.poss.-n.rt-pl.
and	then & there	those	our-word-s

wotaike	enawak	raqanato
Ø-wotaike	enawak	r-qana-to
3s.-v.rt.	mod.	3s.-v.rt.-dual
she-want	all	she-get together-with him

qana	raza	qom
qana	raza	qom
dem.	n.rt.	n.rt.
this	race	Toba

sayšetra	rkat	ne'ena	qa'araqtaka
sa-i-šet-ra	r-kat	ne'ena	qa'a-raqtak-a
neg.-3s.-v.rt.-class.	3-v.rt.	class.	1pl.-n.rt.-s.obj.
not-one-able-present	-lose	this	our-word

qaq	nači	re'era	wo'o
qaq	nači	re'era	wo'o
mod.	mod.	demo.	mod.
and	then & there	this	there was

In Buenos Aires many Toba want to lose their language. They want to lose the Toba language. And this language she [reference to me] wants to get all together. Our race is the Toba race. We can not lose our language. That's why she is here.

This final set of examples consists of three excerpts taken from a conversation between two leaders of an indigenous cooperative. The narrative told within this conversation illustrates the range of intonation contours discussed in section 3.1 as well as a variety of line indicators. It also points out the possibly universal rhetorical device of constant ratification by repetition. Here that reiteration consists of either repeating the same word in a question intonation, or by repeating a key word in the line. The speakers are labeled E.R. and M.G.

(A) E.R.	šiginte	so'onatagatak
	šiginte	so'-onata-aga-tak
	mod.	1s.-v.rt.-intens.-progress.
	morning of today	I-work-hard-+ing

This morning I was working hard.

M.G.	qata	qonte	au'onatagan
	qata	qonte	a-'onata-aga-n
	mod.	adv.	2s.-v.rt.-intens.-punct.-aspect
	also	tomorrow	you-work-hard

Do you work tomorrow also?

E.R.	haha	qata	qonte	so'onatagan
	haha	qata	qonte	so-'onata-aga-n
	part.	mod.	adv.	1s.-v.rt.-intens.-punct.aspect.
	yes	also	tomorrow	I-work-hard

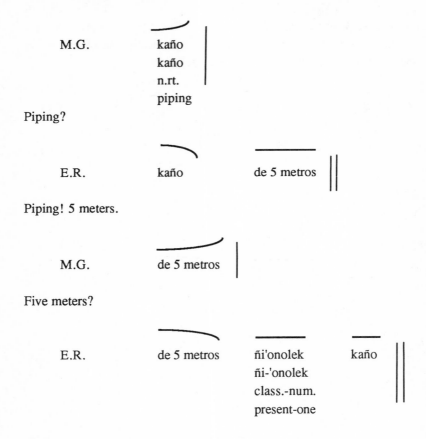

qaɣaǰi	sa'asaq	soɣoñi	kakaño
qaɣaǰi	sa-saq	soɣo-ñi	ka-kaño
mod.	1s.-v.rt.	1s.-v.rt.	class.-n.rt.
because	I-go	I-put-down	not present-piping

Yes, and I work tomorrow also because I am going to put down piping.

M.G. kaño
kaño
n.rt.
piping

Piping?

E.R. kaño   de 5 metros

Piping! 5 meters.

M.G. de 5 metros

Five meters?

E.R. de 5 metros   ñi'onolek   kaño
ñi-'onolek
class.-num.
present-one

Five meters. Each one.

(B)   M.G.

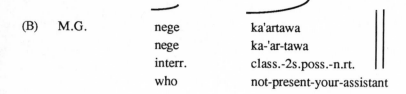

	nege	ka'artawa
	nege	ka-'ar-tawa
	interr.	class.-2s.poss.-n.rt.
	who	not-present-your-assistant

Who is your assistant?

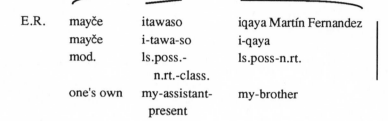

E.R.	mayče	itawaso	iqaya Martín Fernandez
	mayče	i-tawa-so	i-qaya
	mod.	ls.poss.-n.rt.-class.	ls.poss-n.rt.
	one's own	my-assistant-present	my-brother

My own assistant is my (classificatory) brother Martin Fernandez.

M.G.	ah Martin Fernandez	ah	ongaik	qone
			ongaik	qone
			adv.	mod.
			good	then

Ah! Martin Fernandez? Ah, that's good.

(C)	E.R.	qomi	qaq	qomi	20
		1pl.pro	mod.	lpl.pro	
		us	and	we	

Us. And we are 20.

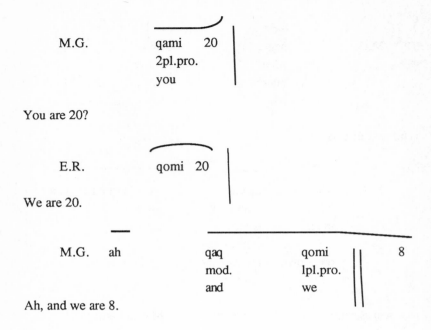

M.G.   qami   20
              2pl.pro.
              you

You are 20?

E.R.   qomi   20

We are 20.

M.G.   ah   qaq   qomi   8
                  mod.   1pl.pro.
                  and   we

Ah, and we are 8.

5.   Conclusion

The aim of this paper has been to analyze Toba discourse and its various styles, using as a common denominator the notion of "line." The line in Toba is a structural element in oratory, narratives and conversation. My initial attempts at analyzing Toba discourse centered on a study of the phonology, morphology, syntax and lexicon. This led to a realization that there was still some additional analysis needed to understand the rationale for the particular types of structures that sentences and larger units took. Relistening to my tapes in terms of prosodic features and the social situation of the various speech events convinced me of the significance of the line for Toba discourse. Thus, using the unit "line" as a basic organizing principle, I was better able to analyze a variety of Toba discourse. Since each style of discourse consists of prosodic features with grammatical markers as well, some of the grammatical issues, such as redundant object morphemes, multiple lexically similar modifiers, and clause word order, which had remained anomalous at the end of my earlier analyses, have become clearer. Finally, the demonstration of the line as primary in analyzing Toba discourse contributes to the body of literature (see References) that already has provided strong evidence that this unit is indeed a universal feature of discourse. [6]

Notes

1. However, my own position has been greatly influenced by the works of McLendon (1981), Sherzer (1981, 1982) and Woodbury (1985).
2. As Sherzer has noted for Kuna, "the line is in several ways the basic ... unit (1982:372).
3. See, for example, the last line of text in Section 4.2 D, in which at the end of the section a falling pitch is replaced by a rising contour to express the drama of the event.
4. Sherzer also notes that this is quite like what happens in Kuna, in which the different line-marking devices interact in different ways in the different styles.
5. The following abbreviations have been used in the interlinear word-for-word and grammatical translations:

adv.	adverb
attrib.	attributive
class.	classifier
dem. (or demo.)	demonstrative
direct.	directional
intens.	intensifier
interr.	interrogative mood
mod.	modifier
n.rt.	noun root
neg.	negative
nom. root	nominal root
num.	number
obj.	object
paragr. part.	paragraph particle
part.	particle
pl.	plural

poss.	possessive
pro.	pronoun
prog. (or	
progess. or	progressive aspect
progr. asp.)	
punct.	punctual aspect
s.	singular
v.rt.	verb root

6. I would like to thank Herbert S. Klein, Joel Sherzer, Greg Urban and Tony Woodbury for valuable criticisms of earlier drafts. The research on the Toba language and texts utilized in this paper was assisted by a grant from the Joint Committee on Latin American Studies of the Social Science Research Council and the American Council of Learned Societies with funds provided by the National Endowment for the Humanities, the Mellon Foundation, and the Ford Foundation, and by grants from Montclair State College Career Development Fund and Released Time for Research.

References

Buckwalter, Alberto
   1980   *Vocabulario Toba*. Chaco, Argentina: Private Publication [Available from the Mennonite Board of Missions, Elkhart, Indiana].
Hymes, Dell
   1981   *"In vain I tried to tell you:" essays in Native American ethnopoetics*. Philadelphia: University of Pennsylvania Press.
Klein, Harriet E. Manelis
   1973   A grammar of Argentine Toba: verbal and nominal morphology. Ph.D. dissertation, Columbia University.
   1974   Enumeration and quantification: linguistic, ethnographic and cognitive reflexes. Paper presented at the annual meeting of the American Anthropological Association, Mexico City.
   1979   Noun classifiers in Toba. In *Ethnolinguistics: Boas, Sapir and Whorf revisited*, M. Mathiot (ed.), pp. 85-95. The Hague: Mouton.

1981   Location and direction in Toba: verbal morphology. *International Journal of American Linguistics* 47: 227-35.

McLendon, Sally

1981   Meaning, rhetorical structure, and discourse organization in myth. *Analyzing discourse: text and talk.* Georgetown University Round Table on Language and Linguistics 1981, D. Tannen (ed.), pp. 284-305. Washington, D.C.: Georgetown University Press.

Sherzer, Joel

1981   The interplay of structure and function in Kuna narrative, or: how to grab a snake in the Darien. *Analyzing discourse: text and talk.* Georgetown University Round Table on Language and Linguistics 1981, D. Tannen (ed.), pp. 306-322. Washington, D.C.: Georgetown University Press.

1982   Poetic structuring of Kuna discourse: the line. *Language in Society* 11: 371-90.

Sorensen, Arthur

1967   Multilingualism in the northwest Amazon. *American Anthropologist* 69: 670-84.

Tedlock, Dennis

1983   *The spoken word and the work of interpretation.* Philadelphia: University of Pennsylvania Press.

Woodbury, Anthony C.

1985   The functions of rhetorical structure: a study of Central Alaskan Yupik discourse. *Language in Society*, 14: 153-190.

Topic Continuity and OVS Order in Hixkaryana

Desmond C. Derbyshire

1. Introduction

The main purpose of this study is to show how third person narrative discourse in Hixkaryana is organized in terms of the use of specific grammatical devices to signal the pragmatic status of participants each time they are referred to in a given text. The pragmatic status relates to degree of topicality. The coding devices, in addition to signalling the topicality of participants, correlate closely with semantic phenomena to divide up the discourse into distinct units, which I call episodes.

A secondary purpose is to throw light on certain issues regarding word order and word order change raised by Givón in his pioneering topic continuity study of Ute (1983b: 197). In particular, I show that Hixkaryana has advanced much further than Ute in its drift from SOV to OVS, to the point where, if any order is to be regarded as basic, it has to be OVS. Moreover, the rigidity of the OV ordering, and the relative rigidity of VS, are evidence that OVS is probably not just an intermediate order, leading to VOS or VSO, but is itself close to the stage of being a fairly rigid basic order in the language. At the same time, the study confirms Givón's (and Hyman's earlier, 1975) prediction that the direction of this drift is determined by the topicality of the major arguments in the clause.

Like the studies in the Givón (ed. 1983) volume, this is a quantitative study, aimed at measuring the degree of topicality of participants and props each time they are referred to in a text. "Degree of topicality" presupposes a scale of topicality, ranging from topics that are highly continuous to those that are low in continuity (that is, are highly discontinuous). For various reasons, discussed in Givón's introduction to the 1983 book, such a scale reflects more accurately the notion of "topic" than the discrete entity idea that prevailed in most earlier work on this pragmatic function. It also leads to more useful insights into certain aspects of discourse structure, and yields more satisfying explanations for the speaker's choice of particular grammatical devices at any given point. This is a quantitative study that is empirically based on data from a single language. Some of the results support the cross-linguistic generalizations and typological predictions proposed by Givón (1983: 30-35) on the basis of the correlations found in the eight languages studied in his book. Other results in this Hixkaryana study are more language specific.

The two sets of phenomena being investigated for the ways in which they correlate are: (1) the grammatical devices used for encoding topics (i.e., referential entities of various kinds, to which I attach the discourse status labels of participants and props); and (2) the position of the topics in the discourse in relation to distance from their last occurrence, persistence in the subsequent discourse, and thematic structuring of the discourse. The grammatical devices used in Hixkaryana are described in section 2; the methodology of the text counting is explained in section 3, and the results of the counts are given in section 4. The results are interpreted and discussed in section 5.

The three texts used for the study are taken from Derbyshire (1965: 28-59). They are origin myths, two of them being stories connected with the creation of the king vulture, the sloth and the land turtle, and the other telling of the creation of the culture hero, Mawarye. They were narrated in 1961 by Kaywerye, who was then nearly thirty years old and a village head. He narrated them on to a tape recorder with only me present and shortly afterwards helped me to transcribe them. I have not seen any evidence of formal public story/myth telling among the Hixkaryana. The normal pattern of transmitting tribal lore, at least during the years I lived with them, was on an individual basis, from parent, other relative, or shaman to a young person.

The total number of clauses for the three texts in the 1965 published version is 513. Some modifcations in transcription and the division of the clauses/sentences were made for this study and this had the net effect of reducing the total number of the clauses to 440. The modified version of the first of the three texts is reproduced as an appendix to this chapter. The original numbering of the clauses of the published version is retained, but the major modification is seen where more than one number appears for what in this version is a single clause/sentence unit but in the earlier version appeared as two distinct sentences. For example:

3-4.   txemtxatxko,   kana txemtxa,   ketxkonï-hatï,
        go poison them, fish go poison, they said,

        kurumyana komo
        vulture   people

appeared in the original version as two sentences:

3.   txemtxatxko.   4. kana txemtxa, ...
        go poison them.   fish go poison, ...

This is a quotative sentence consisting of two main clauses of direct speech, linked together by the quotative margin, " ..., said the vulture people." In the present study, direct speech clauses have been ignored for the major measurements of topic continuity (see section 3), so any sequence of clauses within a direct speech unit was regarded as part of a single clause, which included also the quotative margin.

For one measurement a larger number of texts and clauses was used. This was for the counts of preverbal and postverbal occurrences of independent third person nondeictic forms. There were relatively few such pronouns in the three texts used for the rest of the study, so the data base was extended to cover the first 14 texts of Derbyshire (1965: 13-117). The total number of clauses was 1623. This count disclosed a significant pattern, which is described in sections 4.1.3 and 5.1.5.

2. Grammatical devices

The principal grammatical devices used to encode topics in Hixkaryana are:
        - prefixes, both verbal and nominal, the latter being also used with postpositions;

- independent pronouns, the most important of these being the third person nondeictic forms when they function as subject of the clause;

- full noun phrases, without any morphological or syntactic distinction between definite and indefinite, or referential and nonreferential; and

- in the case of pronouns and noun phrases, the position of the constituent relative to the verb in the clause; this word order parameter is of greatest significance in the case of the pronouns and the subject NP's, but it is a factor also in strategies available for oblique constituents (usually postpositional phrases), whether the referent is signalled by an agreement prefix or by a full noun phrase; word order is not important in the case of direct object NPs, since virtually only one order (OV) is used.

There are a few other grammatical devices which have a very minor part in the signalling of topicality. These are:

- zero anaphora, which is rare in Hixkaryana, occurring only in certain ideophone constructions and very occasionally in "stranded" direct speech clauses (see section 2.1 below);

- clauses in which the subject, direct object, or oblique constituent occurs both preverbally and in a right-dislocated postverbal position, yielding sequences SV, S; OV, O; and Obl-V-Obl; some testing of these was done, but they have not proved to be of any significance for the purposes of the present study and are not included in the results reported here as a distinct device, except for obliques, where one minor pattern of some interest shows up (section 4.3); and

-right dislocation, in general, of subject and object has also been ignored, after preliminary testing which showed that (a) it was often difficult to determine from the phonological features (particularly length of the pause) whether a constituent should be considered as dislocated or not, and (b) no differences of any significance to the measurement of topicality were showing up as between, for example, VS and V, S. In the rest of this section, I briefly introduce and illustrate the grammatical devices that have proved relevant in this study.

2.1 *Zero anaphora*

Although this phenomenon is rare, because of obligatory subject and object prefixes on the verb, it is relevant to the extent that when it does occur it signals a highly continuous topic:

(a) Ideophones. Ideophones are noninflected words which convey the meaning associated with a particular action or sound. They do not give any indication of the actor or recipient of the action, but they usually occur in clauses with main verbs that have agreement affixes that signal such referents, and there may also be pronouns or noun phrases which express the subject and object. (See Derbyshire 1979a: 80-81, 82). There is one ideophone construction, however, in which there is no main verb and no overt signal as to the referents of the subject and object of the action. This is where the ideophone occurs alone or with only an adverbial element. The following example is from the text in the Appendix. (In this paper I identify the source of each example from the texts by using T (Text), followed by two numbers, the first being the number of the page (in Derbyshire 1965) on which the particular text begins, and the second being the number of the clause of that text. The Appendix text is T28 and the clause number of the following example is clause number 88, hence T28.88 identifies the source).[1]

(1)   pow,   owto   hona ha, ...
         descending (IDEO) village   to   INTENSFR
         '(They) descended to the village, ... ' (T28.88)

In clauses like this, the referent of the subject (and usually of the object when there is one) is recoverable from the context. In this particular case, it is the same subject (and topic) as that of the previous five clauses and, apart from one or two very brief background interpolations (76-7, 82), all the clauses back to 69-70, where the referent is clearly identified by a noun phrase as the vulture people. Thus, this subject/topic that lacks overt expression in the ideophone clause, but which is clearly present in the semantics of the discourse, is highly continuous;

(b) Direct speech that is "stranded" in the discourse. This is a direct speech clause that does not have any quotative margin cooccurring with it. A quotative margin, which has some overt expression that signals the speaker-subject of the whole clause, nearly always occurs with the direct speech utterance, which is often just a single clause, but may be a sequence (not usually more than three) of clauses. Where the direct speech occurs without the margin, it is stranded in the narrative, but the identity of the speaker-subject is always recoverable from the context. The phenomenon is rare, and does not occur in the text in the Appendix, but it does occur twice in one of the other two texts. One example is:

(2)   nomokye harha tï, Mawarye.
        'Mawarye came back.' (T44.239)

        uro haka rha wamaxe.
        "'Let me fell it (tree) now again."' (T44.240)

        Mawarye haka rha namekonï.
        'Mawarye was now felling it again.' (T44.241)

The identity of the speaker-subject of the direct speech clause is clearly understood from the preceding and the following clauses. It is also a highly continuous topic in this section of the discourse.

2.2 Prefixes

(a) Verbal prefixes. There are two sets of verb prefixes: the intransitive verb set, which agrees with the subject of the verb; and the transitive verb set, which agrees with both the subject and object in portmanteau forms (see Derbyshire, 1979a: 145ff, which also discusses the collective number (i.e., plural) suffixes, which are also a part of the agreement system). The verbal prefix is obligatory in Hixkaryana, regardless of whether or not there is an independent pronoun or full noun phrase in the clause to express the subject and/or object referent. It is the most common way of expressing the subject and object referents, and in most clauses it is the only way.

(3)   n- ahaye   mak   hatï,   ï-hyaka ha,
        3S-drop +DP COUNTEREXPECT HSY   3-for   INTENSFR

        xofrye hyaka
        sloth   for
        'It (river) dropped for him, the sloth.' (T28.31)

(4)   n-   ahayehkaye   mak   hatï
        3S3O-drop+CAUS+DP COUNTEREXPECT HSY
        'He caused it to drop.' (T28.27)

(5)   mï-   txemnyo, ...
        2S3O-poison+IP ...
        '"You poisoned them," ...' (T28.42)

(6)   ï-   txemnyo
        1S3O-poison+IP
        '"I poisoned them," ...' (T28.43)

(b) Nominal prefixes. There is a set of nominal prefixes that agree with the
person of noun possessors, objects of postpositions, and objects of certain
derived adverbials. They occur also in certain nominalized forms derived
from verbs, and their function is still strictly that of possessor, but for most
nominalizations that possessor represents the underlying subject (if the verb
stem is intransitive) or object (if the verb stem is transitive).

(7)   tï-notxhïrï   wya
        3REFLX-sister by
        'by his own sister' (T28.6)

(8)   ï-rakataka
        3-into: middle: of (Postp.)
        'into the middle of it' (T28.22)

(9)   ï-txempera
        3-poison+NEG (Derived adverb)
        'not poisoning it' (T28.28)

(10)   k-   anïhnoh-nye-   nhï- yamo
     1INCL-destroy- NOMLZR-PAST-COLL
     (Nominalization, trans.)
     'the one who has destroyed us' (T28.114)

(11)   ø-ewakï-   htorï
     3-be:friendly-NOMLZR+NEG
     (Nominalization, intrans.)
     'his being angry' (T44.45)

For a fuller description of the nominal set of person-marking prefixes, see Derbyshire (1979a: 96ff.).

2.3 Independent pronouns

The third person nondeictic pronouns are the only ones that are significant for this study. There are three forms:

noro   '3, animate'
nyamoro   '3 COLL, animate'
ïro   '3 inanimate'

They can occur as any grammatical relation in the clause, but it is only when they occur as subject that they have a distinctive function in relation to topic continuity. This depends on whether they occur preverbally (in fact, sentence-initially) or postverbally. This is discussed in sections 4.1.3 and 5.1.5.

(12)   noro   tho   tï   ïrwomra   n-ehxakonï
     3PRO DEVLD HSY talk+NEG   3-be+DP
     'She was not talking.' (T28.117)

(13)   oske   n-exeye   hatï,   nyamoro
     thus 3-be+DP HSY   3+COLL+PRO
     'That is how they were.' (T28.133)

2.4 Noun phrases

Noun phrases occur as subject, direct object and as part of oblique constituents. No morphological or syntactic distinction is made between definite and indefinite, or referential and nonreferential. (These parameters are referred to, however, in the discussion on the introduction of new referents into a text, in sections 3.5 and 4.6.) The significance of noun phrases in the study of topic continuity relates to two issues: (i) whether or not they are overtly expressed in a clause in which they are clearly part of the semantic interpretation; and (ii) when they are overtly expressed, whether they occur preverbally or postverbally. As will be seen in sections 4 and 5, this latter issue has most significance in the case of subject noun phrases. The examples of verb prefixes in section 2.2 illustrate the absence of noun phrase subject and object where they are semantically present and recoverable from the context. The following examples, taken from the text in the Appendix, show noun phrases occurring as subject, object, or part of an oblique, in various word order patterns: VS (14), SV (15), SOV (16), OVS (17), VO (18), V-Obl (19), and Obl-V (20). In this study, preverbal S includes both SV and SOV.

(14) noseryehokekonï,   xofrye
      he:was:upset   sloth
      'The sloth was upset.' (T28.13)

(15) xofrye heno   n- oseryehokekonï
      sloth   DEAD   3S-was:upset
      'The poor old sloth ("dead" here means disadvantaged, as good
      as dead) was upset.' (T28.14)

(16) kurumyana   komo, xofrye heno   y-   anotometxkonï
      vulture+kin:group COLL sloth DEAD   3S3O-used:to:employ
      'The vulture people used to employ the poor old sloth in their
      service.' (T28.2)

(17) tkokemï   rma   tï   y-   onahyatxkonï   ha,
      rotten+NOMLZN CONT HSY 3S3O-eat+COLL+DP INTENSFR

kurum-yana   ha
vulture-kin:group   INTENSFR
'The vulture people were eating the thing that had already gone
bad.' (T28.98)

(18)   txemko   tï,   epepe   yotï
   .   poison+IMP HSY older:brother meat:food:of
       '"Poison meat food for my brother."' (T28.9)

(19)   tïmko   ha,   oy-eheka   wya
       give+IMP INTENSFR 2- brother   to
       '"Give them to your brother."' (T28.48)

(20)   t-   hetxe wya n-   ekarymekonï
       3REFLX-wife to 3S3O-tell+DP
       "He was telling it to his wife.' (T28.47)

3. Methodology

I have used the same four basic measurements employed by Givón (1938b.
156) and added two other counts. Only the first of Givón's measurements,
referential distance ("look-back"), was used for all grammatical categories
covered in this study. Persistence ("decay") proved significant only for the
subject and direct object categories. The other two - same subject vs.
different subject, and contiguity to major thematic breaks - were relevant
only for the subject category.

   The two additional counts I found useful in interpreting the overall
phenomena of topic continuity were (1) introduction of new referents into
the text, and (2) distribution of subject-marking categories in various clause
types.

3.1 Referential distance ("look-back")

This was a count of the distance, in actual number of clauses, from the
occurrence of the referent in a given clause to the last prior mention of the

referent in the text. The least number of clauses in this count was 1, which applied when the referent was mentioned in the immediately preceding clause. An arbitrary maximum number was 20, which applied whenever the referent was newly introduced in the text in the clause under scrutiny, and also whenever it had not appeared in the preceding nineteen clauses. Anything counted as a previous appearance in the register, including zero anaphora, provided the referent was clearly understood to be a semantic argument of a clause. This applied to all types of clause, including direct speech clauses and nominalized (i.e. relative) clauses. Non-appearances in direct speech and relative clauses were not, however, counted as a gap. All other clause types were treated as main clauses for both gaps and appearances.

Where a referent in one clause appeared as an included part of a group in another clause, the two were treated as separate entities and topics.

3.2 Persistence ("decay")

This was a count of the number of clauses in which the referent continued to appear in the subsequent discourse. In this case, the minimum count was 0, this applying when there was no appearance in the clause next to the one under scrutiny, and there was no upper limit. As noted earlier, I applied this count only to the subject and direct object categories' measurement. In the case of subjects, unlike Givón, I did not restrict the count to subjects of the following clauses, but counted every occurrence, whatever the semantic argument of the entity or the grammatical device used to refer to it.

3.3 Same subject (SS) vs. different subject (DS)

This measurement looked at each clause to see (1) if the subject of that clause was the same as, or different from, the subject of the preceding clause, and (2) which of the grammatical devices was used to refer to the subject of the clause in primary focus. In the following sequence of three sentences from the text in the Appendix, the second clause (22) has the same subject (SS) as the preceding clause (21), and in (22) the subject is indicated only by the prefix in the verb. The subject in (23) is also signalled only by the verb prefix, but it is different (DS) from the subject in the preceding clause(22).

(21) duk,   n-   ahutxownï   hatï, xofrye
      shutting:in 3S3O-shut:in+COLL+DP HSY   sloth
      'The sloth shut them all in.' (T28.76)

(22) tohu ymo   ke   n-   ahutxownï,   duk
      stone AUG INSTR 3S3O-shut:in+COLL+DP shutting:in
      'With a huge stone he shut them in.' (T28.77)

(23) taa,   omohtxok   ha,   ø-
      THEME:CHANGE come+COLL+IMP INTENSFR 3S3O-

      ketxkonï   hatï
      say+COLL+DP   HSY
      '"Everybody come," they said.' (T28.78)

3.4 Contiguity to major thematic breaks

This measurement shows the effect of thematic/action discontinuity on the choice of the topic-marking grammatical devices. There are two main types of thematic discontinuity. One takes place at the boundaries of major thematic units of discourse which I here call episodes. The other type of juncture is at the boundaries of background interpolations, which temporarily interrupt the flow of the action within a thematic unit.

   Criteria used for determining thematic and background breaks are primarily of a semantic nature and include: change of locational or temporal setting in the discourse; change of the type of action in focus; a switch from an action sequence to one of dialogue or repartee; a change of participants or a switch in the roles played by the same set of participants. Background clauses are usually descriptive, or express flashback information or actions which occur simultaneously with the main theme but are not a part of that theme. Such criteria provide a more solid basis than mere "intuitive means," such as Givón talks about (1983b: 158), and they are at least partly independent of the topic-marking grammatical devices. The following two examples, taken from the text in the Appendix, illustrate a major episode break (24) and a background interpolation within a thematic unit (25). In (24), somewhere between sentence 12 and sentence 15 there is a change of theme, evidenced by the following discourse semantic phenomena: there is a change of location from the village (until 12) to the river (from 15); three participants are involved in the episode that closes at 12, whereas only one participant is involved as from 15 (indeed, as from 13); the theme up to 12 is expressed mainly by dialogue, whereas after 15 there is a lengthy action sequence. Sentences 13 and 14 are, in fact, a short background sequence, describing the sloth's feelings, but in this case it has an additional function of separating the two episodes. The grammatical devices that signal the break are found in its two sentences, that is, the postverbal (13) and preverbal (14) subject noun phrases. This two-sentence construction, in which the same semantic information is conveyed in each sentence, is a feature of Hixkaryana discourse, which I have elsewhere called a "sentence cluster" (Derbyshire 1977a). The signalling of a thematic break is just one of its possible functions.

(24) 12. poo,   ø-   kekonï hatï
           DISMAY 3S3O-say+DP HSY
           'He expressed dismay."

      13. n-oseryehokekonï,   xofrye
           3S-be:upset+DP   sloth
           'The sloth was upset.'

      14. xofrye heno n- oseryehokekonï
           sloth   DEAD 3S-be:upset + DP
           'The sloth was upset.'

      15. n- omokye   hatï, ø-txemxe
           3S-come+DP HSY   3-poison+PURP.MOT
           'He came purposing to poison them.'

In (24), both the theme-final clause (12) and the theme-initial clause (15) have only AGR prefixes to signal the subject. As the count shows (Table 14), this is not the only subject-marking category used in these positions in the discourse and is not even the predominant pattern for theme-final clause.

In (25), there is a single sentence (89) background interpolation within a single thematic unit (episode). The whole unit extends from sentences 78 to 98. The theme of this episode is the attempt and failure to light a fire and the consequent decision to eat the rotting fish uncooked. Sentence 89 is the second background interruption in this theme (the other is 82). It breaks into the sequence of actions in 87, 88 and 90 that form a part of the major theme of the episode with the descriptive statement that the sloth was not in the village. This clause is, in fact, a clarification of the final phrase in the preceding clause, '... in his unexpected absence.' The clause-initial, preverbal subject noun phrase is a grammatical device that correlates with the semantic factors to indicate that there is some sort of thematic break at this point. The double fact that it is a copular clause and a negative construction is also a strong signal that it is background information, these being cross-linguistic characteristics of backgrounded material (Grimes 1975).

(25)   88.   pow,   owto   hona ha,   ï-yarïhnaka
            descending village to   INTENSFR 3 in:absence:of

            mak   hatï
            COUNTEREXPECT HSY
            '(They) descended to the village, (arriving) when
            (the sloth) was away.'

      89.   xofrye mah   tï   ehxera   n-ehxakonï
            sloth   COUNTEREXPECT HSY be+NEG 3S-be+DP
            'The sloth was not (there).'

      90.   t-   katxhothïyamo   hatï y-
            3REFLX-goods+PAST+COLL HSY 3S3O-

            arymatxownï   ha,   txow,   fuhtxow.
            throw+COLL+DP INTENSFR throwing falling:to:ground
            'They threw down to the ground their things.'

3.5 Introduction of new referents into the text

This measurement relates to the introduction of new entities into a text, distinguishing three types of discourse entity (for criteria, see Grimes 1975): major participants; minor participants; and props (mostly inanimate items). It discloses certain preferred patterns of correlation between discourse entity types and grammatical constructions used to introduce them. In the text in the Appendix the entities were classified as follows (numbers in parentheses refer to clauses in which they are introduced):

- major participants: king vulture people (1); sloth (2)
- minor participants: vulture's sister, who was also the wife of the sloth (6); village chiefs (35); sloth's sister (59)
- props: fish (3-4); river (11); poison vine (16); assai palm (19-20); village (35); village house (64); fire (69-70); fire stick (72); large stone (77); flies (92).

I took separate counts, shown in the same table, of the semantic status (animate vs. inanimate) and the semantico-pragmatic status (definite vs. referential indefinite vs. nonreferential). Since there is no morphological marking of definiteness, and in texts of this kind most referents are known to the hearer, it is difficult at times to decide whether a referent should be classified as definite or indefinite (cf. Givón 1983b: 153). In the above list of entities from T28 (Appendix), the following categories were distinguished:

- referential indefinite: poison vine, assai palm, fire-stick, large stone, flies
- nonreferential: fish
- definite: all other entities

3.6 Distribution of subject-marking categories in various clause types

This count was concerned with subject categories only, and the restrictions and preferred patterns regarding the choice of preverbal/clause-initial or postverbal/clause-final subject in the six different clause types: intransitive, transitive, quotative, copular, equative, and ideophone.

4. Numerical results of measurements

4.1 Topic-continuity properties of subjects

4.1.1 Referential distance ("look-back"). The average referential distance for the various categories of subject is presented in Table 1. Of the six categories, only three are statistically significant, the other three - Ø and the two with independent pronoun subjects - having a very low number of occurrences in the primary text base. (The result of the study of the occurrence of independent pronoun subjects in a larger text base is given in section 4.1.3.).

The most commonly used device for marking subject is seen to be the agreement prefix. This naturally shows the highest degree of topic continuity, the average referential distance being 1.31 clauses. At the other end of the scale, the preverbal subject noun phrase category clearly has the lowest degree of topic continuity, the average distance to the previous occurrence of the referent being 8.14 clauses. In between the two is thepostverbal subject noun phrase category, which shows an average distance of 5.11 clauses to the last reference to the entity.

Table 1: Average Referential Distance for Subjects

Category	No. of Occurrences	Average Ref. Distance in No. of Clauses
Ø	9	1.33
AGR	298	1.31
$V-S_{NP}$	99	5.11
$V-S_{PRO}$	6	1.67
$S_{PRO}-V$	6	1.50
$S_{NP}-V$	22	8.14
Total	440	

Table 2 shows the variability in referential distance for each category. This highlights a distinctive trend for each of the three major subject-marking categories. The AGR category, in all of its 298 occurrences, never has to go back more than eight clauses for the last reference to the entity. The occurrences of VS are spread out through the

Table 2: Percent Distribution of Referential Distance within Subject Categories

No. of Clauses Since Previous Occurrence of Referent	Ø		AGR PREFIX (only)		V-S_NP		V-S_PRO		S_PRO-V		S_NP-V	
	No.	%	No.	%	No.	%	No.	%	No.	%	No.	%
1	7	0.78	249	0.84	51	0.52	4	0.67	5	0.83	11	0.50
2	1	0.11	29	0.10	11	0.11	2	0.33			1	0.05
3	1	0.11	9	0.03	5	0.05						
4			5	0.02	4	0.04			1	0.17		
5			2	0.01	3	0.03					1	0.05
6			3	0.01	4	0.04					1	0.05
7												
8			1	0.00	3	0.03						
9												
10												
11												
12												
13					1	0.01						
14												
15					1	0.01						
16					1	0.01						
17					1	0.01						
18					1	0.01						
19											1	0.05
20					13	0.13					7	0.32
Total	9	1.00	298	1.00	99	1.00	6	1.00	6	1.00	22	1.00

whole 1 to 20 count range, whereas the SV category is bunched at the two extremes of the range, with a substantial proportion (36%) showing high counts of referential distance. These facts, of course, correlate with the differing degrees of topic continuity noted for each of the categories in Table 1. The more even spread of VS throughout the distance range is one piece of evidence supporting my contention that this is, indeed, the most neutral word order type (section 5.2).

It is noteworthy, however, that in all three categories the highest number of occurrences (50 percent or more in each case) shows the lowest possible referential distance, that is, 1. This alerts us to the fact that no single measurement is sufficient for establishing degree of topicality, but that various factors have to be taken into account. One factor that accounts for some of the 51 VS and 11 SV clauses with the low referential distance count of 1 is the tendency in Hixkaryana to move "from anaphors to fuller identifying expressions," both within a sentence and across sentence boundaries (Derbyshire 1979b: 150, 190-92). This means that, in some cases, before a noun phrase occurs to identify a referent, a prefix is used in the preceding clause. This is discussed further in section 4.6, with respect to the introduction of new referents, but it is not restricted to entities that are being newly introduced. Another factor, also discussed in section 4.6, is the preferred pattern of introducing certain types of discourse entity as a direct object or oblique object rather than a subject. One example of this, in the text in the Appendix, is the subject in clause 8, *xofrye hetxe* 'sloth's wife,' which was introduced in clauses 6 and 7 as *tïnotxhïrï wya* 'to his (vulture's) sister.' This means that some instances of the SV and VS categories could have the lowest referential distance count and still have only a relatively low degree of topicality so far as the preceding discourse is concerned.

The most general characteristic of Hixkaryana discourse that shows up in these first two tables, and which is reflected in others, is the relative number of total occurrences of the three main categories: AGR (298), VS (105, counting both NP and PRO), and SV (28). The significance of these figures is taken up in the discussion on word order in section 5.2.

4.1.2 Persistence ("decay"). The average persistence for the subject-marking categories is presented in Table 3. Again, only the three major categories are of any importance, in view of the low number of occurrences of the other three. The most significant result here is the low persistence count for VS (NP), compared with the other two. When an entity is expressed in a clause by a postverbal subject, it continues in the register for only an average 1.27 clauses. This correlates with the results of the counts relating to thematic junctures (section 4.5), signalling the fact that this category is used frequently at the end of thematic units.

Table 3: Average Persistence for Subjects

Category	No. of Occurrences	Average Persistence in No. of Clauses
Ø	9	1.11
AGR	298	1.85
V-S$_{NP}$	99	1.27
V-S$_{PRO}$	6	2.00
S$_{PRO}$-V	6	2.67
S$_{NP}$-V	22	2.05

The highest average persistence shows for SV. Table 1 shows highest average referential distance also for SV, indicating that this category is used for bringing into the register an entity that has not been on the scene for some time. A fairly natural consequence of this is that, once introduced or reintroduced, it will continue to appear in the register for a while in the following discourse, and this is confirmed in Table 3.

Table 4 shows the actual counts for all degrees of persistence with respect to each category and the distance range within which the greater part of the category is found: 83% of VS falls into the 0-2 clause range; 81% of AGR into the 0-3 range, and 82% of SV into the 0-4 clause range. These figures reflect the same basic facts as Table 3 - the low persistence of VS and the relatively high persistence of SV.

4.1.3 Distribution of nondeictic independent pronouns. The three third person pronouns that constitute this set of nondeictics are listed in section 2.3. Table 5 summarizes all the occurrences of these forms that refer to tangible entities (see end of subsection for dicsussion of abstract usages of

Table 4: Percent Distribution of Persistence within Subject Categories

No. of Clauses in which the Referent Continues	Ø		AGR PREFIX (only)		V-S$_{NP}$		V-S$_{PRO}$		S$_{PRO}$-V		S$_{NP}$-V	
	No.	%	No.	%	No.	%	No.	%	No.	%	No.	%
0	6	0.67	107	0.36	51	0.52	1	0.17	1	0.17	8	0.37
1	1	0.11	67	0.22	22	0.22	2	0.33	1	0.17	5	0.23
2			41	0.14	9	0.09			2	0.33	3	0.14
3	1	0.11	28	0.09	5	0.05	2	0.33			1	0.05
4			18	0.06	5	0.05	1	0.17			1	0.05
5			13	0.04	2	0.02			1	0.17	2	0.09
6	1	0.11	9	0.03	1	0.01			1	0.17		
7			6	0.02	1	0.01						
8			4	0.02	1	0.01						
9			2	0.01							1	0.05
10					2	0.02					1	0.05
11			2	0.01								
12			1	0.01								
Total	9	1.00	298	1.00	99	1.00	6	1.00	6	1.00	22	1.00

iro). Since these occurrences are relatively infrequent, the text base was extended to l4 texts and a total of 1623 clauses (section 1). For the sake of completeness, occurrences as subject, direct object and oblique object in all clauses, including embedded direct speech clauses, are recorded. The result of most significance, however, relates to occurrences as subject in narrative discourse.

Table 5: Distribution of Nondeictic Independent Pronouns
        (in a sequence of 1623 clauses in 14 texts)

		Narrative			Embedded Direct Speech	
		Coreferential with Constituent of Preceding Clause			Coreferential with Constituent of Preceding Clause	
	Total	Yes	No	Total	Yes	No
Preverbal PRO:						
S-V	12	9	3	8	3	5
O-V	5	4	1	1	1	-
Obl-V	3	2	1	1	-	1
Subtotals	20	15	5	10	4	6
Postverbal PRO:						
V-S	21	3	18	8	5	3
V-O	-	-	-	2	-	2
V-Obl	6	4	2	-	-	-
Subtotals	27	7	20	10	5	5
Totals	47	22	25	20	9	11

Note: In the above table, occurrences of the inanimate third person pronoun are recorded only when it referred to a tangible entity. See text for reference to its more abstract usages.

In all, there are 33 clauses in which one of these third person pronouns occurs as subject in the narrative sections of the texts; 12 of these are in the preverbal (and clause-initial) position and 21 in the postverbal position. In general, the determining factor as to the position in which the pronoun occurs is whether it is coreferential with a constituent of the preceding clause. If it is coreferential, that is, a continuous topic, the pronoun occurs in the preverbal position; if it is not coreferential with a constituent in the preceding clause, thus reflecting topic discontinuity, the pronoun occurs in the postverbal position. This is a reversal of the situation that exists when full noun phrase subjects occur preverbally and postverbally. As noted in section 4.1.1, it is preverbal noun phrase subjects that are more highly discontinuous and postverbal noun phrase subjects that show greater topic continuity.

As Table 5 shows, there are a few exceptions to the generalization expressed above: there are 3 cases of PRO-V in which the PRO is not coreferential with any constituent of the previous clause and 3 cases of V-PRO in which PRO is coreferential with a preceding clause constituent. Two of these exceptions occur in the text in the Appendix (in clauses 32 and 65). In both cases it is clear that there are special factors which override the general rule. In T.28.65 (ex. 26), the clause-initial pronoun *nyamoro* is needed for emphatic modification of the statement in the preceding clause, which is expressed as an absolute, but is then immediately modified. Emphatic contrast or modification of this kind always requires the constituent in clause-initial position.

(26)   64.   ïyarhïra nehxakonï nïmno.
                empty   it was   maloca
                'The maloca was empty.'

       65.   nyamoro marma noknomtxownï, asako marma
                they   only   they:were:left two   only
                'They only were left (in the maloca), two only.'

In T.28.32, the clause-final *noro* is coreferential with *xofrye* in the immediately preceding clause, but that clause, ending with *xofrye hyaka* , is the end of a background sequence which begins at clause 27. Clause 32, with *noro* as subject, is a continuation of the main theme line which finishes temporarily at clause 26, and *noro* is not coreferential with any constituent of that clause.

Each of the other four apparent counterexamples are also explainable in terms of overriding factors of this kind, that is, special emphasis or interpolation of a background sequence. This makes the general rule valid and one from which predictions can be made as to the position of nondeictic third person independent pronouns in a clause.

An additional piece of evidence that confirms the rule is the way in which the nondeictic inanimate form, *ïro*, is used when no tangible entity is involved, but only abstract discourse phenomena are being referred to. There are three frequently recurring phrases used as sentence-initial connectives that refer back to whole sections of the discourse: *iro wyaro* 'like that;' *iro ke* 'because of that, so, therefore;' and *iro ti oni ha* '(from) that (to) this.' The *iro* in this usage is invariably preverbal and refers to a part of the discourse that finishes with the preceding clause. This parallels the rule that preverbal nondeictic pronoun subjects express topic continuity with what has immediately preceded in the discourse.

4.2 Topic continuity properties of direct objects

4.2.1 Referential distance ("look-back"). Table 6 shows the average referential distance and Table 7 the more detailed percent distribution counts of referential distance for the direct object-marking categories. There are only two categories of any significance: AGR and OV. VO order only occurs when the subject of the clause refers to first or second person (or both first and second person) and the five occurrences in the three texts all occur in direct speech clauses. For all the counts in the object categories (direct and oblique objects), occurrences in direct speech clauses are included.

Table 6: Average Referential Distance for Direct Objects

Category	No. of Occurrences	Average Ref. Distance in No. of Clauses
AGR	86	2.23
O-V	42	9.43
V-O	5	2.60
Total	133	

The choice between AGR and OV is directly related to degree of topicality. In 88% of the total occurrences in the AGR category, the object has been referred to within the preceding three clauses, whereas the corresponding figure for OV is only 52%. Nearly all the other occurrences of OV (44%) are where the object is being newly introduced or has not been in the register for at least the previous nineteen clauses.

Table 7:   Percent Distribution of Referential Distance within
Direct Object Categories

No. of Clauses Since Previous Occurrence of Referent	AGR PREFIX		O-V		V-O	
	No.	%	No.	%	No.	%
1	56	0.66	20	0.48	2	0.40
2	11	0.14	1	0.02		
3	7	0.08	1	0.02	2	0.40
4	1	0.01				
5	3	0.03	1	0.02	1	0.20
6	2	0.02	1	0.02		
7	2	0.02				
8	1	0.01				
9	1	0.01				
11	1	0.01				
20	1	0.01	18	0.44		
Total	86	1.00	42	1.00	5	1.00

4.2.2 Persistence ("decay"). The OV category is relatively low in topicality, not only in terms of the preceding register, but also in what follows in the discourse (Tables 8 and 9). Average persistence of the referent is only 1.17 clauses, whereas for the AGR category it is 2.17 clauses. This correlates with the fact that OV is the category used most often to introduce the type of entities (props, inanimate) that stay in the register a very short time (Table 16).

These tables show a higher proportion of direct objects occurring as noun phrases (42 out of a total of 133), that is, over 35%) than is the case with subjects (only 27%, calculated from the total figures in Table 2, 121 out of 440). This correlates with the fact that entities are more likely to be introduced into the discourse as a direct or oblique object than as a subject (see section 4.6).

4.3 Topic continuity properties of oblique objects

The only parameter that proves to be of any significance for oblique objects is referential distance. Average referential distance is presented in Table 10

Table 8: Average Persistence for Direct Objects

Category	No. of Occurrences	Average Persistence in No. of Clauses
AGR	86	2.17
O-V	42	1.17
V-O	5	2.00
Total	133	

Table 9: Percent Distribution of Persistence within Direct Object Categories

No. of Clauses	AGR PREFIX		O-V		V-O	
	No.	%	No.	%	No.	%
0	22	0.26	19	0.45	2	0.40
1	24	0.28	5	0.12	2	0.40
2	15	0.18	12	0.29		
3	12	0.14	4	0.09		
4	6	0.07	2	0.05		
5	2	0.02				
6	1	0.01				
7	2	0.02				
8					1	0.20
20	1	0.01				
23	1	0.01				
Total	86	1.00	42	1.00	5	1.00

and the detailed counts for distribution of the distance for each oblique object-marking category in Table 11. The options for expressing oblique objects are: (1) AGR, PRO or NP; and (2) preverbal or postverbal position. The number of occurrences of PRO (that is, nondeictic third person independent pronouns) is insignificant, so the main choice in that parameter is between AGR and NP.

Of the three types of clause constituent -- subject, direct object, and oblique object -- the oblique object is the only one in which NP outranks AGR in number of occurrences, 56 against 31. This outranking by NP's is found in both the preverbal and postverbal positions, but it is more predominant in the preverbal position (27-11) than the postverbal (29-20). This in itself suggests that the preverbal position for oblique object (as for

Table 10: Average Referential Distance for Oblique Object

Category	No. of Occurrences	Av. Ref. Distance in No. of Clauses
Preverbal:		
AGR	11	4.73
PRO	4	1.50
NP	27	7.85
Subtotal	42	6.43
Postverbal:		
AGR	20	4.85
PRO	5	5.40
NP	29	11.55
Subtotal	54	8.50
Sequences:		
Postverbal	6	1.67
Discontinuous (Pre-V-Post)	3	15.67
Subtotal	9	6.33
Total	105	

subject) is more pragmatically marked, since NP's are more likely to be used for giving some kind of prominence to an entity. This is not, however, the whole story, as the two tables show. In Table 10, the average referential distance for preverbal NP's is lower (7.85 clauses since the last reference to the entity) than that for postverbal NP's (11.55 clauses). This indicates rather higher topicality (and, therefore, less pragmatic markedness) for preverbal NP obliques, although both are clearly low in topicality from the overall perspective. Table 11 presents more striking evidence that postverbal NP obliques rate lower on the topic continuity scale than preverbal NP obliques: 55% of the preverbal NP's refer to the same entity in the preceding clause, as against only 14% of the postverbal NP's. Both NP positions, however, show high counts for maximum referential distance of 20 clauses or more: preverbal with 33% and postverbal with 46%.

For completeness, sequences of oblique phrases in a single clause have been included in the counts in the two tables. These sequences are of two types: postverbal; and discontinuous, in which one phrase occurs

Table 11: Percent Distribution of Referential Distance within Oblique Object Categories

No. of Clauses Since Previous Occurrence of Referent	Preverbal Oblique						Postverbal Oblique						Sequences of Oblique Phrases Postverbal		
	AGR		PRO		NP		AGR		PRO		NP				
	No.	%	No.	%	No.	%	No.	%	No.	%	No.	%	No.	%	
1	6	0.55	3	0.75	15	0.55	10	0.50	3	0.60	4	0.14	4	0.45	AGR/PRO-NP
2	1	0.09	1	0.25	1	0.04	2	0.10			1	0.03	1	0.11	AGR-PRO-NP
3							3	0.15			3	0.10			
4	1	0.09					1	0.05	1	0.20	1	0.03	1	0.11	NP-AGR
5											1	0.03			
6											2	0.07			Preverbal-V-Postverbal
7	1	0.09			1	0.04					3	0.10	1	0.11	PRO-V-NP
8					1	0.04									
9											2	0.07			
10															
11															
12															
13	1	0.09					1	0.05							
14															
15															
16															
17							1	0.05							
18															
19															
20	1	0.09			9	0.33	2	0.10	1	0.20	13	0.46	2	0.22	AGR-V-NP
Totals	11	1.00	4	1.00	27	1.00	20	1.00	5	1.00	29	1.00	9	1.00	

before the verb and the other(s) after the verb. In both types, each phrase in the sequence gives the same information, but with an increasing degree of specificity regarding the referent, which is normally expressed by moving from AGR and/or PRO to NP. This pattern is seen in clause 31 in the Appendix: ... *ïhyaka ha, xofrye hyaka* ' ... for him, for the sloth.' In clause 22, the NP oblique phrase precedes the AGR oblique, but the increasing degree of specificity is still in the same direction, from left to right: ... *ukuthonï ymo kwaka, ïrakataka* ' into the lake, into the middle of it.' The results of this study show the postverbal sequences as having much higher topicality than the discontinuous ones, but the total number of occurrences is too small to warrant any firm conclusions.

4.4 Distribution of same subject (SS) and different subject (DS)

This measurement shows the significance of interference of another subject-topic in the preceding clause on the choice of subject-marking category. Tables 12 and 13 both show the same basic counts regarding distribution of SS and DS occurrences with each subject-marking category. Table 12 focusses on each category, showing the percentage of that category that is either SS or DS. Table 13 shows the percentage of total SS and total DS that applies to each category. In both tables, only three of the categories have a sufficient number of total occurrences to make them significant: AGR, V-S (NP), and S(NP)-V (cf. section 4.1).

The category showing the highest proportion of DS is the postverbal subject NP (63%, Table 12). This was to be expected in comparison with the AGR category (32%), but it is somewhat surprising that it is also higher than the preverbal subject NP category (59%), which has been seen to be high in topic discontinuity (section 4.1). This suggests that there is no direct correlation between topic continuity/discontinuity and the switch reference parameter for full NP's. It is, however, additional evidence that the VS category is used in a wider range of contexts than any of the others, and that this establishes it as the most neutral of the word order patterns (section 5.2).

Table 12: Relative Distribution of SS vs. DS Occurrences with Each Subject-
Marking Category

Category	SS		DS		Total	
	No.	%	No.	%	No.	%
Ø	5	0.56	4	0.44	9	1.00
AGR	202	0.68	96	0.32	298	1.00
V-S$_{NP}$	37	0.37	62	0.63	99	1.00
V-S$_{PRO}$	1	0.17	5	0.83	6	1.00
S$_{PRO}$-V	3	0.50	3	0.50	6	1.00
S$_{NP}$-V	9	0.41	13	0.59	22	1.00
Total	257	0.58	183	0.42	440	1.00

Table 13 shows that the AGR category has a higher percentage
(53%) of total DS occurrences than any other category. Only the VS
category comes close to it (34%). AGR has a much higher percentage
(78%) of total SS occurrences, as was to be expected.

Table 13: Prototype Distribution of the SS and DS Functions across the
Entire Subject-marking Category Range

Category	Percent of Total SS in Various Categories		Percent of Total DS in Various Categories	
	No.	%	No.	%
Ø	5	0.02	4	0.02
AGR	202	0.78	96	0.53
V-S$_{NP}$	37	0.14	62	0.34
V-S$_{PRO}$	1	0.01	5	0.03
S$_{PRO}$-V	3	0.01	3	0.01
S$_{NP}$-V	9	0.04	13	0.07
Total	257	1.00	183	1.00

4.5 Distribution of subject-marking categories at thematic junctures

Table 14 shows the number of occurrences of each topic-marking grammatical device at the crucial points of thematic divisions and background interpolations. In the case of major thematic divisions, there are two crucial points that always occur: the theme-initial clause and the theme-final clause. There is a third that may or may not occur: the presence of a transitional sequence (never more than two clauses in the three texts of this study) at the boundary between the end of one theme and the beginning of the next. In the case of the background interpolations, there are four crucial points: the initial clause of the background sequence; the final clause of the sequence (where there is more than one clause of background); and the clauses that occur on the main theme line immediately before and after the background material. These seven points of the discourse are presented in the columns of Table 14 for the purpose of showing the number of times each grammatical category appears at each point.

There are just two categories that are prominent at thematic breaks: AGR and VS(NP). This shows in both total number of occurrences (55 and 42 respectively) and also in the fact that these are the only two categories that occur on a number of occasions at each one of the seven crucial points relating to thematic junctures. AGR occurs more often than VS at the theme-initial point (14-8), but the reverse holds true at the theme-final point, where VS outnumbers AGR (13-10). The total number of major thematic units in the three texts was 26, and the background interpolations numbered 14.

The VS category outnumbers SV at every point including, somewhat surprisingly, but in a most emphatic way, the theme-initial point (8 VS to 3 SV). This is yet another factor confirming VS as the most neutral and basic of the word order types in the language (section 5.2).

One other fact of interest that emerges from Table 14 relates to the percentage of each category's total occurrences that are found at thematic junctures. Both VS and SV show almost equally high figures: VS has 42% of its 99 occurrences and SV 40% of its 22 total occurrences at these boundaries. AGR, on the other hand, has only 18% of its 298 occurrences appearing at these points of the discourse.

Table 14: Distribution of Subject-Marking Categories at Thematic Junctures

	TOTAL: All Clauses	TOTAL: Thematic junctures		Theme-initial	Theme-final	Transition between	Background-initial	Background-final	Pre-background	Post-background
Ø	9	1	0.11						1	
AGR	298	55	0.18	14	10	6	4	5	7	9
V-S$_{NP}$	99	42	0.42	8	13	3	8	3	4	3
V-S$_{PRO}$	6	4	0.67	1	1			1		2
S$_{PRO}$-V	6	2	0.33					1		
S$_{NP}$-V	22	9	0.40	3	2	1	2		1	
Total	440	113	0.26	26	26	10	14	10	13	14

Table 15 gives a different percentage measurement.   The figures shown here give the percentage of the total number of crucial thematic points (113) that pertains to the number of occurrences in each category. In this case, AGR (48% of the 113) and VS(NP) (36%) have significantly higher scorings than any of the other categories.

Table 15:   Percent Distribution of Each Category Occurring at Thematic Junctures across the Entire Range of Subject-marking Categories

	Total Occurrences in All Clauses	Occurrences at Thematic Junctures	Percent
Ø	9	1	0.01
AGR	298	55	0.48
V-S_{NP}	99	42	0.36
V-S_{PRO}	6	4	0.04
S_{PRO}-V	6	2	0.02
S_{NP}-V	22	9	0.09
Total	440	113	1.00

4.6 Introduction of new referents

Table 16 is a summary of the number of times each grammatical category is used in the three texts to introduce new referents.   The first section presents the numbers from the standpoint of the discourse status of the entity: major participant, minor participant, or prop.   The second section shows the numbers according to the semantic status of the entity, and the third section according to the semantico-pragmatic status of the entity (section 3.5).

Major participants are never introduced by oblique categories and, in the more straightforward cases, are only introduced as subject or direct object noun phrases.   The less clear cases all occur in the story of the origin of the hero, Mawarye.   The hero is introduced in two stages: first, as a human being who pops out of a turtle egg, and here a verb form is used, with the word for human being incorporated into it; second, as Mawarye (who turns out to be something more than just a man), and here there is simply the exclamatory use of the name in a nonverbal, direct

Table 16: Introduction of New Referents

	No.	SV	VS	OV	VO	Obl-V	V-Obl	Noun Possr.	Incorporated in V	V-less Clause	Vocative
Discourse status of entity:											
Major participants	9	2	2	2				1	1	1	
Minor participants	16	3	6	1			5			1	
Props	30	3	2	12	1	7		1		2	2
Totals	55	8	10	15	1	7	5	2	1	4	2
Semantic status of entity:											
Animate	31	7	8	5		2	3	1	1	2	2
Inanimate	24	1	2	10	1	5	2	1		2	
Totals	55	8	10	15	1	7	5	2	1	4	2
Semantico-pragmatic status of entity:											
Definite	24	3	6	5			2	2	1	3	2
Referential-Indefinite	25	5	4	8	1	4	2			1	
Non-referential	6			2		3	1				
Totals	55	8	10	15	1	7	5	2	1	4	2

speech utterance. The third atypical form of introduction of a major participant, found in the same text, is when a noun possessor form is used: 'the jaguar people's trail.'

Minor participants are also typically introduced by means of subject or direct object noun phrases. Props, on the other hand, are much more likely to be introduced in direct or oblique object noun phrases. Animate entities are more likely to be referred to initially by subject or object noun phrases, and inanimate by object or oblique phrases, but there is no unique way of referring to either category. In the semantico-pragmatic categories, the nonreferential entities are introduced only as direct or oblique object nominals. There is no significant difference in the ways definite and indefinite referents are introduced.

As I noted in section 4.1.1, in Hixkaryana entities are often introduced or reintroduced in a two-sentence sequence. In the first sentence, the entity is expressed simply by an anaphorical device, usually a prefix, and only in the second sentence is a full noun phrase used. One example of this occurs in the first two sentences of the text in the Appendix. In the first sentence the sloth is referred to by the prefixal form *n-* '3S3O' in *nanotometxkonï*. In the second sentence, the full noun phrase is used, *xofrye heno*. In that example, the entity is the direct object in both sentences. In sentence 89, *xofrye* occurs as the subject in an SV construction; in the preceding sentence he is referred to by means of a prefix in an oblique phrase, *ïyarïhnaka* 'in his absence.' Before that he had been off the scene since 77, except for a reference in an embedded direct speech clause in 84. This pattern of bringing entities (back) into the register -- anaphor first, then noun phrase -- tends to obscure the degree of topicality of the entity and it could also skew the pattern of introducing new referents. In fact, in my analysis here of new referents I have treated such sentence sequences as a single unit and taken the noun phrase as the crucial device for introducing the referent. Thus in T28.1-2, I counted this in the summary in Table 16 as OV (sentence 2), not AGR (sentence 1).

4.7 Distribution of subject-marking categories in various clause types

Table 17 highlights three interesting facts. One is that in each of the six clause types, there are more occurrences of VS than SV. The other two

Table 17: Distribution of Subject-Marking Categories in Various Clause Types (S = NP or PRO)

Clause Type	SV		VS		Other		Total	
	No.	%	No.	%	No.	%	No.	%
Intransitive	7	0.08	13	0.16	64	0.76	84	1.00
Transitive	9	0.10	13	0.14	72	0.76	94	1.00
Quotative			53	0.39	81	0.61	134	1.00
Copular	10	0.11	19	0.22	55	0.67	84	1.00
Equative			1	0.20	4	0.80	5	1.00
Ideophone	2	0.05	6	0.15	31	0.80	39	1.00
Totals	28	0.06	105	0.24	307	0.70	440	1.00

are facts about quotative clauses. First, SV does not occur at all in these, and second, there is a much higher ratio of the VS construction (39%) than in other clause types. The embedded direct speech component can be regarded as equivalent to a direct object, so that OVS can be considered as fairly normal for quotative clauses. It is, however, a special construction and I ignore it in my discussion of OVS word order in section 5.2, and also, more generally throughout this paper, when referring to the category OV.

The greater frequency of a noun phrase subject (rather than simply an AGR prefix) may be due to the fact that quotative sentences are relatively long and complex. There is normally at least one full clause of embedded speech, and this is often repeated after the quotative margin, that is, the VS part of the sentence (which may also have an addressee phrase added). Examples of this kind of complexity can be seen in the text in the Appendix: clauses 8-9, 59-60, 69-70. Quotatives are also often followed by a clause in which there is a change of speaker or other subject-topic. This results in a low rate of topic persistence for the subject of the quotative clause, and this has already been noted as a general characteristic of the VS category (section 4.1.2).

5. Discussion and conclusions

5.1 The organization of third person narrative discourse
    in Hixkaryana

The principle characteristics of the organization of third person narrative discourse are:[2]

(1) a very small set of grammatical devices used to express a wide range of discourse pragmatic functions (5.1.1);

(2) general adherence to the crosslinguistic topicality hierarchy established by the studies in Givón (ed. 1983), with one coding device (AGR) that consistently expresses a high degree of topicality, another (preverbal S) that is used relatively infrequently but, when it is used, expresses a low degree of topicality, and a third device (postverbal S) which is intermediate in the degree of topicality it shows, and is especially prominent at the close of thematic units, but is also used to express so

many different discourse-pragmatic functions that it must be considered the most neutral of the coding devices (5.1.2);

(3) in the switch reference parameter, a strong correlation between same-subject occurrences and degree of topicality, but an absence of the expected correlation between different-subject occurrences and low degree of topicality, with all three major coding devices, AGR, postverbal S and preverbal S, being used relatively frequently in clauses in which the subject is different from that of the preceding clause (5.1.3);

(4) discourse thematic units, both major (episode) and minor (background interpolations), at the boundaries of which a high proportion of the total occurrences of both preverbal and postverbal subject noun phrases occurs (5.1.4);

(5) a distinct pattern for the occurrence of nondeictic third person independent pronouns, with preverbal (clause-initial) pronouns being emphatic and high in topic continuity, and postverbal pronouns being contrastive and low in topic continuity (5.1.5); and

(6) the use of any of the categories in which a full noun phrase occurs to introduce new referents into the discourse (5.1.6).

5.1.1 Grammatical coding devices. There are only three grammatical devices used for encoding the primary pragmatic functions relating to topics: agreement prefixes, noun phrases, and word order (section 5.1.2). One other device, the set of nondeictic third person independent pronouns, is used for another function that is related to topicality but is primarily one of emphasis and contrast (section 5.1.5).

Zero anaphora and particles, although they sometimes occur, are not significant devices for marking topicality. With regard to zero anaphora, Hixkaryana is thus different from the OV languages described by Givón (ed. 1983), where Japanese, Ute and, to a lesser extent, Amharic all use this device as an important indicator of topic continuity. The explanation is that in Hixkaryana there are verb prefixes that agree with both subject and object and they are obligatory. For all clauses having verbs, therefore, there is no possibility of zero anaphora, and there are very few clauses that do not have verbs (or nominals or adverbs derived from verbs that also have prefixes agreeing with underlying subjects and/or objects).

There are other devices frequently referred to in the topic continuity studies in Givón (ed. 1983) which have not proved relevant for Hixkaryana: dislocation of noun phrases; and markings for referentiality vs. nonreferentiality and definiteness vs. indefiniteness (but these are examined with respect to the introduction of new referents (Table 16)).

Since all verbs have the agreement prefixes, the first option for topicality marking is the presence or absence of noun phrases in the clause. There is a slightly higher ratio of direct object noun phrases (35%) than subject (27%). A comparison of clauses that have at least one nominal, subject or object, as against clauses having only the agreement prefixes, shows 32% with nominal and 68% without. In all the 440 clauses in the text base there are only 4 that have both subject and object nominals (see 5.2 below for further discussion).

Verb agreement does not carry over to oblique constituents. Obliques that make reference to topics are all postpositional phrases, and the choice here is between (i) noun phrase plus postposition and (ii) postposition with a prefix that substitutes for the noun phrase. This is the only category where noun phrases outnumber prefixes (by 64% to 36%).

The third device that is relevant to topic continuity is word order. This is primarily a distinction between preverbal and postverbal occurrences of the categories, although in most clauses this is equivalent to clause-initial vs. clause-final. All obliques are affected, whether they have noun phrases or prefixes. For the other two categories, it is only when they are expressed by noun phrases (including pronouns) that the position in the clause is relevant. Direct objects are found to be almost rigidly preverbal, the only exceptions being in clauses where there is a first or second person subject, and in the text sample used there are only five of these, always in direct speech clauses. Obliques are fairly even in their distribution, with slightly more postverbal (56%) occurrences than preverbal (44%). For the subject category, there are significantly more instances of postverbal (105) than preverbal (28).

5.1.2 Pragmatic motivation for selection of particular coding devices . The most general and pervasive motivation for selecting a particular grammatical device relates to degree of topicality of the referent. The results of this Hixkaryana study in general support the topicality hierarchy that emerges from the studies of the eight languages in Givón (ed. 1983). This is most clearly seen in the referential distance measurement. For all three categories, the agreement-only device reflects the highest degree of topic continuity. In the major category, subject, where the position of the noun phrase is significant, the postverbal noun phrase is a more continuous topic than the preverbal noun phrase. In the case of obliques, the preverbal noun phrase is more continuous than the postverbal noun phrase, although both are generally low in topic continuity compared with the AGR category.

The persistence measurement for subjects shows a sharp difference from the referential distance count. It is the preverbal subject device that has the greatest persistence in the following discourse and the postverbal subject that has the least. The agreement category falls in between the other two for degree of persistence. This result is not surprising when considered in relation to other measurements. Preverbal subjects show high referential distance counts, signalling that they have not been in the register for some time. Once in the register, it is reasonable to suppose that they will continue for a while, which is what this persistence count shows. Postverbal subjects, on the other hand, are especially prominent at theme-final boundaries (Table 14) and this is where one would expect topics to be discontinued.

Nondeictic third person independent pronouns pattern quite differently from noun phrases. Preverbal (always clause-initial) pronoun subjects show very low referential distance and, therefore, high topic continuity, whereas postverbal pronouns show relatively high referential distance and low continuity. Topic continuity is not the crucial pragmatic motivation in this case (see section 5.1.5 for further discussion). The functions and patterns of Hixkaryana pronouns are thus quite different from those in the languages reported in Givón (ed. 1983). For example, Hinds (Japanese) says (p.77): "the category 'pronoun' is shown to have an intermediate functional status between ellipsis and full nouns" (cf. also Givón on Ute, p. 182). In no sense can the Hixkaryana pronouns be said to have an intermediate status between AGR and NP's. The functions and patterns are totally different. There are other languages reported in that volume in which independent pronouns do seem to have some distinct pragmatic function that is only partly related to degree of topicality, but the patterns are still quite different from those found in Hixkaryana (see section 5.1.5).

5.1.3 Switch reference and topic continuity. There is close correlation between the same-subject count (Tables 12 and 13) and the referential distance measurement of topic continuity. The agreement category has low referential distance (1.31 clauses) and a high percentage of total same-subject occurrences (78%). The next highest percentage of same-subject is VS(NP) (14%), which is also the second lowest for referential distance among the major devices (5.11 clauses).

The correlations do not extend to the comparison of different subjects with low topic continuity. In terms of referential distance, the preverbal subject, S(NP)V, has the lowest degree of continuity (8.14 clauses, see Table 1), and one would have expected this to be reflected in a high different-subject count. In fact, it comes behind the postverbal subject in both kinds of percentage rating: within the category itself, there are 59% of all S(NP)V occurrences that have different subjects, against 63% of all VS(NP) occurrences (Table 12); and, taking the percentage of all different-subject occurrences, the preverbal shows only 7%, against postverbal 34%, and agreement 53% (Table 13).

5.1.4 Thematic organization and boundary phenomena . Based primarily on semantic criteria (see section 3.4), there appear to be, in Hixkaryana, two types of thematic unit above the sentence level (or, possibly, the sentence cluster level; see Derbyshire 1977a, and the "two-sentence sequence" to which I refer in section 4.6, cf. section 4.1.1). The two units are: episode, which is the whole theme sequence; and background interpolation, which is a temporary interruption (often only a single clause, and rarely more than four or five clauses) within an episode. It is the boundary phenomena that are of greatest interest, and both types of thematic units show the same basic characteristics.

A high percentage of the total occurrences of both SV (40%) and VS (42%) occur at the boundaries of these thematic units (Table 14). As might be expected, VS is more predominant at the end of theme units (both episodes and interpolations). But VS also outnumbers SV at theme-initial position, by 16 occurrences to 5 (including background interpolations). Theme-initial is where one would expect a high degree of discontinuity and, therefore, the SV device to predominate, since it has the lowest continuity by the referential distance measure. This lack of correlation, here and elsewhere with respect to SV, is largely due to the infrequency with which SV occurs.

The reverse also holds true with respect to the agreement device. This occurs much more frequently than any other coding device, so it shows strongly in some places where one would not expect a device that is generally high in topic continuity. This applies at thematic boundaries, where the agreement device is used in 48% of the total possible occurrences at boundary points, although it is not too far ahead of VS(NP), which has 34% of the total. VS actually occurs more often than AGR at theme-final points (Tables 14 and 15). This theme-final preference for VS correlates strongly with the low persistence value of that device (Tables 3 and 4).

5.1.5 The pragmatic functions of nondeictic third person independent pronouns. The primary functions of these pronouns are distinct from, but related to, the question of topic continuity. There are two distinct functions for the subject pronouns, depending on the position of the pronoun: if preverbal, this signals emphatic continuity (or, occasionally, emphatic contrast) with a topic in the preceding clause; if postverbal, this signals a subject that is different from that of the preceding clause, and a topic that has been referred to earlier in the discourse, and it is thus a clear signal of discontinuity. As noted earlier, these signals of continuity and discontinuity for pronouns are the reverse of what happens when noun phrases occur as subjects.

This functional pattern for independent pronouns is also something quite different from the patterns described for languages in Givón (ed. 1983). In Amharic, independent pronouns are contrastive and continuous (Gasser 1983: 128 and examples), and in Biblical Hebrew they are "largely contrastive and discontinuous" (Fox 1983: 223). In neither case are they said to be both continuous and discontinuous, as they are in Hixkaryana. Nor does either author refer to distinct functions that depend on position of the pronoun in the clause. Givón's study of pronouns in spoken English (Givón 1983c) appears at first sight to approach most closely to what occurs in Hixkaryana. He distinguishes two types of function: (i) anaphoric/continuative; and (ii) contrastive/topic changing. But he goes on to equate the first type with unstressed pronouns and the second with stressed pronouns. The stress distinction does not apply in Hixkaryana, and what does apply in that language - the preverbal and postverbal positions for subject pronouns - does not apply in English. (See also section 5.1.2, where I refer to pronouns in other languages reported in the same volume).

5.1.6 Topic continuity and the introduction of new referents. The results of this count are largely negative. The AGR category is rarely used, otherwise any category (S, O, Obl., etc.) or grammatical device may be selected for the purpose of introducing new referents into the register. While a few preferred patterns show up, there are no absolute constraints on the devices that may be used for referring to participants vs. props, major vs. minor participants, animate vs. inanimate entities, or definite vs. indefinite entities. Such gaps as there are may be accidental, due to the limited number of occurrences in the various subgroupings.

5.2 Word order issues

5.2.1 Basic word order in Hixkaryana. I have in earlier works presented the evidence, mainly on intuitive and syntactic grounds, for postulating OVS as the basic constituent order in Hixkaryana (Derbyshire 1977b, 1979a,b, 1981; cf. Derbyshire & Pullum 1981). I now summarize the facts in the present study which bear on the matter. My conclusion is that these facts support OVS as the basic word order in the language. The only reservation I have relates to the issue of whether any language which has so few transitive clauses with both subject and object noun phrases can be said to have a basic order of constituents for that clause type. I return to this question below.

I consider the evidence in three stages: OV; VS; and OVS. The first concerns the position of the direct object in relation to the verb. There is no doubt here that OV is a very rigid order. There are only five occurrences of VO and in all five the subject is first or second person (or both), always in embedded direct speech clauses. Even when the subject is first/second person, the object more often precedes the verb (for example, in sentences 3-4, 7, 10, and 69-70 in the text in the Appendix). When the subject is third person, the object almost invariably precedes the verb (the very few exceptions, involving complex constituents, are discussed in Derbyshire 1979a, 40-41, 76-78).

The second stage of the evidence relates to the position of the subject. The cumulative evidence of this study, summarized below, leads inevitably to the conclusion that VS is a more basic order than SV:

(1) A comparison of the total occurrences shows VS to outnumber SV by 99 to 22 (105 to 28 if third person independent pronoun subjects are included).

(2) The occurrences of VS range over almost every possible dimension of topic continuity and discontinuity: Table 2 shows them more evenly spread with respect to referential distance than any other category; with respect to persistence (Table 4), although VS characteristically shows low persistence and a high rate of decay compared with all other categories (section 4.1.2), it still occurs more often than SV at the higher persistence levels; VS has a higher percentage than SV of the total number of different-subject occurrences, even though SV is characteristically high in topic discontinuity (section 4.4); and at thematic junctures VS occurs more often than SV at every possible boundary point, including both the theme-initial and theme-final clause positions (Table 14).

(3) Table 17 shows that in every clause type VS occurs more often than SV. From this table it is clear that a large proportion of VS occurrences are due to the fact that it is virtually the obligatory order of quotative clauses, which happen to be the most frequently recurring clause type in third person narrative discourse and also the clause type in which a noun phrase most often occurs as subject. Even if we ignore quotative clauses, however, VS is still the predominant pattern in every type of clause.

It is clear from this study that SV is a pragmatically marked order that is used sparingly even for the restricted functions which primarily characterize it. VS, on the other hand, is used for a wide range of functions, including those associated with SV. All this adds up to VS being the basic, unmarked order of a fairly rigid type in clauses that have a noun phrase subject.

The third and final stage is the consideration of transitive clauses in which both subject and object noun phrases occur. The major factor here is that there are so few of them. Of the 440 clauses of the text base, 94 are transitive. Only 4 of these have both subject and object nominals: 3 OVS and 1 SOV. This seems far too small a numerical base on which to postulate a basic order. The earlier evidence in this section, however, showing the predominance of OV and VS, suggests strongly that if we examined a larger number of noun phrase transitive clauses from a greater quantity of text material, we would find at least the 3 to 1 ratio in favor of OVS, and probably more likely a 4 to 1 or 5 to 1 ratio.

The main issue relates not to the ratio of OVS to SOV but rather to the very low count of clauses that have both subject and object nominals -- a little over four percent of transitive clauses and less than one percent of total narrative clauses. Is this not totally inadequate for postulating any basic constituent order for this clause type? The only argument I can see for doing so, and one I accept, is this. Transitive clauses with subject and object nominals do occur in the language and it is feasible, looking at the evidence from both those (relatively few) clauses, and also the (many more) clauses that have either the subject or object nominal, to make a reasonable hypothesis about their constituent order. I submit that, on this evidence, OVS can be considered the basic order of full noun phrase transitive clauses in Hixkaryana. I would add, however, that Hixkaryana is one of those languages with respect to which any statement about word order must be qualified by reference to other special typological characteristics of the language.

These characteristics for Hixkaryana are: obligatory person-marking verb prefixes which agree with subject and object; and the consequent scarcity of noun phrase subjects and direct objects in most discourse contexts. Within this typological framework, Hixkaryana can be said to have OVS as its basic order in clauses that have subject and object noun phrases.

In order to account for languages of this type, and at the same time preserve a uniform concept of basic word order that can be applied to languages of all types, Doris Payne (1986) proposes that we view the concept as:

> composed of two separate typological parameters: (1)
> the least marked word order when full noun phrases

are employed, and (2) the most neutral clause type within discourse. In some languages these two parameters converge on a single clause type, but in others ... they distinguish two orders of 'basic' clauses.

Hixkaryana is one of those languages with two orders of basic clauses: (1) the neutral clause in discourse, which is the clause without subject and object nominals and in which the verb prefixes signal the two major arguments; and (2) the clauses in which the nominals occur and the least marked word order is OVS (which includes clauses with a single nominal, either OV or VS).

5.2.2 Word order change. At the end of his study of Ute topic continuity, Givón (ed. 1983b: 197) calls for further studies in ex-SOV languages "to assess the relative viability of SVO, VSO or OVS as the most likely targets in the natural drift from SOV." This study of Hixkaryana makes a contribution in that area of research.

In an earlier paper (Derbyshire 1981), I described the likely stages in the drift from SOV to OVS in Hixkaryana, comparing that language with two others in the Carib family (Carib of Suriname and Macuxi), which appear to be changing in the same direction but have not advanced so far as Hixkaryana. I can now compare Hixkaryana with Ute on the evidence that Givón (1983b) provides on that language of the Uto-Aztecan family.

Hixkaryana has clearly advanced further than Ute in the drift to OVS. It is more rigidly OV and more predominantly VS than Ute. In fact, in Ute there are still many more occurrences of SV and SOV than there are of VS and OVS, although these latter orders are the second most frequent in the language. In Hixkaryana, as we have seen, VS occurrences outnumber SV by 4.5 to 1, and OVS outnumbers SOV by 3 to 1. On the basis of the Hixkaryana evidence, we can say with confidence that OVS is a natural target for drift from SOV. We can go further than that and say that OVS is probably not just an "intermediate word order," which is as far as Givón could go in the case of Ute. The rigidity of OV and the dominance of VS in the current synchronic state of the language suggest that OVS may be here to stay for a long time. (Of course, other factors, such as contact with Portuguese, may radically affect the situation).

It is difficult to know just where to place Hixkaryana on the word order rigidity scale. As I have suggested earlier in this study, it is probably best described as rigidly OV and "fairly rigidly" VS. (I am not prepared to make any classification of OVS in terms of rigidity since there are so few full noun phrase transitive sentences.) As Givón (1984: 188, 204) points out, "word order flexibility is used in most languages," both so-called "rigid-order" and "flexible-order" languages. This variation is pragmatically motivated in both types of language, the only difference being in the degree to which certain orders are determined by discourse-pragmatic factors, rather than being more fully grammaticalized and relatively indifferent to the contextual factors. In Hixkaryana, the selection of the OV or VS order rather than AGR-only is heavily motivated by the discourse-pragmatics. On the other hand, the choice of OV or VS rather than VO or SV is much less pragmatically motivated, since OV and VS can, and do, occur in all kinds of discourse-pragmatic environments. These two orders have become virtually grammaticalized with respect to clauses in which noun phrases occur, but obviously not in the more "neutral" clause in which the noun phrases do not occur (see section 5.2.1).

Hyman (1975) first suggested that pragmatic considerations motivate word order change, and specifically that the high topicality of the object constituents motivated the change from OV to VO in Niger-Congo languages, via "afterthought" types of constructions. In Derbyshire (1981) I followed this suggestion of Hyman's, but demonstrated from Hixkaryana that in some languages the subject, not the object, would be the constituent that drifted to the postverbal position, first as an "afterthought" constituent, but later becoming grammaticalized as (O)VS. Givón's Ute study (1983b) supported this particular direction of drift and emphasized the significance of the pragmatic motivation for the change from SOV to OVS. This quantitative study of Hixkaryana provides further evidence of the influence of pragmatic factors, especially those relating to degree of topic continuity, in determining diachronic change of basic word order patterns.

Appendix

The Origins of the King Vulture, the Sloth, and the Land Turtle:
A Hixkaryana myth told by Kaywerye (Candinho)

1. kurumu   n-   anotometxkonï
    king vulture   3S3O-employ +COLL+DP
    The king vulture (people) employed him in their service.

2. kurum- yana   komo, xofrye heno
    vulture-kin group   COLL sloth   DEAD

    y-   anotometxkonï
    3S3O-employ+COLL+DP
    The vulture people employed the poor old sloth in their service.

3-4. Ø-   txemtxatxko,   kana Ø-   txemtxa,
      2S3O poison+MOT.IMP+COLL   fish 2S3O-poison+MOT.IMP

      Ø-   ketxkonï   hatï,   kurum- yana   komo
      3S3O-say+COLL+DP HSY   vulture-kin group COLL
      "Go poison them, go poison fish," said the vulture people.

5. ïï,   Ø-   kekonï- hatï
    RESP 3S3O-say+DP-HSY
    "O.K.," he said.

6. Ø-   txempekonï   tï   tï-   notxhïrï wya
    3S3O-poison+CAUS+DP HSY 3REFLX-sister   by
    He (vulture) caused him to poison them through his (vulture's)
    sister.

7. rotï   Ø-   txempoko,   ø-   kekonï   tï,
    my meat food 2S3O-poison+CAUS+IMP 3S3Ø-say+DP HSY

kurum-yana,   tï-   notxhïrï   wya ha
vulture-kin group   3REFLX-sister   by   INTENSFR
"Cause (him) to poison food for me," said the vulture to his
sister.

8-9. Ø-   txemko   tï,   Ø-   kekonï hatï,   ïro ke,
      2S3O-poison+IMP HSY   3S3O-say+DP HSY   that because

      xofrye hetxe, ø-   txemko   tï,   epepe   yotï
      sloth wife of 3S3O poison+IMP HSY older brother meat food of
      "Poison them," said the sloth's wife, therefore. "Poison meat
      food for my brother."

10. hentano   tho   ï-   txemyano
      where+NOMLZR DEVLD   1S3O-poison+NONPAST+UNCERT

      ha,   Ø-   kekonï   hatï
      INTENSFR   3S3O-say+DP   HSY
      "Where is the thing I shall poison?,"he said.

11. ehnï tho   ymo   mak   hatï,
      river DEVLD AUG   COUNTEREXPECT HSY

      Ø-   kekonï hatï,   ï-hetxe
      3S3O-say+DP HSY   3-wife of
      "The big river," said his wife.

12. poo,   Ø-   kekonï hatï
      DISMAY 3S3O-say+DP HSY
      He expressed dismay.

13. n- oseryehokekonï,   xofrye
      3S-be upset+DP   sloth
      The sloth was upset.

14. xofrye   heno   n- oseryehokekonï
    sloth   DEAD   3S-be upset+DP
    The sloth was upset.

15. n- omokye   hatï,   Ø-txemxe
    3S- come+DP HSY   3-poison+PURP.MOT
    He came purposing to poison them.

16. bawa   y-   otahaye   hatï,   ukuthonï   ymo
    poison vine 3S3O-beat+DP HSY   lake   AUG

    hatï,   e-nytxemnyïrï,   xofrye nytxemnyïrï
    HSY   3-poison+OBJ.NOMLZN   sloth poison+OBJ.NOMLZN
    He beat poison vine ("timbo") (for) the big lake he, the sloth,
    was going to poison.

17. poo,   krïk,
    DISMAY stopping and looking (IDEO)

    e-hokoso   n- exeye   ha
    3-at edge of 3S-be+DP INTENSFR
    (He expressed) dismay, stopping and looking. He was at the edge
    of (the lake).

18. poo,   Ø-   kekonï hatï
    DISMAY 3S3O-say+DP HSY
    He expressed dismay.

19-20. txaray,   manaka   y-   amaye
       felling (IDEO) species of palm   3S3O-fell+DP

    hatï,   txea
    HSY   falling (IDEO)
    He felled an (assai) palm tree, and down it came.

21. fom,   krow,   Ø-   kaye   hatï
    throwing (IDEO) piercing water (IDEO)3S3O-do+DP   HSY
    Throwing (it), he caused it to pierce the water.

22. manaka y-   arymaye,   ukothonï ymo kwaka,
    palm   3S3O-throw+DP lake   AUG into

    ï-rakataka
    3-into middle of
    He threw the palm tree into the lake, into the middle of it.

23. krow,   txekruk
    piercing water (IDEO) piercing river bed (IDEO)

    tkaxero   n- exeye
    do+ADVBLZR   3S-be+DP
    He was making it pierce the water and the river bed.

24. xwax,   Ø-   wakaye   hatï,   xofrye
    pulling out (IDEO)   3S3O-pull out+DP HSY   sloth
    The sloth pulled it out.

25. sïïy,   n- ahaye   hatï,   ukuthonï
    falling of river level (IDEO) 3S-drop+DP HSY   lake

    ymo tho,   thenyenohnï ymo tho   mak
    AUG DEVLD big+NOMLZR AUG DEVLD   COUNTEREXPECT

    hatï,   sïïy
    HSY   falling of level (IDEO)
    The level of the huge lake area dropped.

26. tapa tapa tapa tapa   kana heno
    floundering (IDEO)   fish   QUANT
    All the fish were floundering around.

27. n-   ahayehkaye   mak   hatï
     3S3O-drop+CAUS+DP COUNTEREXPECT HSY
     He caused it to drop.

28. ï- txempera   mah   tï
     3-poison +NEG   COUNTEREXPECT HSY

     n- exeye   ha
     3S-be+DP   INTENSFR
     But he didn't poison it/them at all.

29. oske rma   n-   ahayehkaye
     thus CONT 3S3O-drop+CAUS+DP
     Yet thus he caused it to drop.

30. ï- txempera   rma   n- exeye
     3-poison+NEG   CONT   3S-be+DP
     He didn't poison it/them.

31. n- ahaye   mak   hatï,
     3S-drop+DP   COUNTEREXPECT HSY

     ï- hyaka   ha,   xofrye   hyaka
     3-for   INTENSFR   sloth   for
     It dropped for him, for the sloth.

32. n-   ahosïye   hatï,   noro   ro   xak
     3S3O-take hold+DP HSY   3PRO EXCLUS DISADVAN

     mak   hatï
     COUNTEREXPECT HSY
     He took hold of them, just he all by himself.

33. towenyxa   tï   n- ehxakonï
     one   HSY   3S-be+DP
     He was alone.

34. koho   mah   tï   n- ehxatxkonï
    many   COUNTEREXPECT   HSY   3S-be+COLL+DP

    haryhe,   kurum- yana   komo haryhe   tï
    CONTR.EMPH   vulture-kin group   COLL CONTR.EMPH HSY
    The vulture people on the other hand were a great many.

35. ï- nyakheranye   mah   tï
    3-send+NEG+COLL   COUNTEREXPECT   HSY

    n- ehxatxkonï   ha,   owto yohï ha
    3S-be+COLL+DP   INTENSFR   village chief of INTENSFR
    But the village chief(s) were not sending them.

36. ïtohra   Ø- ehtxoko,   Ø-akoro,
    go+NEG 2S-be+COLL+IMP   3-with

    Ø-   ketxkonï   mak   hatï
    3S3O-say+COLL+DP   COUNTEREXPECT   HSY
    "Do not go with him,"they said.

37. ï- xehranye   n- ehxakonï
    3-DESID+NEG+COLL   3S-be+DP
    They did not like him.

38. xofrye heno   xehra   n- ehxatxkonï
    sloth   DEAD DESID+NEG   3S-be+COLL+DP
    They did not like the poor old sloth.

39. n-   arïye   hatï, xofrye
    3S3O-take+DP HSY   sloth
    The sloth took them (the fish).

40. ïhpo,   n- ahatakaye
    coming into open (IDEO) 3S-come out+DP

    hatï   owto   hona   harha
    HSY   village   to   back
    He arrived back at the village.

41. txoow   kana   heno   y-   arïye
    dropping fish   QUANT   3S3O-take+DP
    He took the great quantity of fish and dropped them down.

42. mï-   txemnyo   Ø-   ketxkonï   ha
    2S3O-poison+IP   3S3O-say+COLL+DP   INTENSFR
    "You have poisoned them?," they said.

43. ïhï   ï-   txemnyo,   Ø-   kekonï   hatï
    RESP   1S3O-poison+IP   3S3O-say+DP   HSY
    "Yes, I poisoned them," he said.

44. n-   enkuhtetxkonï
    3S3O-deceive+COLL+DP
    He was lying to them.

45. tï-   wya Ø-ahayehka-   txhe   rma
    3REFLX-by   3-drop+CAUS-after   CONT

    oske   n-   kekonï
    thus   3S3O-say+DP
    Even though he had caused the river to drop, that is what he said.

46. ï-   txemnyo   ha,   noro   ha
    1S3O-poison+IP   INTENSFR   3PRO   INTENSFR

    Ø-   kekonï   hatï
    3S3O-say+DP   HSY
    "I poisoned them," he said.

47. t-   hetxe wya n-   ekarymekonï
    3REFLX-wife   to   3S3O-tell+DP
    He was telling it to his wife.

48. tïmko   ha,   oy-eheka   wya
    give+IMP   INTENSFR   2- brother to

    Ø-   kekonï   hatï
    3S3O-say+DP   HSY
    "Give them to your brother," he said.

49. ïtono   mokï   n- ahko   ha,
    there+NOMILZN that one 3S-be+IP INTENSFR

    kana heno,   Ø- kekonï   hatï   xofrye
    fish QUANT   3S3O-say+DP HSY   sloth
    "There is a heap of fish over there," said the sloth.

50-51. henta ha   Ø- ketxkonï   hatï,
       where INTENSFR   3S3O-say+COLL+DP   HSY

    kurum- yana   komo
    vulture-kin group COLL
    "Where?," said the vulture people.

52-53. ïtono   mokï   n- ahtxok   ha,
       there+NOMLZN   that one 3S-be+COLL+IP INTENSFR

    thenyenohnï   xak   mak   ha,
    much+NOMLZR   DISADVAN   COUNTEREXPECT INTENSFR

    ï-matanïrï   hampïnï, Ø- kekonï   hatï xofrye
    3-go bad+NOMLZN WARNING 3S3O-say+DP HSY sloth
    "There is a great lot of fish over there that is going bad," said the
    sloth.

54. eten hamï   Ø- ketxkonï
     what DEDUCT 3S3O-say+COLL+DP
     "What should (we do)?," they said.

55. awanaworo, Ø- ketxkonï   hatï
     tomorrow   3S3O-say+COLL+DP HSY

     kurum- yana   komo, ïpa   txowï
     vulture-kin group COLL let's go   COLL
     "Tomorrow," said the vulture people, "let's go."

56. awanaworo ïpa   txowï t-   eh-   txe,
     tomorrow let's go COLL 1INCL-look for-MOT.IMP

     kana heno,   Ø- ketxkonï   hatï
     fish QUANT 3S3O-say+COLL+DP   HSY
     "Tomorrow, let's go, let's go look for the fish," they said.

57. sa,   n- enmahye hatï
     dawning (IDEO) 3S-dawn+DP HSY
     The next day came.

58. n- omohtxownï   hatï
     3S-come+COLL+DP HSY
     They came.

59. ïtohra   exko,   wawa   y,
     go+NEG be+IMP older sister VOC

     Ø-   kaye   hatï,   tï- notxhïrï   wya,   xofrye
     3S3O-say+DP HSY   3REFLX-sister to   sloth
     "Don't go, older sister, " said the sloth to his sister.

60-61. ïtohra   exko   omoro, nyamoro   marma
       go+NEG be+IMP you   3PRO+COLL only

Ø- totxowi,   Ø-   kekonï hatï,   xofrye
3S-go+COLL+IP   3S3O-say+DP HSY   sloth
"Don't you go, just let them go," said the sloth.

62.   Ø-   totxownï   hatï   tïtotïhkaxero
3S-go+COLL+DP HSY   go+COMPL+ADVBLZR
They all went, the whole lot of them.

63.   tkatxehkaxero   Ø-   totxownï
do+COMPL+ADVBLZR   3S-go+COLL+DP
They went, all of them.

64.   ïyarhïra   n-   ehxakonï   nïmno
empty   3S-be+DP   maloca
The maloca (village house) was empty.

65.   nyamoro   marma   n-   oknomtxownï
3PRO+COLL   only   3S-REFLX+leave+COLL+DP

asako   marma
two   only
Only they were left, only the two of them.

66.   ïsna   n-   ehtxownï   ha,   e-hokoso
to there 3S-be+COLL+DP   INTENSFR 3-at edge of
They were there, at the edge of (the river).

67.   aaa,   onokna rma   kana   heno   y-ehtoko   hatï
SURPRISE creature CONT fish   QUANT 3-be+when   HSY
Sound expressing surprise, (at) their being so many fish.

68.   say say say say say say   Ø-   katxownï   ha,
gathering up (IDEO)   3S3O-do+COLL+DP INTENSFR

kurum- yana   komo
vulture-kin group   COLL
The vulture people gathered up the (fish).

69-70. taa,   k-   wehetorï   komo arymatxoko,
       THEME CHANGE 1INCL-fire   COLL throw+COLL+IMP

Ø-   kekonï   hatï, Ø-   ketxkonï   hatï,
3S3O-say+DP   HSY 3S3O-say+COLL+DP HSY

kurum- yana   komo,   k-   wehetorï   komo
vulture-kin group   COLL   1INCL-fire   COLL

arymatxok   ha
throw+COLL+IMP   INTENSFR
"Everybody make a fire for us," he said, said the vulture people.
"Everybody make a fire for us."

71. hï,   Ø-   ketxkonï
    RESP 3S3O-say+COLL+DP
    "O.K.," they said.

72. weryeko   hoko   n- ehxatxkonï
    fire stick   occupied with 3S-be+COLL+DP
    They worked on the fire stick.

73. weryeko   y-   arymetxkonï,   xïk xïk xïk xïk xïk xïk
    fire stick   3S3O-throw+COLL+DP rubbing fire stick (IDEO)

    xïk xïk xïk xïk xïk xïk
    They were rubbing the fire stick between their hands.

74. atahohsïra   mak   n- ehxakonï
    REFLX+catch+NEG   ADVERS   3S-be+DP
    But it was not catching alight.

75. ehurkahra   mah   tï   n- ehxakonï,
    fall+NEG   ADVERS   HSY   3S-be+DP

    wereko   ha
    fire stick   INTENSFR
    The fire stick just wasn't falling as it should have done.

76. duk,   n-   ahutxownï   hatï,   xofrye
    shutting in (IDEO) 3S3O-shut in+COLL+DP   HSY   sloth
    The sloth shut them all in.

77. tohu   ymo ke   n-   ahutxownï,   duk
    stone AUG INSTR 3S3O-shut in+COLL+DP   shutting in (IDEO)
    With a huge stone he shut them in.

78. taa,   omohtxok   ha,
    THEME CHANGE come+COLL+IMP INTENSFR
    Ø-   ketxkonï   hatï
    3S3O-say+COLL+DP   HSY
    "Everybody come," they said.

79. ïto   xak   t-   onyetxowï
    there DISADVAN 1INCL.S3O-eat+COLL+NONPAST

    hamï,   owto ho, Ø-   ketxkonï   hatï
    DEDUCT   village at   3S3O-say+COLL+DP   HSY
    "We will have to eat them there, at the village, " they said.

80. n- omohtxownï   hatï, sïh sïh sïh sïh sïh sïh sïh sïh
    3S-come+COLL+DP HSY   walking (IDEO)
    They came.

81. ïto   tohu ymo   y-ehtoko   hatï, poo
    there stone AUG   3-be+when   HSY   DISMAY
    When (they came to where) the big stone was, (they expressed
    their) dismay.

82. eten na   rma   haxa   mak
     what UNCERT CONT   CONTR   COUNTEREXPECT

     hatï, ïhï   ymo haryhe   tï,   tohu ymo
     HSY mountain AUG FRUSTR HSY stone AUG

     haxa   hama   rhye   tï
     CONTR ABNORMAL EMPH   HSY
     What a huge thing (it was), bigger than anything (they had seen
     or could imagine), (like) a great mountain, a stone of abnormal
     size.

83. eten onï ha   Ø-   ketxkonï
     what this INTENSFR 3S3O-say+COLL+DP
     "What (is) this?," they said.

84. k-   ahutxowï
     3S1INCL.0-shut in +COLL+IP

     hamï,   xofrye,   Ø-   ketxkonï   hatï
     DEDUCT sloth   3S3O-say+COLL+DP HSY
     "The sloth must evidently have shut us in," they said.

85. ïto   n- ehxatxkonï
     there 3S-be+COLL+DP
     There they were.

86. n-   awnukyatxkonï   hatï
     3S3O-climb+COLL+DP HSY
     They were climbing it.

87. n-   awnuhtxownï   hatï, sayk sayk sayk sayk sayk sayk
     3S3O-climb+COLL+DP HSY climbing (IDEO)
     They climbed it.

88. pow,   owto   hona   ha,
    descending (IDEO) village to   INTENSFR

    ï- yarïhnaka   mak   hatï
    3-in absence of COUNTEREXPECT HSY
    (They) descended to the village, (arriving) when (the sloth)
    was away.

89. xofrye   mah   tï   ehxera   n- ehxakonï
    sloth   COUNTEREXPECT HSY be+NEG 3S-be+DP
    The sloth was not (there).

90. t-   katxhothïyamo   hatï y-   arymatxownï
    3REFLX-goods+PAST+COLL   HSY 3S3O-throw+COLL+DP

    ha,   txow,   fuhtxow
    INTENSFR throwing (IDEO)   falling to ground (IDEO)
    They threw down to the ground their things (i.e. the carrier-
    baskets containing the fish).

91. ïto   kana   heno   n- ehxakonï ha
    there fish   QUANT 3S-be+DP   INTENSFR
    There the fish was.

92. peryem peryem peryem perye   weryewerye
    buzzing of flies   (IDEO)   fly

    heno,   ï-hoko,   n- ehxatxkonï
    QUANT   3-occupied with   3S-be+COLL+DP
    Flies were buzzing around, occupied with it.

93. ehxera   mah   tï   n- ehxakonï
    be+NEG COUNTEREXPECT HSY 3s-be+DP

    ha,   weheto hatï
    INTENSFR   fire   HSY
    But there was no fire.

94.   ehxera   n-aha   ha,
      be+NEG   3S-be+NONPAST   INTENSFR

      Ø-   ketxkonï   hatï,   kurum- yana   komo
      3S3O-say+COLL+DP   HSY   vulture-kin group   COLL
      "There isn't any," said the vulture people.

95-96. ïsoke t-   eryatxowï,   t-
       how   1INCL.S3O-fix+COLL+NONPAST   1INCL.S3O-

      enahtxe   hama,   onï wyaro rma   xako,
      eat+COLL+IMP   ABNORMAL   this like   CONT DISADVAN

      Ø-   katxownï   hatï
      3S3O-say+COLL+DP   HSY
      "How shall we fix it? We shall have to eat it just like it is
      (uncooked), " they said.

97.   dom dom dom dom   oskeno   rma   y-   onahtxownï
      eating (IDEO)   thus+NOMLZN   CONT 3S3O-eat+COLL+DP
      They ate it just like that.

98.   tkokemï   rma   tï   y-   onahyatxkonï
      rotten+NOMLZN   CONT   HSY   3S3O-eat+COLL+DP

      ha,   kurum- yana   ha
      INTENSFR   vulture-kin group   INTENSFR
      The vulture people were eating the thing that had already gone
      bad.

99.   oske n- atakïhtotxownï
      thus 3S-REFLX+create+COLL+DP
      Thus they were created.

100. kurumu   me   xah   tï   ø- totxownï
     vulture   DENOMLZR   DISADVAN   HSY 3S-go+COLL+DP

     ha
     INTENSFR
     They went in the form of vultures (i.e., king vulture).

101. bo fofo   ø-   katxownï   hatï
     wing-flapping (IDEO) 3S3O-do+COLL+DP HSY
     They flapped their wings.

102. too   kunto kunto kunto   ø-   katxownï   hatï
     wing action in flight (IDEO) 3S3O-do+COLL+DP HSY

     mak   hatï
     COUNTEREXPECT HSY
     They flew away.

103. ïsok make   xak   mah   tï
     in every direction DISADVAN   COUNTEREXPECT HSY

     ø- totxownï   ha
     3S-go+COLL+DP INTENSFR
     They went off in all directions.

104. n- osomtatkatxownï   xako
     3S-disappear+COLL+DP   DISADVAN
     They disappeared (or, ceased to exist as people).

105. kurum me   harha   mah   tï
     vulture DENOMLZR CHANGE STATE COUNTEREXPECT HSY

     ø- totxownï   ha
     3S-go+COLL+DP INTENSFR
     They now went in the form of the king vulture.

106. toto   me   n- ehxakonï amnyehra haka, kurumu
     human DENOMLZR 3S-be+DP   in the past then   king vulture
     At that time in the past the king vulture was a human being.

107. henta ha   ø-   ketxkonï   hatï
     where INTENSFR 3S3O-say+COLL+DP HSY
     "Where?" they said.

108. henta k-   wahathïrï   ha,   xofrye   tho
     where 1INCL-murderer+PAST INTENSFR sloth   DEVLD

     xa   n- aye,   henta, ø-   ketxkonï   hatï
     CONTR 3S-be+NONPAST where 3S3O-say+COLL+DP HSY
     "Where is the sloth, the one who murdered us, where?" they
     said.

109. wee   ø-   kekonï hatï,   xofrye
     SOUND (made by a sloth) 3S3O-say+DP HSY   sloth
     The sloth was saying "wee."

110. ehutwahra   n- ehxakonï
     REFLX+know+NEG 3S-be+DP
     He was (doing it) unconsciously.

111. ehutwahra   tï   oske n-   kekonï
     REFLX+know+NEG HSY thus 3S3O-say+DP
     He was doing/saying it like that unconsciously.

112. wee ø-   kekonï   hatï
          3S3O-say+DP   HSY
     He was saying "wee."

113. henta xak   oske n-   keno,
     where DISADVAN thus 3S3O-say+NONPAST

ø-   ketxkonï   hatï
3S3O-say+COLL+DP   HSY
"Where is he saying it like that?" they said

114. henta oske n-   keno,   xofrye tho   xako,
     where thus 3S3O-say+NONPAST sloth   DEVLD DISADVAN

k-   anïhnohnyenhïyamo   tho,
1INCL-destroy+NOMLZR+PAST+COLL DEVLD

ø-   ketxkonï   hatï
3S3O-say+COLL+DP   HSY
"Where is he saying it like that, that sloth who has destroyed
us?" they said.

115. ï-notxhïrï   xarha, wayamo   me   mak
     3-sister   also   land turtle DENOMLZR COUNTEREXPECT

harha   tï,   wayamo me   tï   n- exeye
CHANGE STATE HSY turtle   DENOMLZR HSY 3S-be+DP

noro   ha
3PRO INTENSFR
His sister also, she had now become a land turtle.

116. wayamo   me   n- atakïhtoye   ha
     turtle   DENOMLZR 3S-REFLX+create+DP INTENSFR
     She was created in the form of a turtle.

117. noro   tho   tï   ïrwomra   n- ehxakonï
     3PRO DEVLD HSY talk+NEG 3S-be+DP
     She was not talking.

118. ïrwomra   n- ehxakonï
     talk+NEG 3S-be+DP
     She was not talking.

119-20. osonyhera   w- ehxano,   ø-   kekonï hatï,
REFLX+see+NEG 1S-be+NONPAST 3S3O-say+DP HSY

t-   eheka wya, osonyhera   w- ehxano
3REFLX- brother to   REFLX+see+NEG 1S-be+NONPAST
"Am I not able to be seen?" she said to her brother. "Am I not
able to be seen?"

121. ïhï,   osonyhera   m- anaha,   ø-   kekonï
RESP REFLX+see+NEG 2S-be+NONPAST 3S3O-say+DP

hatï ø-eheka
HSY 3-brother
"Yes, you are not able to be seen," said her brother.

122. uro, uro xarha, osonyhera   w- ehxano,
    I   I   also   REFLX+see+NEG 1S-be+NONPAST

ø-   kekonï hatï, xofrye, tï-   notxhïrï wya
3S3O-say+DP HSY   sloth   3REFLX-sister   to
"And I also, am I not able to be seen?" said the sloth to his
sister.

123. m?m,   osonyhera   m- anaha,   ø-   kekonï hatï
RESP REFLX+see+NEG 2S-be+NONPAST 3S3O-say+DP HSY
"Yes, you are not able to be seen," she said.

124. noro   tho   tï   ïrwomra   n- ehxakonï
3PRO DEVLD HSY talk+NEG 3S-be+DP
She was not able to talk.

125. ïsoke xah   tï   n- ïrwonakonï
how DISADVAN HSY 3S-talk+DP
Then how was she talking?

126. n- ewnatxhunakonï   xah   tï
     3S-blow through nose+DP DISADVAN HSY
     She was blowing through her nose.

127. xwoo, xwoo   ø-   kekonï hatï
     blowing through nose (IDEO) 3S3O-do+DP HSY
     She was blowing through her nose.

128. ehutwahra   tï   oske n-   kekonï
     REFLX+know+NEG HSY thus 3S3O-do+DP
     She was doing it like that unconsciously.

129. fss   ø-   kekonï tï   wayamo
     SOUND (made by a turtle) 3S3O-say+DP HSY   turtle
     The turtle was saying "fss."

130. ehutwahra   oske ï-   keno,
     REFLX+know+NEG thus 1S3O-say+NONPAST

     ø-   kekonï hatï
     3S3O-say+DP HSY
     "Am I saying it like that without knowing it?" she said.

131. ehutwahra   oske mï-   kehe,
     REFLX+know+NEG thus 2S3O-say+NONPAST

     ø- kekonï   hatï   ø- eheka
     3S3O-say+DP HSY   3-brother
     "You are saying it like that without knowing it," said her
     brother.

132. oske tï   n- otkukmetxkonï,   ï- yarïhnawo,
     thus HSY 3S-RECIP+try out+COLL+DP   3-in absence of

     omokhïra   haka ø-ehtokonye   haka, kurum- yana
     come+NEG   then 3-be+when+COLL   then   vulture- kin group

komo   y-omokïhtotoko   haka
COLL   3-come+NEG+when   then
Thus they were practicing on each other in their absence, during
the time when the vulture people still had not returned.

133. oske n- exeye hatï,   nyamoro
     thus 3S-be+DP HSY   3+COLL+PRO
     That is how they were.

134. tï-   notxhïrï   rma   y-akoro n- exeye, oske
     3REFLX-sister   CONT 3-with   3S-be+DP thus
     He was with his sister just like that.

Notes

1. The key to abbreviations used throughout this paper is as follows:

ADVBLZR	adverbializer
ADVERS	adversative
AUG	augmentative
CAUS	causativizer
COLL	collective
COMPL	completive
CONT	continuative
CONTR	contrast
COUNTEREXPECT	counterexpectancy
DEDUCT	deduction
DENOMLZR	denominalizer
DESID	desiderative
DEVLD	devalued
DISADVAN	disadvantaged
DP	distant past
EMPH	emphasis
EXCLUS	exclusive
FRUSTR	frustrative
HSY	hearsay
IDEO	ideophone

IMP	imperative
INCL	inclusive
INSTR	instrument
INTENSFR	intensifier
IP	immediate past
MOT	motion
NEG	negative
NOMLZN	nominalization
NOMLZR	nominalizer
O/OBJ	object
PRO	pronoun
PURP	purpose
QUANT	quantity
RECIP	reciprocal
REFLX	reflexive
RESP	response
S	subject
UNCERT	uncertainty
VOC	vocative
1	first person
2	second person
3	third person

2.   The particular texts on which this study is based are all of the traditional myth genre, but my long observation of other genres, such as personal experiences, written letters, and input of native speakers into the translation of materials into their language, makes me confident that these conclusions more generally reflect all discourse genres in which there is reference to third person participants.

References

Derbyshire, Desmond C.
1965   *Textos Hixkaryana*. Belém: Museu Paraense Emílio Goeldi.
1977a   Discourse redundancy in Hixkaryana. *International Journal of American Linguistics* 43: 176-88.

1977b   Word order universals and the existence of OVS languages. *Linguistic Inquiry* 8: 590-99.

1979a   *Hixkaryana.* Lingua Descriptive Studies 1. Amsterdam: North-Holland.

1979b   Hixkaryana syntax. Ph.D. thesis, University of London. (To appear as: *Hixkaryana and linguistic typology.* Dallas: Summer Institute of Linguistics and University of Texas at Arlington (1985)).

1981   A diachronic explanation for the origin of OVS in some Carib languages. *Journal of Linguistics* 17: 209-20.

Derbyshire, Desmond C. and Geoffrey K. Pullum

1981   Object-initial languages. *International Journal of American Linguistics* 47: 192-214.

Fox, Andrew

1983   Topic continuity in Biblical Hebrew narrative. In *Topic continuity in discourse: a quantitative cross-language study*, T. Givón (ed.), pp. 215-254. Amsterdam: John Benjamins Publishing Company.

Gasser, Michael

1983   Topic continuity in written Amharic narrative. In *Topic continuity in discourse: a quantitative cross-language study*, T. Givón (ed.), pp. 95-139. Amsterdam: John Benjamins Publishing Company.

Givón, Talmy

1983a   Topic continuity in discourse: An introduction. In *Topic continuity in discourse: a quantitative cross-language study*, T. Givón (ed.), pp. 1-41. Amsterdam: John Benjamins Publishing Company.

1983b   Topic continuity and word-order pragmatics in Ute. In *Topic continuity in discourse: a quantitative cross-language study*, T. Givón (ed.), pp. 141-214. Amsterdam: John Benjamins Publishing Company.

1983c   Topic continuity in spoken English. In *Topic continuity in discourse: a quantitative cross-language study*, T. Givón (ed.), pp. 343-363. Amsterdam: John Benjamins Publishing Company.

1984   *Syntax: a functional-typological introduction*, Vol. I. Amsterdam: John Benjamins Publishing Company.

Givón, Talmy, ed.
1983   *Topic continuity in discourse: a quantitative cross-language study.* Amsterdam: John Benjamins Publishing Company.

Grimes, Joseph E.
1975   *The thread of discourse.* The Hague: Mouton.

Hinds, John
1983   Topic continuity in Japanese. In *Topic continuity in discourse: a quantitative cross-language study,* T. Givón (ed.), pp. 43-93. Amsterdam: John Benjamins Publishing Company.

Hyman, Larry M.
1975   On the change from SOV to SVO: evidence from Niger-Congo. In *Word order and word order change,* C. N. Li (ed.), pp. 113-148. Austin: University of Texas Press.

Payne, Doris.
1986   Basic constituent order in Yagua clauses: implications for word order universals. In *Handbook of Amazonian languages,* Vol. 1, D. C. Derbyshire and G. K. Pullum (eds.). Berlin: Mouton.

The Decline of Dialogue: Ceremonial and Mythological Discourse among the Shuar and Achuar

Maurizio Gnerre

In this paper I will focus on two forms of discourse found among the Shuar and the Achuar (Jivaroan) of the Upper Amazon. These are the ceremonial visiting dialogue and the narrative discourse dialogue with mythological content. Both of these forms of verbal interaction are highly salient for native speakers, who are conscious of them as distinctive types of language use.

Ceremonial conversations, both the visiting dialogue on which I will focus and the war party ritual dialogue, were and still are perceived as special speech forms. They were once known to Shuar men and are sometimes still used by Achuar men, who volunteer to "reproduce" them as a significant example of their speaking abilities. Some simplified forms of dialogue are occasionally taught in Shuar bilingual and bicultural schools as a facet of the traditional way of life that boys are supposed to master.

If these forms of ceremonial dialogue reach the level of consciousness of speakers because of their special formal features, mainly prosodic and rhythmic, the narrative with mythological content reaches the consciousness of speakers because of its content, perceived as a set of stories characteristic of traditional Shuar and Achuar beliefs and way of life. Significant changes have taken place both with regard to ceremonial conversation, which has almost disappeared among the Shuar, and with regard to mythological narrative, which, at least in some social settings, has undergone a general switch from direct discourse to a widely used quotative form. In this paper, these changes are viewed as factors in the development of native speaker consciousness of ceremonial dialogue.

My main focus will be on Shuar forms of verbal interaction. Achuar data on ceremonial visiting dialogues will be used, since these are the closest possible example of the ceremonial conversations which are no longer available for observation and recording among the Shuar.

Traditionally, all Jivaroan groups lived in isolated houses in the forest, situated several hours from one another by travel on foot. Two or three nuclear families lived in a house. During the last two decades the Shuar and the Aguarana groups, which were most subject to the influence of missionaries and contact with Ecuadorian and Peruvian settlers, have to some degree abandoned their traditional settlement pattern and now live in single-family houses located close to one another, although these are at times brought together into a village. More recently, similar changes are taking place among the Achuar and the Huambiza groups of the Jivaroan language family.

Since 1964, the Shuar, one of the largest groups in the Amazon basin, have been organized into a Federation with an economic and educational program. Literacy and schooling in the Shuar language have triggered a process of language standardization. With socio-economic changes, and the changes in settlement patterns, major transformations have come about in Shuar ways of interpersonal communication and language use.

As Shuar schools, at both the primary and   secondary levels, are bilingual and bicultural, and as biculturalism is obviously most difficult to pursue in a context of massive cultural change in the direction of western-mestizo patterns of life, the emphasis in new Shuar consciousness is on the Shuar language as the main extant diacritic of ethnic identity. The leaders of the Shuar Federation stress their language as an effective instrument for communicating both traditional and modern content, and tend to use it to demonstrate to themselves and to the whole group that their culture is truly alive. Obviously, however, the new cultural content and functions of verbal interaction, related to economic and overall social change, bring about new forms of verbal interaction, new forms of discourse, which imply some kind of training outside the traditional settings of language use and cultural reproduction.

For every man from a Jivaroan group, it generally was, and still is, very important to visit other men in order to carry out commercial exchanges and to maintain or create alliances, or to obtain information concerning other potentially hostile groups. During contacts among men from different houses, and at times among men from the same house, the use of language is of decisive importance. Among the Shuar, when a man occupies a position of low prestige, the form used to express the low esteem in which he is held is *chichatsui*,[1] "doesn't talk," which is to say he doesn't know how to use language (*chicham*). Traditionally, the Shuar, as well as other Jivaroan peoples, had almost exclusively one-to-one verbal interactions, as an early writer, Vacas Galindo (1895: 84) pointed out a century ago. Such a dialogic orientation is encoded even in Shuar morph-syntax, where we find a special status accorded the addressee-referent.

With the changes in settlement patterns, the practice of public speaking has become common in settings such as village meetings, schools, or general political assembly. Furthermore, since 1967, the Shuar Federation has operated a broadcasting station. Besides its educational functions, the station is used several hours a day to broadcast messages to the villages in the backcountry. Many Shuar men and women speak daily into the radio microphones to send messages to their relatives. Obviously, communication by radio establishes a new perception of language. Face-to-face interaction is eliminated and every single speech, even a speech of an unknown person, can be heard by thousands of Shuar in the whole Shuar country.

With all these changes and with the drastic reduction of feuds and war, the intense visiting activities described in the literature (Harner 1972: 105-111, 125-132) are either reduced or restructured into new forms of visiting. Shuar culture, as described during the last hundred years, included, as an outstanding feature, a set of speech events which were basically ceremonial conversations and greetings related to feuding and visiting. These were explicitly identified both by the Shuar themselves and by non-Shuar observers. These speech events have undergone many complex changes in different Shuar groups, as well as in other non-Shuar Jivaroan groups, in the short span of time for which we have evidence. One linguistic consequence of the new socio-economic conditions is that in the last twenty years these speech events have almost completely disappeared from Shuar socio-cultural behavior.

Two often cited speech events were (1) a ceremonial dialogue performed during visits and (2) a ceremonial dialogue performed at the beginning of a war party. Both of them were one-to-one interactions between visitor and host. These speech events have both been described by Vacas Galindo (1895: 79-80 and 82), Karsten (1935: 245-246, 248-249,

283-287), and Stirling (1938: 97-98), among others . Stirling describes the visiting conversation as follows:

> At about 3 o'clock in the afternoon, or 24 hours after our arrival, Caneros pulled his seat in front of Ambusha and began a vigorous ceremonial conversation, very loud, and delivered in a sort of syncopated rhythm, beating time with his feet and gesturing with his arms, while Ambush replied in similar vein, each of them punctuating the talk with ejaculations of "Casa," "Casa," (So that's it!), "Ho," "Ha," (Good! Fine!), "Tsa," "Tsa," "Tsa," (No, no, no!), "Tcah," Tcah," (I don't know) (Stirling 1938:97).[2]

In the most recent monograph on the Shuar, by Harner (1972), only one of these two speech events, the war party dialogue, is described:

> all members of the war party, normally numbering about thirty or forty, arrive at the house of the *wea*.[3] As each enters the house, he engages in a ritualistic shouting chant (*enemartin*)[4] with the *wea*. During the chanting each man stamps back and forth in turn, thrusting his shotgun in rhythm as though threatening the other speaker. This chant, which primarily focuses on establishing the identity and demonstrating the supernatural power of the speakers, is also used when complete strangers happen to encounter one another on a trail (Harner 1972:184).

Harner does not mention the visiting ceremonial dialogue. I would assume that it was already in decay in 1956-57 among the groups he visited. Some ceremonial features can still be observed in present-day visiting, even if young men tend to move towards a kind of informality that they perceive in the mestizo and white settler's behavior under similar circumstances. However, in myth telling even today, the pattern of formality associated with visiting activity is sometimes stressed. As an example of this I translate a segment of a narrative recorded by Pellizzaro in 1978 in which we are told of a young Shuar man visiting the old Tsunki, a supernatural being living in a special environment deep in the water:

The aged Tsunki, who had the appearance of being a good man, watched him, sitting on his throne as a man of worth. Indeed, how do we elderly Shuar usually behave? Is it not usual for us to remain seated before the visitors to our house? And when a visitor approaches, do we not usually ask: "Who is that man approaching?" It is precisely in this manner that Tsunki carefully observed the man who approached his house. The latter, after having called at the door saying "I am coming," entered and sat down (Pellizzaro 1979:27-28).

Ceremonial conversations traditionally represented perhaps the most important abilities of male speakers and were central activities in social life. Although some varieties of traditional ceremonial conversations are still in use on some occasions among the Shuar, and in some cases war party and visiting dialogues are represented as "folklore" or taught in a classroom setting, it is clear that a basic displacement has taken place with regard to the social relevance of these conversations. Until recently, they represented one of the most formal uses of the language. Achuar, and even present-day Shuar, still perceive these conversations as something worth being heard and seen by non-Jivaroan visitors, who very likely will be able to appreciate them as an outstanding example of speech ability.   A missionary, Father Luis Bolla (Yankuma'), who has lived in the Achuar country for many years and who speaks the Achuar language very fluently, some years ago prepared himself to perform a ceremonial dialogue on special occasions. Some Achuar men appreciated his ability, although others had the feeling that he was learning too much of their traditions and knowledge.

What follows is an exposition of personal observations concerning a type of ceremonial dialogue still in use among the Achuar.[5] During three field trips among Achuar groups, I recorded many examples of ceremonial dialogues.[6] Furthermore, I carried out some interviews with Achuar men, focusing on their competence in the use of language and on the social importance they attributed to such competence. The verbal event I describe here was relatively common ten years ago among the Achuar living in Ecuador. In order to describe this event, it is necessary to consider the entire social act of the visit.   Through the observation of many cases of ceremonial visiting and from the interviews , it was found that many non-linguistic aspects of the visit are significant and that they form a continuum with the central verbal act, the visiting ceremonial dialogue. The fundamental components of this continuum are : (1) the distribution of silence and speech; (2) body position and the direction of looking; (3) the rhythm and prosody of the dialogue; (4) the quantity and quality of information communicated.

A visit begins with an (acoustic) announcement by the visitor, which is frequently repeated some twelve hours later, before dawn on the following day. The visit may last until later in the day or through subsequent days. Usually the information the visitor wishes to acquire or communicate is exchanged almost at the end of this sequence. There is thus a total event - including linguistic and non-linguistic behavior - which must take place in order for the visit to achieve the goal that the visitor originally intended. The ceremonial dialogue can occupy a relatively brief period of time, from 10 to 40-50 minutes. Yet, there is no doubt that this dialogue is of central importance, and some interviews indicated that its performance is indeed the part of the visit which is the object of most concern on the part of youth who undertake visits to other houses for the first time. Without knowing how to perform this verbal act, a youth can not make visits. Children play at trying to express fragments of ceremonial conversations. Adolescents follow their fathers in their visits and listen in silence. A youth may be sent by his father to make a formal visit, and so will be obliged to engage in a ceremonial dialogue with the head of the house he visits.

The duration of the dialogue, as already noted, is variable. It seems to vary in relation to both spatial distance (visitor's place of origin) and social distance (solidarity and kinship). As the performance of the ceremonial dialogue has the overall function of lessening potential social tension existing between the interlocutors, its duration is variable but not arbitrary. The rhythm and the prosody as well as the formulaic organization and the rather archaic type of language used all make the mastery of this dialogic discourse the most demanding part of the communicative continuum of the visit.

When an Achuar man goes to visit another house, he arrives in its vicinity between three in the afternoon and sunset. After three o'clock, the men return from hunting or other activities in the forest. If the visitor arrives earlier in the vicinity of the house he intends to visit, he can wait nearby in the forest for a suitable hour to begin the visit. He prepares for the visit in the forest by painting his face red with achiote (*Bixa orellana*), donning a crown of yellow and red toucan feathers, and putting on his best clothing. When he is ready and feels that the time is appropriate for the start, he gives the acoustic signal of his arrival, blowing into a shell or into the barrel of his rifle.

At that moment, the visitor's interaction with the residents of the house begins. The latter immediately change all their activities and their relations. The men, women, and children do not speak any longer, nor do they laugh. Children interrupt their playing. A period of tension and silence begins. The only noise is the barking of dogs. The visitor (V), after having given the acoustic signal of his arrival, approaches the house with a decisive and proud bearing, with his rifle or spear in a slightly oblique horizontal position. When he reaches the limit of the house, which consists of a large oval roof supported by poles, without walls, he stands there firmly waiting for the children to bring him a wooden stool which is placed exactly under the limit of the roof. Part of the house, more than half, is reserved for women, for children, for the preparation of food, and for sleeping. The other part, called *tankámash'*, is reserved for normal and ceremonial conversations between the men of the house, and between them and visitors, who also sleep there. The place of the head man (H) of the house is on the boundary between the *tankámash'* and the rest of the house. The distribution of the stools, bed, and jars of fermented drink in an Achuar house is represented in Figure 1.

When the stool has been placed on the perimeter, the visitor sits down and places his rifle or spear across his knees in an oblique horizontal position. H sits at this place and with exaggerated slowness begins to paint his face. He dons the crown of toucan feathers and the other ornaments he possesses. V waits in silence as H prepares himself. After a long period of silence H addresses V. The direction of the look, especially for V, is important. To look one's interlocutor in the face means to behave as a strong man. Some youths have told me that during their first ceremonial visits they keep their eyes downwards. In such cases it is possible for H to exempt his young visitor from performing the ceremonial dialogue. Even older men and famous warriors have told me that if they receive a visit from a youth who does not raise his eyes, they avoid engaging him in a ceremonial dialogue. Some have said that in such circumstances they may begin the dialogue but that they try to terminate it at once if they find that V is in difficulty. In this case V ends up with no prestige and can be derided not only by the men but also by the women of the house. All of this shows that in Achuar visiting set eye contact signals negotiation of relative position. In less formal talk, both Achuar and Shuar men, at the beginning and at the end of a visit, carefully avoid eye contact, to a degree that western observers often find quite remarkable.

The first sentence H utters is *winyámek* ("did you come?"), preceded by the address form he finds appropriate to use with V : *saér* ("my brother-in-law"), *yatsúr* ("my brother"), or, if V is more distant in terms of social relations, *amíkur* ("my friend").[7] Kin terms are always used in a broad sense. The personal name of the interlocutor is never used in verbal interactions of this type. Knowing how to use one's voice and having a strong voice are considered important qualities.

The distance between the two is typically ten meters or less. If two or more men live in the house, a ceremonial dialogue between the second man of the house and the second visitor may begin while the dialogue between H and V is going on. In this case one generally finds conversations between interlocutors seated in crossed positions in relation to the side of the house.

It seems that physical distance between interlocutors is privileged, at least for the first ceremonial dialogue, in the event that two or more take place simultaneously. Men maintain a physical distance which is overcome only several hours after the start of the visit. The visitors, after their arrival, are approached only by children and by women. During the entire conversation H and V keep one hand on their mouths, or are occupied with a cup of fermented manioc drink which women start to serve after the dialogue begins. During the conversation, the men sip the fermented drink and spit on the ground between one sentence and another, or between one reply and another. The speakers thus punctuate their discourse with projectiles of saliva ejected through two fingers placed in a vertical postion over the lips.

Immediately after the initial phrase pronounced by H, V also begins to speak. The two thus speak together without bothering to listen to their interlocutors. After a few moments H begins his rapid and rhythmic

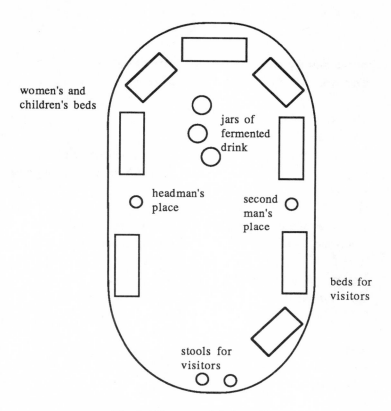

Fig. 1: Diagram of Achuar House

speech. What follows is a ceremonial visiting conversation volunteered by
two Achuar men, Nayásh and Chiriáp, in the house of the first, settled on
the upper Setuchi river, on September 22, 1974:[8]

	Nayásh	Chiriáp
1	Yatsúru winyámek	
	my brother did you come?	
1a		jm
2	tse warí ántsarik	
	even what without doing anything	

pujákrisha
we stay too

2a   jai

3   tse warí jiímkyachu   ántsarik pujákrisha aushá
    even what without visiting   without doing anything we stay
                                            too

    kétkursha
    stays at home

4   warí jiímtsuk keémtaka   jiímkyachu kétkursha
    what without visiting staying   without visiting stays at home
    keémtainkya
    at home staying at home

5   ya warí áush tímya juyá   kémtaka kémtainkya aushá
    who what   like this   staying at home staying at
                                            home

6   yá tímya júsh tímya jauyá   warí jiímtsuka
    who like this like this   what without visiting
                                            ekémtainkyaitya
                                            staying at home

7   warí ekétsuk áusha yá   tú tukin wekájai
    what without staying at   so saying I go
    home who

7a   jai

8   warí áush jiímkyachu
    what   without visiting

8a   chua

9   warí jiímkyachu keemtá
    what without visiting staying

9a   jm

10 warí tú tukímtsukuk áusha ya
    what so saying this   who

10a   nekása
                                            true

11 tú tukímtsuk wekátash
    so saying so you go also
    wekámtiya
    going

11a		jm
12	warí aéntsarik kétkurish	
	what without anything stays	
	áusha ya	
	at home who	
12a		jai
13	ya káme áush jiímkyachu	
	who this without visiting	
	(who can stay without visiting)	
13a		chua
14	warí jiímkyachu keemtá	
	what without visiting staying	
14a		nekása
		true
15	warí tú tukin áusha yá	
	what so saying this who	
15a		jm
16	wekátash wekámtaiyá	
	you go going	
16a		chua
17	tú tukin áusha yá	
	so saying who	
17a		jm
18	wekátash wekámtai	
	you go also going	
	wekámtai wekámtaya	
	going going	
19		warí áush áusha yá
		what who
19a	jai	
20		warí tímyaju áusha yá
		what that much who
20a	jentá	
21		warí tímyaush aushá
		what that much
21a	jm jm	

22   warí túmashtainkyá
     what it is done this way

23   warí ántsar pujákrisha
     what this way staying
24   jiímkachuka kémtainkya
     without visiting staying at
     home

25   warí kémtaka kémtainkya
     what staying staying
26   warí tú tútukimtsuk wekátash
     what so so saying this you go
     wekamtaiya
     going
27

27a ja jai
28

28a maa
29

29a jm
30

30   jai
31

31a ja warí tumashtainkyá
     what it is done this way

warí ántsar kétkurish áusha
what this way we stay at home
ya
who
warí jinískeka kémtainkyá
what without visiting staying
warí tímyaju tsúru
what that much my

áusha ya
brother who
yá kémtaka áusha
who staying
 warí tímyajuka
what that much staying
kémtainkya
at home
tú tútukimtsuk áusha yá
so so saying   who

wekátanash wekájaiya
going   I go

warí tímyaju tsúru aushá
what that much my brother

nuíkya nuíkya tsúru aushá
before before my brother

júnik pujákminkya
without anything if you stay
tsúru aushá
my brother

32   káme ántsarik kétkursha   ya wayásan tsúru aushá
       this way staying at home   who I am entering the
                                             house my brother

       jiímtsuka keemtá
       without visiting you have to stay

33   irásmin ayátkun tútunish   warí jínyantá wísha
       visiting begin able around   what without seeing I
       wekékini   kináchkun
       there going   also am leaving

34   wayása jiímkyachu   já wéakun jiímtsuk
       entering the house without   sick I am going without
       ekét wéajai   pujú wéajai
       visiting the house staying I go   visiting staying I go

35   ja warí ántsar kétkursha   warí warí tímya áusha yá
       sick what this way staying   what what said   who

36   jiímkyachu kémtainkya   warí tímya tsúru áusha yá
       without visiting staying   what said my brother who

37   yatsúta tímyaujainkiá   warí trúakun tsúru áusha yá
       between brothers with such   what I am doing so my
                                             brother who

       inyáischamuka awítya
       without seeing it should not be
       (how is it possible for brothers
       to live without visiting?)

38   warí ekéttutikyá aushá   ekéttutikya áusha tá
       what I stay in my house   I stay in my house

39   wajaté wajaté wajaténkyaityá   warí ekéttutikya aushá
       stop and wait stop and wait   what I stay in my house

40   warí túra wekátsumeash   warí imyá
       what so doing you come to visit   what that
                                           (u)ntsuríchuka aushá
                                           much many

41   warí tímyajush áawitya
                                what that much has to see

41a   jm jm

42		tú tútukin yatsúru so saying this my tímyaju aushá brother that much
42a	jm	
43		yá yamáya juí se aushá who now here
43a	jai	
44		twí twí tukí áusha yá where where I am saying
44a	jm	
45		ya aé akunchá who this way áusha ya although he stays
45a	chua	
46		ma aé akunchá áusha this way although he stays
46a	jentá	
47		wainyásan jínanta (u)kúakun entering seeing leaving (going back without seeing)
47a	jentá	
48		yá túrusan tímyaju satá who the same like this you stay
48a	jm jm	
49		wi túnantaku tsúru aushá I saying this way my brother
49a	jae	
50		yá tsúrnash ukumajá who saying I left
50a	jentá	
51		tú tútnyaku tsurú áusha yá so saying my brother who
51a	jm	

52   yamáya juí tímyau áusha yá
                                              now   here that much who

52a   jaei

53   penké nankámniaksha se áusha
                                              completely without
                                              anything asking

53a   túmashtainkyái
       it is done this way

54   jái wayása iísan aushá
                                              entering seeing

54a   jentá

55   wayása jiistajá
                                              entering I want to see

55a   jai

56   tú tútukimtsuk aushá
                                              so so saying this

56a   jentá

57   yamáya juí yamáya juí
                                              now here now here
                                              wekajaiyá
                                              I am going

57a   tumatáinkyai
       so doing

58   warí ántsa eketúti ausha yá
       what without anything
       staying at home

58a   jai

59   ya káme áush jiímkyachu
       who   without seeing

59a   tsaa
                                              no

60   warí jiímkyachuk keemtá
       what without seeing you
       have to stay

60a   jm jm

61   warí tútukimtsuk ausha yá
       what so saying   who

61a   nekása
                                                 true
62   wekátesh wekámtayá
      you go   going
62a   jai
63   warí aéntsek tímya juyá
      what the same like this
63a   jaa
64   warí áush ketútikya
      what   staying at home
64a   jm
65   warí jiínkachu akemtá
      what without seeing you
      have to stay
65a   tsaa
                                                 no
66   tú tútukim áusha yá
      so saying this you who
66a   jm
66b   wajérchi pái
                                                 my little sister-in-law good!
                                                 (he is giving back the
                                                 bowl with the manioc beer)

67   warí kákmincha áusha yá
      what while you pass   who
67a   jai
68   warí áush túrusan
      what   this way
68a   nekása
                                                 true
69   warí ekémtaka kémsata
      what you have to stay
69a   jm jm
70   warí aénstikya tímya juyá
      what we the humans like this

70a		jm
71	warí tíntya áush jeámtaya	
	what the day when comes	
71a		nekása
		true
72	inyújai inyáisar	
	with our (people) visiting	
72a		chua
73	warí áush kéchakur	
	what without going out	
73a		jai
74	warí rúktaka ruktaimpyái ‾	
	what has to be done at home	
74a		jm
75	warí tú túkimtsuk áusha yá	
	what so so saying who	
75a		jm
76	wekátesh wekámtaya	
	you go also going	
76a		nekása
		true
77	kámtai kámtai kámtaya	
	going going going	
77a		warí áush áusha yá
		what who
78	jai	wíkya tsúru áusha yá
		I myself my brother who
78a	jm	
79		yá aéntsar kétkurish áusha
		who this way staying
		we at home also
79a	jae	
80		ya warí tímya juyá
		who what like this
80a	jae	

81		warí ekémtaka
		what somebody has
		áusha ekémtainkya
		to stay always at home
81a	jm	
82		yá tútutkin áusha yá
		who so saying
82a	jm	
83		warí tímyaju tsúru áusha ya
		what like this my brother
83a	chua	
84		warí tímyau áusha
		what like that
84a	jai	
.		.
.		.
.		.

The end of the conversation is similar to the beginning and consists of two speeches, uttered at the same time by the two interlocutors, and ending simultaneously. Another period of silence follows this, during which the interlocutors remain seated, sipping the fermented drink. If there are two or more visitors, after a short silence, H will begin a ceremonial dialogue with the second V, while the first remains silent or is engaged in another ceremonial dialogue with a second man of the household.

The most outstanding features of Shuar and Achuar ceremonial conversations are prosody and rhythm. The typical intonational contour of the main speaker's utterance in Achuar visiting dialogue consists in a rapid rise to and fall from a single intonational peak. The interval between the rise and fall corresponds to a minor third. The second speaker replies with expressions such as *jai* ("yes"), *nekása* ("true"), *chúa* ("wow!"), *tsa* ("no"), *mákete* ("its enough") and a few others drawn from a closed set.

As the main speaker gathers rhythm and intensifies the prosodic pattern, some significant phonological changes occur - stress shifts, apocopes, and vowel reductions. The utterances are pronounced with great rapidity and while the number of words and the semantic content may vary, the rhythm and the prosody become more uniform. Each utterance of the main speaker lasts two seconds or less.

With regard to the lexical and grammatical selection of forms, some forms are used only to complete the rythmic and prosodic pattern, but with scarce or non-existent semantic function, such as *áusha, káme*. In addition, many words are used which in themselves carry a clear meaning but in this context are little more than generic forms used to fulfill the rhythmic and prosodic pattern. Examples, among others, are *warí* ("what"), *ya* ("who"), *juníkya* ("like this"), *júsha* ("this also"), *ju* ("this"), *timyajuya* ("that far away"). The variation in the forms used is quite remarkable and the degree of variation is not directly related to semantic difference, but much more to adjusting phonology to rhythm, prosody, and formulaic patterns. Many utterances completely lack semantic content beyond the possible translation of individual words. An example is (77a): *warí áush áusha yá*. No Achuar man has been able to suggest an interpretation for this kind of utterance. Other utterances, even though translatable, are highly redundant, such as (18): *wekátash wekámtai wekámtai wekámtaya*. Both redundancy and formulaic pattern reflect an implicit folk theory of language efficacy. By repeating the same forms and even the same utterances many times, the speaker not only fills out the pattern of the ceremonial dialogue; he also states beyond any doubt some basic and constitutive concepts of the whole cultural system.

During the period of silence that follows the end of the ceremonial conversation or series of conversations, and depending on how many men are present, one man at a time may get up and leave the house for a moment to urinate. After the silence, conversations begin which may last several hours, until after dusk. During these conversations information of secondary importance may be communicated. The interlocutors laugh. The women serve food. An hour or two after dusk the visitors and the residents of the house go to sleep. The visitor is usually accompanied by one of his wives. She sits on the ground behind her husband, beyond the limit defined by the roof of the house. Her integration with the other women of the house only begins after the end of her husband's ceremonial dialogue.

About two or three in the morning, the women get up and begin to heat the water used to prepare the infusion of *guayusa* leaves which the

Achuar drink at that hour. Shortly thereafter, the men, both residents and visitors, get up and sit together and converse in an informal manner. The conversations can last as long as three hours, until dawn. During this period, the men communicate news which they hold to be important and visitors reveal the reason for their visit and their aims. At dawn the minimum sequence of the visit ends. If V remains in the house through the day, he may be invited by H to help him in some activity in the forest (cleaning the plantation ground, preparing for construction of a new house, participating in collective fishing) or go hunt in the forest. When V leaves, the leave-taking conversations begin after dawn and may last several hours.

Not only the new living pattern and consequent new forms of visiting, but also self-consciouness with respect to the special form of ceremonial visiting dialogue contributes to the decline of this verbal form. It is already becoming less and less used among the Achuar, as they change their living pattern, their visiting activity, and their awareness of language and language use. Furthermore, for the Achuar, the Shuar, their neighbors, constitute an example of social change, and the radio broadcasting station in Shuar is widely heard by the Achuar, so that the Shuar language is becoming a model for the widely nonliterate and isolated Achuar of Ecuador.

Among the Shuar a basic transformation has taken place with regard to the relevance of ceremonial visiting conversations. Until a few decades ago, these conversations represented one of the most important uses of language. Now, even if some kind of reduced or simplified form of the visiting dialogue is still practiced, it is clear that there are other uses of language in school and in bureaucratic settings, which are more important. In this sense a transformation has occurred in terms of what really counts in language use and linguistic knowledge. The main feature of this set of changes is the decline of the exclusive dialogic pattern of verbal interaction.

The decline of the visiting ceremonial dialogue, among the Shuar and the Achuar, is related to the restructuring of other forms of discourse and verbal interaction. Narration is a verbal activity which often occupies a special status, in that while it establishes a dialogic relationship between narrator and interlocutor, it also establishes a more or less defined indirect relation with the protagonists of the narrative. The narrative activity thus articulates relations between the narrator, the listener/interlocutor, and the referents, persons, beings, and objects described in speech.[9]

If we listen to a narrative as produced by a Shuar or an Achuar for another individual (not for a researcher) we observe that a dialogic verbal interaction takes place. The listener participates at all times in the narrative discourse, either repeating the last word of a paragraph (a set of sentences) of the narrative, asking rhetorically: *nekása* ? ("is that true?"), or using expressions which manifest his or her agreement with or involvement in the narrator's performance. However, in the narratives of myths or traditional stories as recorded by researchers we find repeated use of the verb *t-i/a/u-*, "to say." Each paragraph, or sometimes even sentence, of the narrative is closed by a form of that verb. We should interpret such a form of myth telling as a kind of reported speech. As an example of this myth telling style, I provide a segment of the Shuar text of the myth of Tsunki as narrated by Pitiur in 1978, and recorded and transcribed by S. Pellizarro. Part of this segment of the narrative was given above in free translation:[10]

1. Tsek jeá   nuyánka   juní   tímiaju
    soon arriving   afterward over here the very outstanding
    pénker únt,   nu shuár   winiákui, íimia
    the good elder, that Shuar coming,   watching
    pujúmia,   tímiayi.
    was seated,   it was said.

    Soon after he arrived here, after that person came, the very powerful and good elder (Tsunki) was seated (on his throne) watching him, it was said.

2. Ma   úntti   uruktaimpiáit ?
    Truly we the elders how is it done ?

    Indeed, how do we the elders usually behave?

3. Ii jéen   pujákrisha naka   pujúshtainkiáit ?
    In our house sitting also in front   is it not usual to be seated?

    Is it not usual for us to be seated in front (of the visitors) in our house?

4.   Ma   nu   shuár   winiákuish   páant: -   Ma shuar   winiáwai,
     Truly that person coming also clearly: -Indeed a Shuar comes,
     ya   shuár   winiá? -   tuchatainkiáit?
     which Shuar   comes? - is it not what is said?

Indeed, when that person comes, (one says) clearly: "Indeed someone
is coming; which person is coming?" Is that not what is said.

5.   Aíntsank Tsunkísha   winiákui,
     Likewise Tsunki also while he was coming,
     íimia   pujúmia   tímiayi.
     watching he was seated   it was said.

In this way, Tsunki was seated, watching him while he approached, it
was said.

6.   -Winiájai - tínia,   waniá,   pujús,   nuí
     -I come- saying,   entering,   sitting down, there
     waniámujai métek pánkikia: juka nu   Tsunkí
     at the entrance   the anacondas: these that   Tsunki
     kuchirí   tíniu   ármiayi   pankínkia.
     his pigs they   were called the anacondas themselves.

After saying, "I am coming," he entered and sat down. There at the
entrance were anacondas, which Tsunki used to call his pigs.

7.   Tsunkí   kuchirínkia   áawini   taníshmarma
     Tsunki's pigs   towards outside   within a fence
     ániunam   tepétar   ajármia   tímiayi.
     like this   lying   they were   it was said.

Tsunki's pigs were lying down just outside the door, surrounded by a
fence, it was said.

From: Pellizarro (1979: 27-28)

In lines 1,5, and 7 we find the form *tímiayi*, "it was said," which closes the paragraphs of the narrative. When we read the texts of myths as transcribed by researchers in the past, however, we find that such forms of the *t-i/a/u-* verb do not occur with the same paragraph-closing function.

Rafael Karsten, a Finnish ethnologist, who travelled among the Shuar and other Jivaroan peoples between 1916 and 1919 and in 1928-29 and who knew the Shuar language, transcribed many myths under dictation. Consider the following short text as transcribed by him[11]:

1.   Yountsu unta hī atsúmasa whuétta shuāra eini tsukáppi
     In primitive times, fire not existing, ancient Jibaros under the
     arms.

2.   tsuira hásma nu yúoma. Tákkea hī ríntinyu. Ni Tákkea noa
     (the food) made tender, ate it. Takkea alone fire possessed.
     Takkea's wife

3.   áhana wui,   wakítka   himbui   weinikama.   Tura,
     going to the plantation and returning a humming-bird saw.
     Thereupon

4.   hukīma, tánguchi nahána, hīna anáaru   huhúrtitsa.
     she took him (home), tame to make him, at the fire placed him
     to dry him.

5.   Huhúrma sɨri hīna huáka ákasa
     Having got dry, he shook his wings, took of the fire, having
     caught it

6.   uhúki. Tura numa áka ikyúkma.   Noa
     with his tail. Thereupon in a tree, which caught fire, he left it.
     A woman,

7.   áha wīni tu   weinika hukima. Hi ikyámsata,
     returning from the plantation, seeing it thus, took it with her,
     "Light the fire"

8.   timya, yamai hī wéinikahei. Yurúma awita painikatārum
     she said, "now fire I have found. Place the pots (on the fire) to
     cook the food,

9.   pīngera   yúotinyu.
     so that we may eat nicely."

From: Karsten (1935 : 516)

In this text, we find reported speech which is part of the narrative, followed by *timya* ("(she) said") in line 8, but not a single occurrence of the verb in paragraph-final position. To explain this absence, which is puzzling when compared to the contemporary frequent occurrence of the *t-i/a/u-* verbal forms in paragraph-final position, in narrations recorded and transcribed by researchers, I offer three possible hypotheses:

1) Karsten's Shuar informants performed a simplification or a restructuring of the way they would have otherwise told the myth to a non-Shuar listener, because they were using a variety of contact Shuar,[12] or because they were dictating the text and the extremely artificial situation led them to drop the *t-i/a/u-* verb forms;

2) Karsten edited the texts to make them "cleaner" as he was focusing primarily on their content as myths and not on their linguistic and stylistic form;

3) in those years the *t-i/a/u-* forms were not used in paragraph-final position.

In what follows, I will show that the last of the three hypotheses receives strong support from some more recent evidence. The same researcher who collected most of the Shuar myths, S. Pellizarro, recorded some texts in 1955.[13] One of the few texts transcribed from those early machine recordings is the following one, told by Shakai, who at that time was 20 years old.

1.   Saú   shuaráuyayi.
     Sau   was a Shuar.

     Sau was a Shuar.

2. Ti yajáuch' asa, nuarín tuke katsumniúyayi.
    Very bad   being, his wife alway he was accustomed to beating.

    Because he was very bad, he was accustomed to beating his wife all the
    time.

3. Ti   tunamatkíyayi.
    Much he was one who made her suffer.

    He was one who made her suffer much.

4. Ayamprúkmataj-sa   wáin   achíkmiayi.
    Saying I have to defend myself, digging stick   she took.

    In order to defend herself, she carried a digging stick.

5. Ajánam   taká   puján   shiáshia
    In the garden working while she was   a jaguar
    núweram   tarímiayi.
    fat (strong) came to her.

    While she was working in the garden, a strong jaguar came to her.

6. Tuma,   núaka   wari   chankínnium mamán chumpiámiayi.
    So doing, the woman quickly in the basket yuca   she put.

    So doing, the woman quickly put the yuca in the basket.

7. Uchirín achík, úmak weak,   chará chará
    Her child taking, hiding going,   screaming
    tsekénkmiayi: - shiáshia winiáwai- tusa.
    she run: -the jaguar comes-   saying.

    She took her child and after hiding him, she ran shouting: "the jaguar
    is coming."

8. Tuma,   unt yawá   amaniákmiayi.
   So doing,   the jaguar   reached her.

So doing, the jaguar reached her.

9. Shuar nua   numíjai   ayamprumakámiayi.
   The Shuar woman with the stick   defended herself.

The Shuar woman defended herself with the stick.

10. Iniashínkia   numpák   ajásmiayi.
    His body itself   only blood   was made.

His body became only blood (from the wounds).

11. Tuma   unt yawáka   nuíntusha   ajámiayi.
    So doing   the jaguar himself   following her also   he was.

In spite of that, the jaguar continued to follow her.

12. Níi   áishrin   untsúkmiayi.
    Her husband   she called.

She called her husband.

13. Tura, áishmankka   níi nankíríjai ta,   shiáshia
    Then, the man himself with his lance   arriving,   the jaguar
    awákak,   etsenkékmiayi.
    overcoming,   made it to run away.

Then, the man arriving with his lance overcame the jaguar and made it
run away.

14. Shuár   núaka   ti   pimpikín asa   numpán imiákmiayi.
    The Shuar woman   very tired   being blood   she vomited.

Because the Shuar woman was very tired, she vomited blood.

15. Turámtai,   Etsa wáit   anentáimtus,   útmiayi.
    She being thusly,   Etsa having pity for her,   he cried.

She being thus, Etsa cried, having pity for her.

16. Saú   wáit   anentáimtuschámiayi.
    Sau   did not have pity for her.

Sau did not have pity for her.

From: Pellizarro (1977: 132-35)

This short mythological narrative is traditional in its structure. It is told as an exemplary story. Etsa's good behavior, as a man who had pity on the woman who was not even his wife, is opposed to the woman's husband's (Sau's) pitilessness. In the whole text, not a single *t-i/a/u-* form is used.

Other evidence of the absence of these verbal forms from narratives with mythological or traditional content can be provided. The same researcher in 1975 tape-recorded the narrative of the myth of Nunkui from a very old woman, Tatsémai. Her text is quite long but the *t-i/a/u-* forms are used only infrequently:

1. Kunka nua,   áishri   wématai,   yawá
   Snail woman,   her husband going away,   the dogs
   ewekámumtai   unkúchan,   juúk,   penú
   making to go hunting unkuch leaves, collecting, rolling up
   wekás, penú   wekás ímianai   entsa ápunam jeá.
   going   rolling up going far away to a large river   she arrived.

The woman, Kunku, after her husband left to hunt with the dogs, walked through the forest collecting unkuch leaves, rolling them up as she went, until she arrived at a wide river.

2. Mamán yankisári   jákekin   winínian   wáiniak,
   Little branches of yuca floating   which came   seeing,
   nuna   júukin júukin.
   those ones   she collected.

Seeing little branches of yuca which came floating, she collected them.

3. Wesa   Nunkui nua   pujámunam,   nua   jujajáitium
   Going   Nunkui woman   where she was,   women   letting out laughter
   ajamunam   jeá.
   where they were   she arrived.

Going, she arrived at where Nunkui was, where the women were letting out bursts of laughter.

4. Tsekeárkuta   jeá: -   máanku,   winiásha
   Running a little   she arrived: -my sister   with me also
   mama   ajámprusia!-
   yuca   share!-

She came to them almost running: "my sisters, share the yuca with me also!"

5. Tu   tai: -nu   mámachua   tepá
   Thus saying: -that one which is not yuca   lying there
   jurúmkikia!-
   take!-

Thus saying: "take that one (the girl) lying there which is not yuca.

6. Tu tai,   júkin   tímiai.
   Thus saying, that she took her,   it was said.

   Thus saying, she took her, it was said.

From Pellizarro (1971 : 11-12)

The first section of the narrative is quoted here. One of the very few occurrences of *t-i/a/u-* verb forms delimits this section. This evidence supports the hypothesis that the *t-i/a/u-* forms used as quotatives in paragraph-final position are an innovation in the way of narrating. Their meaning in the narration is either a legitimation of the knowledge the informant is transmitting or the expression of some distance that he or she is taking from the narrative content. The two meanings could converge with a sense something like: "it is not me the one who is saying this, somebody else (more reliable, more knowledgeable than me) told this." With the use of the *t-i/a/u-* forms, mythological narrative becomes embedded into a temporal/aspectual frame of reference: "it was said, they used to say." This embedding into an indefinite past increases the distance between the narrator (in his function as "informant") and the narrative content and actually states that somebody (or everybody) once said or used to say that. It is possible that consciousness of the fact that a traditional story is being told out of its normal context (i.e., for a researcher) plays an important role in triggering the use of the *t-i/a/u-* forms.

An alternative interpretation, which we might call a "formal," as opposed to a "semantic" one, is that these forms show up only in the special interaction which is established with an outsider (the researcher) who is silent most of the time and who does not interact in a dialogic way with the narrator, in the usual Shuar manner. These forms would be, according to this interpretation, a substitution for the dialogic interchange. There is, however, counter-evidence to this exclusively formal interpretation. When in 1975, for the first time, a Shuar researcher, Ricardo Tankamash', tape-recorded traditional narratives, most of his informants produced texts with an outstanding amount of *t-i/a/u-* forms. He was obviously able to interact with his "informants" and in most cases he did interact in the narration of the myth of Nunkui as told by Rosa Tankamash':

1. Yaunchu   yurúmak   atsú   timiaja,
   Long ago food   there was not it was said,
   pénke   tsúka asamtai núwa ajana   ishiniu
   completely hungry being   women to the gardens they used to go
   timiaja.
   it was said.

Long ago there was no food, it was said. Being completely hungry, the
women used to go to the gardens, it was said.

2. Túramu   entsá   inchí   chuchíkchiri   champiarach'
   So being on a river sweet potato small pieces   plantain
   ajéksamu kaúnu   timiaja.
   peel   were carried together   it was said.

So being, small pieces of sweet potato and plantain peel were carried on
a river, it was said.

3. Tura   yurúmak   kaúnkui   nuka nuka wekátukin,
   So being the food   by being gathered that that walking,

   núna   jurí jurí   núwa   jujajái! jámunam
   that   following   woman laugh   to where it was
   tsekén   jeá   timiaja.
   running she arrived it was said.

So being, walking to that food being gathered, following that, she
arrived running to the place of the woman's laugh, it was said.

4. Tura   tsenkén jear   nuyá   yurúmak,   uchi
   Then   running arriving after that food,   a child
   mankarú tepá   timiaja.
   fat   lying   it was said.

Then, after arriving running, the food lying there was a fat child, it was said.

From: Rueda (1983 : 85)

In this short segment of the narrative (which corresponds approximately to the segment quoted above from Tatsemai's narrative) we find five occurrences of the form *tímiaja* ("it was said"). The frequency of *t-i/a/u-* forms even in narratives recorded by a Shuar researcher leads me to prefer the semantic interpretation rather than the formal one. The Shuar researcher was interacting with his informants, but in the artificial recording setting the dialogue had to shift into a monologue incorporating the dialogue. In the monologue the informant establishes a relation with previous times when traditional Shuar really knew about things. In this way, the narrative incorporates within itself, when produced in an artificial setting, a meta-narrative, and any myth or traditional story becomes an opportunity to repeat the general story concerning changes in knowledge and beliefs in the community. The narration of each myth becomes a discourse about change in the cultural system. Dialogue becomes a monologue about the process of decline of dialogue.

When a myth is written in the Shuar language, the *t-i/a/u-* verb forms are not used as quotatives. This fact is not to be interpreted as a return to the traditional way of narrating. The few Shuar who have written mythological narrative constitute a group that is quite advanced in the process of critical consciousness and distance from an "internal" perspective on the content of myth. They have all spent many years in school, some of them outside of Shuar country. For them, the proper way to narrate orally a myth is by using the *t-i/a/u-* forms, but for written narrative they are strongly influenced by the western (Spanish) model.

We have seen two ways in which socio-cultural change and forms of discourse are related to one another. General trends of socio-cultural change have brought to speakers' consciousness one type of dialogue (the visiting one) because of its outstanding formal features, and the other type (the narrative mythological one) because of its content.

The visiting conversation involved a ritualized representation of dialogue. Its disappearance and replacement by other, less formal forms of dialogue should be seen as an indication of a general shift towards more flexible forms of verbal interaction. This decline took place in a context of social change in which the formalized representation of dialogue became too emphatic and excessive for Shuar auto-representation. The special form of verbal interaction became consequently less functional with respect to the emerging forms of social stratification. These require forms of verbal interaction allowing for more flexibility and adaptability in turn-taking and a more westernized way of interaction, in which the relative social position and prestige of speakers can be constantly negotiated.

Parallel to the decline of formalized dialogue is the increasing distance between traditional knowledge and current Shuar beliefs, values, and ways of life. Literacy, schooling, and even the presence of researchers among the Shuar play an important role in the process of establishing a consciousness of that increasing distance. The new way of performing traditional narratives, especially in the presence of researchers, reflects that consciouness through the use of quotative forms. Of course, it is not at all by chance that the presence of a researcher, either a white man, a "gringo," or a Shuar, triggers the use of the quotative forms. These manifest the consciousness the narrator has of the different world views and beliefs of his listener. But even further, in most cases they represent the different world view and beliefs of the narrator himself or herself in relation to those expressed in the narratives. In this way, the narratives with *t-i/a/u-* forms become a discourse about the change of the whole cultural system. Ultimately, they become a monologue in which traditional, or even contemporary, dialogue is represented.

Notes

1. Shuar and Achuar forms and texts are given here using the standard alphabet adopted by the Shuar Federation. This alphabet is very similar, with regard to phonetic value, to contemporary South American Spanish. Thus *ch* represents a palatal affricate [č], *ts* represents an aleolar affricate [ts], and *sh* represents a palatal fricative [š]. Two major differences from the usual Spanish value of the

graphemes are *j*, which in the Shuar and Achuar alphabet represents a velar, soft, spirant fricative, between [h] and [x], and *e*, which represents a high, back rounded vowel [ɨ]. For a description of Shuar phonology (with some interesting problems related to the interpretation of the phonemic system of the language) see Turner (1958).

2. M.W. Stirling, an American ethnologist, was among the Shuar in a "rather hasty trip" (Stirling, quoted by Harner 1972: 3) in 1930-31. The most puzzling aspect of the description he gives of a ceremonial conversation is the moment at which it was performed- 24 hours after arrival at the house. In general, these conversations among the Shuar as well as among the Achuar were (and still are, sometimes) performed immediately after the visitor's arrival at the house.

3. A *wea* is the oldest man of the household, who behaves as a master of ceremonies.

4. The verb *enéma-* or *anéma-* can be analyzed as a causative, from the verb *nemá-s-* or *nemá-k-* ("to join, to go together"). If this interpretation is correct, its meaning would be "to cause to join," a meaning which fits the social context and the general purposes of the speech event.

5. Other ceremonial speech events that were in use among the Achuar were the *yá yá chícham*, performed when an unknown person was met (*yá* "who?") and the *já já chícham*, performed when a known person was met (*ja, jaa,* and *jai* are different expressions used to call someone's attention).

6. The data presented here were collected during field work conducted in 1970, 1971, and 1974.

7. This term of address is obviously derived from Spanish *amigo* "friend," which in Shuar-Achuar phonology becomes *amíkiu* .

8. Numbers identify statement and response cycles. Where there is no overlap between statement and response, letters are used to differentiate the two.

9. These ideas have a long history in the fields of literarary theory and the philosophy of language. I might mention here at least the works of two major thinkers active in the first half of this century: V.N. Voloshinov (otherwise known as M. Bakhtin) and E. Cassirer.

10. The editors and author are grateful to Janet Wall Hendricks for providing English translations of the Shuar texts taken from Pellizarro.
11. I have not modified Karsten's orthography, which is very different from that of the current writing system .
12. A variety of pidginized Shuar was in use, at least since the nineteenth century, in the area of the old mestizo village of Macas. Karsten was travelling with interpreters and guides from Macas.
13. The recordings were made with early wire recorders. Most of the original wires have been destroyed but fortunately the researcher had already transcribed the recordings.

References

Benveniste, Emile
    1971 *Problems in general linguistics*, Mary E. Meek (trans.). Coral Gables: University of Miami Press.
Harner, Michael J.
    1972 *The Jívaro: people of the sacred waterfalls.* Garden City, New York: Doubleday Anchor Press.
Karsten, Rafael
    1935 *The head-hunters of western Amazonas: the life and culture of the Jibaro Indians of eastern Ecuador and Peru.* Helsingfors: Societas Sciantiarum Fennica.
Pellizarro, S.
    1977 *Shakaim. Mitos de la selva y del desmonte.* Quito-Sucúa: Mundo Shuar.
    1978 *Nunkui. El modelo de la mujer Shuar.* Quito-Sucúa: Mundo Shuar.
    1979 *Tsunki. El mundo del agua y de los poderes fecundantes.* Quito-Sucúa: Mundo Shuar.
Rueda, M.V.
    1983 *Setenta mitos Shuar recogidos por R. Tankámash'.* Quito-Sucúa: Mundo Shuar.

Stirling, M.W.
  1938 *Historical and ethnographical material on the Jivaro Indians.*
         Bulletin of the Bureau of American Ethnology., No. 117.
         Washington: Government Printing Office.
Turner, Glenn D.
  1958 Alternative phonemicizing in Jívaro, *International Journal of*
         American Linguistics 24 : 87-94.
Vacas Galindo, Enrique
  1895 *Nankijukima: religión, usos y costumbres de los salvajes del*
         oriente del Ecuador. Ambato: Imprenta de Teodomiro Merino.

Guide to Tape Selections

Side A:

1. Shokleng (see G. Urban, "Semiotic Functions of Macro-parallelism")

    a. *Wãñēklèn* dyadic performance: discussed but not transcribed
    b. *Wãñēklèn* narration: B.1.1 (1975), B.2.1 (1975), B.2.2 (1975), B.2.3 (1975), B.2.1 (1981), B.2.1 (Wãñēkï 1982): transcribed (pp. 42-49)

2. Suyá (see A. Seeger, "Oratory Is Spoken, Myth Is Told, and Song Is Sung")

    a. Examples 1-6: discussed but not transcribed
    b. Example 7 (*Sangére* for a Child with Fever): transcribed (pp. 72-75)

3. Shavante (see L. Graham, "Three Modes of Shavante Vocal Expression")

    a. *dawawa* (ritual wailing): transcribed (pp. 101-107)
    b. *dañoʔre* (collective singing): transcribed (pp. 108-111)
    c. political oratory: partially transcribed (pp. 112-113)

Side B:

1. Kalapalo (see E. Basso, "Quoted Dialogues in Kalapalo")

    Myth of Fitsagu the Cuckoo: the tape contains a portion of the text transcribed on pp. 137-167; the tape begins with the text on p. 137

2. Kuna (see J. Sherzer, "The Report of a Kuna Specialist")

    The Report of a Kuna Specialist: a portion of the text transcribed on pp. 180-194; the tape begins with the text on p. 180

3. Toba (see H. Klein, "Styles of Toba Discourse")

    a. Most formal style: transcribed (pp. 221-224) (Note: Examples D and E from the text do not appear on tape; however, a sample of murmured dialogue that has not been transcribed is included to illustrate descriptions in the text)

Index